INSIDE FATHER HOOD

a guide for
becoming the dad
God created
you to be

DR. ROY SMITH + ROBERT AMAYA

ISBN: 978-1-942292-39-5

Published by LiveUp Resources
200 North 7th Street
Lebanon, PA 17046

Printed in the United States of America

Cover and book design by Jory Kauffman

CONTENTS

PART III: FATHERHOOD REFINED

To Kim, Mike, Silas, and Jorah.
May I always be there for you even when I'm not.

To Nick, the Professor (1988–2020).
Thank you for all the lessons you've taught me. You
are loved and missed.

To Jan, who said, "Let's do this thing and become
parents," and was a faithful partner throughout
the journey.

To Roy Smith Sr., who gave me a love for God's Word,
an interest in discovering who I am, and a desire to
help others. You were a very interesting man.

—Roy

To my dad, who would have benefited greatly from a
book like this. None of us is perfect, but I wouldn't
be where I am if it weren't for your example and
sincere love for God, Mom, Arlene, and me.
¡Te quiero, Papá!

—Robert

A WORD FROM ROBERT

"Fathers, do not provoke your children to anger, but bring them up in the discipline and instruction of the Lord." Ephesians 6:4 (ESV)

I've been deeply affected by this passage of Scripture ever since my eldest daughter, Sophia, was born. Growing up in church, I thought I understood exactly what it meant, and I'd attempt to use it against my own dad whenever I was agitated with him. "Don't provoke me, Dad!" I'd say. "The Bible says so." You can imagine how well that sat with him.

After having Sophia, however, I realized that this passage was never intended to be understood that way. In my ignorance, I was reading it as if "do not provoke your children" was all it said, which meant I was missing so much of its depth and intention. What I didn't see was that the Apostle Paul's words are actually laying the entire responsibility of raising children upon the father's shoulders. Don't believe me? Read it again. It says, "Fathers... bring them up."

This eye-opening moment changed me forever. I began to comprehend that, according to the Apostle, provocation happens when you *don't* raise up your child. It's not when a father disciplines his child for wrongdoing or doesn't do what they want that he sets them up for terrible anger and resentment—it's when he's too busy, too lazy, or too anything that keeps him from spending quality time with them.

The more I kept digging into this verse, the further it clarified a sobering truth. It's essentially telling us that the person or thing that has the greatest influence in a child's life, whether intentional or unintentional, is the one acting as their father. Now, that person is meant to be us. It's our God-given duty to teach, guide, and develop our children. But when we *don't* step up to that duty, when we allow them to stare at a screen for hours a day and spend only minutes with us, when they spend most of their days in a classroom and only an hour at dinner with us, when they spend five days a week away from us and only two days with us, well... it means we're letting someone or something else do the raising. It means we have handed over, in every meaningful way, our role as fathers.

That was mind-blowing to me. And I knew that as far as I was concerned, things needed to change. But here's the kicker: I spent months frustrated after understanding this verse. I knew I needed to do more in my relationship with my daughter, but I kept losing my internal drive and focus, kept running out of gas. I spent so much time feeling guilty and useless, aware of what needed to be different but unable to do anything about it. It was absolutely exhausting.

Then I finally looked up. I recalled the words from John's first Epistle: "We love because he loved us first" (1 John 4:19). That was the missing key. Something needed to happen within me first. I needed to become aware of how much my heavenly Father loved me and what He did for me through His Son. In essence, feeling that embrace from God is what fuels us to be passionate fathers. And that begins inside.

Years later, now with two young girls, I find myself wanting to put into words so much of what I've learned as a father. So when my dear friend Dr. Roy Smith approached me with his idea for a book about the internal development needed to become an effective father, I was more than ready to contribute. While he poured his research and expertise into the body of the work, I contributed real stories and experiences with my dad and with my children. In the end, I could not be more proud of our work. It honors God, His role as our Father, and His calling upon us to be fathers.

I wish I'd had this book years ago. I may have avoided much pain and frustration with myself. However, I believe in God's perfect timing in all things. So I pray that you are radically blessed and encouraged with every page. This isn't your typical fatherhood book. It's not about the ten steps to better fathering. It's about experiencing your heavenly Father. It's about letting that experience open the depths of your inner person, insecurities and all, and getting changed by a love that surpasses all understanding (Ephesians 3:19).

Thank you for letting us speak into your life. May you and your family be richly blessed.

A WORD FROM ROY

I'm sure it won't surprise you to hear that life is unpredictable. We've all experienced it, whether it was a small, unexpected change that altered your plans for the day or an unforeseen path that redirected the course of your whole career. Looking back on my own life, I can see countless ways the unpredictable parts of it have shaped where I am today. When I began a counseling practice out of my living room nearly forty years ago, my biggest dream was to one day expand into a real office. But God blessed me beyond my greatest expectations, and since that humble beginning, Pennsylvania Counseling Services has expanded into eleven counties, employing over 650 individuals and providing just about every type of counseling you can imagine.

Unfortunately, however, not every surprise in life is quite this positive. In early 2020, the entire world was unexpectedly hit with the most physically and culturally devastating event most of us will experience in our lifetime—COVID-19. All of a sudden, everyone had to make drastic life changes in an attempt to keep ourselves and others safe. I myself was lucky enough to have stayed healthy, but like many of you, I still had to experience quarantine, isolation, and even months of separation from my own family. Since my company was mandated to stay open to continue serving thousands of clients during this challenging time, I had a higher risk of contracting or passing on the disease. And that meant I had to take extreme precautions to keep my loved ones safe.

To my dismay, what I thought would be a brief week away from them quickly turned into two weeks, then three, and the end of the tunnel still was nowhere to be seen. This cruel separation made me miserable, and watching the news didn't exactly help. I quickly realized I needed something to do when I wasn't working on therapy outreach programs, just to stay sane, so I turned to a hobby that has always brought me comfort—writing.

This may sound odd, but writing is actually a form of prayer for me. It's a special time where I can focus wholly on God and listen as He speaks through His Word, my memories of inspiring counseling sessions I've had, and new ideas that could help other men. So as I settled into quarantine, I turned on some jazz, pulled out my yellow legal pad, and looked to God. And He led me right to fatherhood.

I can't help but laugh that it took a global pandemic for me to write this book, because I've actually been talking about it with God for quite some time. Every December, I participate in Fatherhood CoMission's leadership summit in Rome, Georgia, where a group of Christian leaders extol the importance of fatherhood and work together to encourage the various fatherhood ministries in attendance.[1] The wisdom they share and their dedication to helping others do fathering right always makes me think about my own journey with my father and my experience counseling clients through their issues with their fathers. Each year, I can't help but feel God's tug on my heart to put my own ideas regarding fatherhood into writing.

The problem is, fatherhood isn't as simple as I wish it were. I could give you step-by-step instructions on what to do or say to your child, but that isn't what will make you a great father. That's because fatherhood isn't just about providing structure for your

---

1   Check out all of Fatherhood CoMission's resources and information for dads at fatherhoodcomission.com.

child to live by. It's also about how your relationship with them reflects your relationship with God, our ultimate Father whose character, love, and principles we must practice in our own fathering. It's about your relationship with your earthly father, whose influence you must evaluate so you know which lessons of his to pass on to your own child. And it's about your internal development, as it's only through changing with God's guidance that you can become the man you need to be to help your child develop themselves in the same way.

That's a lot to tackle in one book! Maybe now you can understand why it took me so long to write it. But with a pandemic and God's help, I got it done. And now it's your turn to put in the work. Life may be unpredictable, but I have absolute faith that with God's guiding hand, you will fully step up into the most holy role of fatherhood.

INTRODUCTION

I want you to take a moment to think about your life. Specifically, think about how you got to where you are. But don't focus on the obvious parts, like where you went to college or how you met your wife. I want you to go back even further—to your childhood, to all those experiences that shaped you without you even realizing it.

Think about the class field trip or family vacation that first inspired you to dream. Think about your first experience with fear and what it revealed to you about your insecurities. Think about the first challenge you had to really push yourself to overcome. Think about the strength it unleashed within you when you finally did.

All of these experiences helped you become the man and father you are today. And your child is on that same journey of self-discovery right now. God created them with great potential, and He wants them to achieve it. But to do that, they need you. They need your guidance to help them sharpen and develop all of their God-given skills and capabilities. And they need your love so they can feel safe enough to do so.

But in order to successfully guide and love our children, we must first develop our own identities. After all, we can't give our children what we don't have ourselves. If we let our own potential fall to the wayside, how can we hope to teach them to pursue theirs?

The good news is that it doesn't matter what ruts you've fallen into or what negative behaviors you've let become habits. You can still become a godly father, because as soon as you decide to prioritize that calling, God will take you on a journey of spiritual growth. He is always working within you to fulfill His great plan (Philippians 2:13). That means that even without much knowledge or experience in being a good father, you will begin to change simply by engaging in the various aspects of fathering discussed in this book and opening yourself up to your child.

As you take your own growth further, you'll find that you can do so most effectively when you fully tune in to God and invite Him into every area of your life. However, whether because of busyness, shame, or even ignorance, we often don't include God in certain aspects of our day-to-day experiences. But in reality, each goal we achieve or struggle we face, no matter how small, is an opportunity to deepen our relationship with Him. This kind of full immersion in God's will is especially important when it comes to fatherhood. As our ultimate Father, God serves as our greatest example for how we should father our own children. The closer we grow to Him, the more we will recognize how He fathers us, and the more capable we will become of reflecting His standards in our own fathering efforts.

As you're beginning to see, the journey of fatherhood is a very personal one. For this reason, this book will focus more on how to *be* a father than how to *do* fathering. First we'll discuss the general role of fatherhood and how it should positively influence the physical, mental, emotional, and relational developmental challenges every child faces. Then we'll turn the focus inward to explore the ways you must develop yourself in order to father your child successfully. Finally we'll delve into the specific areas you'll need to guide your child through to help them establish a strong, godly identity. Along the way, you'll see how God's Word can help you better understand His view of fatherhood and how to integrate His teachings into your daily life as you walk with Him on this amazing journey.

You may notice that some of these topics are approached from the perspective of a biological father for simplicity's sake. But it's important to understand that these lessons apply to *all* types of fathers, whether you're a stepfather, a grandfather, or a non-biological guardian, whether you're married, divorced, or widowed, or whether you adopted your child or are a foster parent. The application of the principles will just look different based on your specific fathering role, circumstances, and unique child.

So as you read through this book, throw out what isn't helping and write in what you think would work better for your personal situation. All I ask is that you interact with every chapter. Even if you wind up finding a specific topic completely useless, you will still grow just by thinking through it and making that determination for yourself.

In the same way, this book will also at times discuss a topic as it applies to a young child, especially with some of the more foundational concepts. In an ideal world, a man will start integrating these fatherhood concepts into his life the moment he becomes a father. However, this world is anything but ideal, which is why God's grace allows us to grow and change at any point in our journey. So even if your "child" is no longer an actual child, they will still benefit from your guidance in these areas. The nature of that guidance will just change over time. However, there's one thing that never will—your duty to love them like God does.

To help understand these nuances, I will at times provide a variety of examples of how a certain issue may manifest in a young child versus in adolescence or even young adulthood. While these examples may not always apply to you, thinking through them will help you begin to understand how to recognize an issue in your own fatherhood so you can step in and guide your child toward a better way.

This book may or may not be the first step in your fatherhood journey, but it hopefully won't be the last. Fatherhood is a lifelong job, and it's one that you must continually and intentionally work at. You may never feel like you have it all figured out. And that's okay! For one thing, no one does, so you certainly aren't alone. But more importantly, being the perfect father matters less than being a loving father. As long as you trust in God and rely on His guidance, both you and your child will find the path to success. Even better, your relationship will become everything it's meant to be.

part I

FATHERHOOD DEFINED

"You will have a son of your own. He will get everything you have."
—Genesis 15:4

01

BECOMING A FATHER

I remember the exact moment my wife came to me and said the two words that can immediately fill any man with a mind-boggling mix of pure joy and sheer terror: "I'm pregnant."

Over the following weeks, I found myself latched into the same roller coaster of questions and doubts that so many fellow fathers-to-be experience. One moment I'd feel totally empowered and excited to tackle the challenge of being a dad. The next I'd feel like jumping in my car and driving aimlessly through the streets to try to outrun the overpowering anxiety that often comes with any responsibility you can't get out of. The questions would flood in out of nowhere. What does taking care of a baby even look like? Would my child love and trust me? How could I guide someone else through life when I had already failed so many times? And the big one: can I really do this?

I'm a problem solver, though. So instead of sinking into misery, I got to work. I read about the dos and don'ts of child rearing, studied what the Bible has to say about fatherhood, and did a lot of praying. And here's the most important truth God revealed to me: God created each man for fatherhood, whether he ever becomes a father or not.

No matter how inadequate you may sometimes feel as a father, the reality is that you're already fully equipped for the job. As long as you're willing to try, God will be there to walk you through the process. He'll guide you through the struggles, show you the lessons you need to teach your child, and above all, demonstrate the love He wants you to reflect to them. Love is the single most important piece of fatherhood. When there's love, a father and his child will have everything they need (1 Corinthians 13:13).

So keeping this truth in mind, let's start at the beginning and look at what fatherhood means at its very core. Before we get to the more in-depth processes that will help you build a strong, lifelong bond with your child, we must first understand what exactly binds you together. And that requires turning a deliberate eye to something we often overlook the importance of—biology, science, and basic instinct.

EARLY CHANGES[1]

Everyone knows and can even physically see evidence of the changes a woman undergoes during pregnancy. But what is less recognized is that as her body changes, so does her husband's. And I'm not talking about a sympathetic pregnancy (though some men do experience nausea and weight gain along with their wives). I'm talking about the subtle hormone changes that happen in the father-to-be. During pregnancy, women produce and emit chemicals called pheromones that their partner instinctively senses and responds to on a hormonal level. For instance, a man's prolactin will increase quite a bit over the duration of the pregnancy. In the mother, prolactin is responsible for initiating and maintaining lactation. But in the father, it begins to prepare him to bond with his child.

The biggest effect, however, is on a man's testosterone. This hormone typically decreases more and more the closer a couple gets to the due date. Now, that may seem like a bad thing, since

---

1   Much of the research and information referenced in this chapter is taken from: Louann Brizendine, *The Male Brain* (New York: Harmony Books, 2010).

you're probably aware that testosterone is essential to being a man. However, it's also what makes us impulsive, territorial, and aggressive—all of which limit our ability to bond with others. So a drop in testosterone during your wife's pregnancy also means a drop in these self-centered tendencies. Combined with a prolactin increase, these changes allow you to become both a better husband during the pregnancy and more emotionally connected to your child after they're born.

And these biological changes don't end after birth. Remember those powerful feelings of love and passion you felt at the beginning of your relationship with your wife? Well, that was due to a sudden activation in certain brain circuits, which will kick in once more when you first lay eyes on your child. Every time a parent holds their child or gazes into their adorable face, they experience a rush of oxytocin, the bonding hormone, and dopamine, the feel-good hormone. In other words, their child makes them really, really happy, deepening the connection between them even further.

As you can see, fatherhood is an innate part of every man—and that means it's a part of you too. The scenario described above is one way God prepares men for fatherhood, but it certainly isn't the only way. No matter where your journey started, God is standing by ready to support you as you become a father. And once you accept this part of His great plan, it won't be long before fatherhood begins to feel like a natural, inseparable piece of you.

A FATHER'S ROLE

One helpful way of understanding the essence of fatherhood is to look at how it's different from motherhood. As we just saw, many of those early hormonal changes happen to both you and your wife during the pregnancy, just in different ways. However, it's hard to deny that the physical and hormonal changes are a little more intense for her, which means things will return to normal much faster for you after your child is born. This is why mothers often take charge during early parenthood, changing all the diapers, comforting the child whenever they cry, or tucking them snugly into bed every night. It's not that the fathers don't want to help. It can just be intimidating to see motherhood come so naturally to their wives, and it feels easier to let them take over and do it all.

But the truth is, you're just as equipped for the job as she is. Like her, you also have natural instincts for fatherhood, such as when you become spontaneous and creative as you play with your child. You have an amygdala and insula, the parts of the brain relating to emotional responses and gut feelings, which cause you to jump into action when you hear your child cry. And that little smile, even in the middle of the messiest diaper change, is enough to trigger your brain's reward center to make you feel fulfilled and content in your role as a dad.

However, just because men and women are both equally designed for parenthood doesn't mean their approach to it will be the same. While mothers are typically praised for being gentle and comforting, fathers are often criticized for being too aggressive or even harsh. And while it's certainly possible to cross that line, for the most part they are just fulfilling the specific job God created them for—to protect and guide their children in a sinful world.

We all have a responsibility to be like Jesus, who stood up against a culture that encouraged spiritual compromise (Matthew 21:12-13). When it comes to fatherhood, part of that responsibility means teaching your child to take care of themselves, express and guide their emotions, set boundaries, and develop perseverance and resiliency. Thankfully, your nature as a man is perfectly suited to teach your child these exact skills.

For one, you are likely to be more direct with your child when they need it. When it comes to discipline or confrontation, mothers often emotionally guide their children through conversation and support, while fathers prefer to give clear orders. Although such an approach can seem abrupt and distant, being strict doesn't mean being unloving, and such structure can actually help your child learn self-control and internalize high standards for themselves. A father's directness will also enhance his child's own transparency in communication, which will help them navigate the real world. After all, others won't be able to read their minds or anticipate their needs in the same way their mother can.

Another way you help your child is through your tendency to connect through physical play, like a wrestling match or a tickle fight, instead of through conversation alone. The creative, spontaneous, and even risky nature of this style of play feeds a child's curiosity and improves their ability to learn. Researchers have even found that those whose fathers played with them safely but roughly as children have more self-confidence as teenagers. Similarly, verbal teasing, when playful and good-natured, can teach a child how to sense what others are feeling and determine when someone is being deceptive, further increasing their self-reliance and relational abilities.

Regardless of their natural tendencies, men are also good at being flexible in their fathering approach, especially between daughters and sons. For instance, daughters typically don't like to be teased as much and prefer more structured play, such as a tea party or make-believe. To make them happy, fathers are usually more than willing to accommodate, especially if it allows them to help their daughters in some way. Fathers feel closest to their daughters, no matter their age, when they can solve problems together or fix something for them. Engaging in your daughter's style of play allows you to do exactly this by helping improve her relational skills and ability to get along with men later in life.

Fathers also like to help their sons, but in different ways. While there is more softness in a father's interactions with his daughter, he is more likely to be firm when guiding his son, even during play. Because he views his son as more like himself, he

demands of his son what he would require of himself. Being physical and unrelenting as you roughhouse together or teach him a
sport will help develop the same perseverance and work ethic in
your son that you try to express yourself.

Of course, that doesn't mean daughters won't also need a
firm hand at times or that sons won't benefit from compassion in
certain moments. But adjusting to those nuances is just a part of
fathering, as is adjusting to the ways your children will grow and
change. Just remember that you are more than capable of handling
it. No matter how difficult, intimidating, or downright frightening
this role may sometimes seem, God has already equipped you with
the exact tools you need to help your child shape their identity and
create a future filled with success.

However, fatherhood isn't all about discovering your role and
learning how to care for your child. It's just as important to understand what you will reap as a result. As you give to and bond with
your child, you will receive several blessings that will enhance your
life beyond what you could ever imagine. When you can recognize
and focus on the following blessings, you'll find yourself stepping
more and more into the amazing role of being a dad.

THE BLESSING OF LOVE

One of the biggest problems men struggle with is accepting
the love others give them. It's so much easier to do the bare minimum by keeping our friendships with other men shallow or even
by avoiding friendships completely. But this approach to life denies
our basic need for emotional affirmation and support. By attempting to protect ourselves, we actually limit our ability to internalize
and benefit from the love of others, which is essential to achieving
all of our potential.

However, a child changes all of this. As a father, you automatically have some type of relationship with your child, making it

impossible to maintain your isolation. And as you relate to them, even through something as small as fulfilling their basic needs, they will respond with an appreciative love you can't help but take in. When your little girl calls you daddy for the first time, your heart will melt in an instant. When you catch your son watching and imitating your actions, you will instinctively smile with pride. It's these special moments with your child that make the weariness of the world temporarily disappear, leaving you with a sense of complete contentedness, peace, and love. Embrace that love and internalize it, and then return it to them tenfold (Jude 1:2).

THE BLESSING OF PERSPECTIVE

Each man naturally seeks meaning in life. We want to make a difference, even be heroes if we can. But being a hero doesn't always mean saving the world. It starts in the mundane, with just being present with your family and actively loving them like God does. This is where you'll discover your true value—in your child's shouts of joy as you walk in the door, or in your wife's sigh of relief as you finish the dishes for her.

Along with reminding you of your own value, time spent with your child also gives you perspective on your priorities. Where life tells you to speed up to reach the end goal, your child asks you to slow down to be present in the moment. Despite how some jobs or aspects of life require routine with little room for creative thought, life isn't meant to be boring or success-oriented. Your child will be the one to enliven it, encouraging you to become spontaneous and flexible. As you engage with them and see them grow and change each day, you will rediscover the joy and inspiration that comes from something as simple as drawing a picture with crayons.

THE BLESSING OF GROWTH

As much as we may not like it, much of our growth comes

from the unforeseen challenges of life. And what greater challenge is there than fatherhood? In the course of their life, your child will explore parts of themselves you may have never thought about. They'll experience situations you never went through. They'll exhibit behaviors you don't like or make choices you never would have. Responding well in these moments may require words or behaviors you've never engaged with before. And that means you're naturally going to change.

There are three specific aspects of fatherhood that foster growth within a father as he experiences them. The first is basic child-rearing. The task of taking care of another human being can be a huge adjustment. There will be times when you get tired of the demands your child places on you, whether it's the nonstop crying at the baby stage or the endless back talk during adolescence. You may feel like you want to just block it out and do nothing about it—but you can't.

Just as you have to push yourself beyond your limit at the gym to get bigger muscles, you must also stretch yourself to the edge of your relational comfort zone and then courageously take one step further. In this way, when you comfort your wailing infant or discipline your unruly teen, you don't just help them. You also help yourself by developing your perseverance, leadership, and ability to self-sacrifice.

The second aspect is relational connection. Your child may be like you in many ways, but they will still be their own person. In helping them discover their unique identity, you'll naturally develop a variety of social and emotional skills. For instance, when you don't understand your child, you'll have to learn to slow down and listen to their perspective in order to see where they're coming from. Not only will this help you work with your child better, but it will also teach you how to understand your own internal processes. And the better you understand your thoughts and responses, the easier it will be to communicate with others, including your child.

The last aspect of fatherhood that pushes you to grow is teaching, which is one of your most important and enduring tasks. As your child encounters and explores the world, they will find themselves with countless questions, most of which you've probably never thought about before, at least not for many, many years. When they turn to you to ask "why?" for the millionth time, and as you try to dig up an answer to give them, you will find yourself really thinking about topics you may have never considered or always took for granted. As a result, you and your child will both get to explore a new area of life and enhance your thought processes, allowing you to better understand and navigate the world.

Besides increasing your knowledge, teaching your child will also further your internal development. As you give your child specific instructions, like what principles they should live by, you'll both help them create structure to build their identity on and discover how you can do the same. And given the way children mimic their parents' actions more than their words, you'll quickly learn to adjust your behaviors to ensure your child takes your lessons to heart, which will in turn help you become more of the man God wants you to be.

Depending on your current level of maturity, you may be pushed to grow in only one of these aspects of fatherhood or all of them—but you will grow. The only father who has no need for growth is God (Deuteronomy 32:4). His greatness doesn't change, but our relationship with Him does. Success in fatherhood can only be achieved when we learn to feel God's presence guiding us. When you rely on Him, He will show you exactly what you need to do to become the father your child needs.

A FINAL THOUGHT

So what happens to a male who chooses to ignore the importance of fatherhood? The answer is simple—he ends up being less of a man. A male who simply goes through the motions of fatherhood misses out on all the resources and benefits God has to offer. The biological changes discussed above are less likely to impact him, and he blocks himself from receiving the blessings of fatherhood and the growth God intends for him. In other words, by denying his full responsibility as a father, he ends up denying an essential part of himself. And worst of all, he hurts his child, creating a legacy that will lead them to make the exact same mistakes in their own life.

Of course, I don't need to tell to tell you this. The fact that you're reading this book already means you've chosen a different path from such a male. You understand that Jesus died for your child and that you have been chosen to help them discover this truth (1 Peter 2:24). The job won't be easy, but with strength, perseverance, love, and God's guidance, you will find yourself fully prepared to help your child grow into the amazing person God created them to be.

 ROBERT'S STORY

In the wee hours of one seemingly normal morning, my life was changed forever... my daughter was born. I remember the volcanic bursts of emotions more than the facts, but what I know is that nothing could've prepared me for such a moment.

My wife, Colleen, being the strong warrior that she is, chose to give birth naturally. My job as her partner in this journey was to be as knowledgeable about the process as possible. So I went to as many parenting classes and trainings as I could attend. I learned about feeding, bathing, and changing diapers. I learned about football holds, baby carriers, and the beauty of white noise. I read all the classic pregnancy books and convinced myself I knew exactly what to expect for my expecting wife.

Inside, however, I was terrified. How could anyone trust me with the life of another human being?

On the evening of April 19, while my wife and I enjoyed a warm chocolate brownie topped with vanilla ice cream and fudge, the inevitable began: contractions. Out came the stopwatch. "Tell me when it stops," I exclaimed, as if I was in control in any way. "I have to write down the duration times."

Back and forth we played this game as the contractions got steadily longer and closer together until, finally, we realized we really needed to go. I drove to the birthing center in record time, and an attendant promptly took us to our room. So far, everything was unfolding as planned for my wife.

As for me, however, I was quickly becoming an anxious mess. Worried thoughts flooded my head: Am I going to be good dad? What if my daughter doesn't like me? What if I'm a disappointment to her? Does she deserve better?

After a few hours of this foolish internal dialogue, the glorious moment came. With one final burst of determination, our firstborn daughter, Sophia, had arrived. And that's when everything finally changed for me.

When those tiny eyes squinted at the lights above me, I suddenly believed in love at first sight. There in my arms was a person I had met only a few seconds ago. And yet for reasons beyond my comprehension, I knew with absolute, unwavering certainty that I would willingly offer my life for her safety. I knew that no one would bring her harm as long as she remained in my hands. I knew she needed me and that I would always be there for her. She and I were simply meant to be.

At that same moment, a heavenly clarity came over me. I realized that this is how God sees us. When that divine appointment with His Spirit opens our eyes to His good news and we truly see our Father for the first time, we are in His hands—safe, innocent, and fully dependent on Him

I thought I had no idea how to be a father, but I failed to see that the best example of a Father had always been with me, training and developing me all along. God equipped me for fatherhood. He called me to this. The proof, for me, was found in Him, in the wee hours of one seemingly normal morning.

💬 DISCUSSION QUESTIONS

1   Why do you think the role of fatherhood is so important? How has God prepared you for such a task?

2   Describe the child or children you are a father, grandfather, mentor, or other father figure to. What do you need to do to be the best example for them to follow?

3   What aspects of fatherhood have helped or could help your personal growth? What areas could you improve on to become a better father?

4   Discuss what Psalm 127:3-5 reveals about how God views children and the role of fatherhood. How can you rely on His perfect example to better father your child?

Children are a gift from the LORD.
    They are a reward from him.
Children who are born to people when they are young
    are like arrows in the hands of a soldier.
Blessed are those
    who have many children.
They won't be put to shame
    when they go up against their enemies in court.

02

YOUR GREATEST WEAKNESS

I just spent a lot of time telling you how naturally fatherhood can come to a man, detailing all the ways God has already equipped you to be a great dad. While this is all true, however, it won't automatically make the difficulties go away. Being a dad takes a lot of hard work and intense effort, and some days you will feel like you just don't have the energy to rise to the challenge. And to make it even worse, you have a part of yourself working directly against you—your sin nature.

We all have something within us that pushes us toward doing what we want when we want, no matter how it may hurt us or the people we love. Even as fathers, we are constantly fighting between our own selfish desires and what we know is best for our children. As hard as it may be to admit, sometimes we're tempted to just shrug our shoulders, do what's easy, and move on.

This internal battle can be exhausting, and I'm sure we all wish it would just end. But let me tell you, as long as it's still raging within you, you're actually on the right track. Later on in this book, we'll talk more about the self-destructive nature of sin and how you can manage it and help your child manage theirs. In this chapter, I want to focus specifically on the impact your sin nature has on your fatherhood. The better you can understand and accept this internal struggle, the less control it will have over your ability to become exactly the father your child needs.

THE STRUGGLE

On a fundamental level, sin isn't all that complicated. Paul lays it out pretty simply in Romans 7:15-16: we don't always do what we want to do, and we often do what we hate to do. This tendency exists in all areas of our lives, but it can be especially intense when it comes to fatherhood. That's because, to be frank, our children can bring out the worst in us. They try our patience, exhaust us beyond repair, and often don't even know or care that they're doing it. In those moments, our first response isn't often to teach them self-control or emotional regulation. Instead, we're tempted to take the easy route, whether it's exploding in anger, numbing ourselves through addiction, or simply stuffing it all down.

However, the problem isn't that this sinful part of us exists—it's that we try to pretend it doesn't. We are all fairly adept at putting on social masks and acting like someone we aren't. We try to hide away the narcissistic, self-centered parts of ourselves to avoid judgment and negative consequences. We hope that if we can convince others that we're perfect and in control, we will become just that, and then we'll never have to worry about changing what we know deep down that we need to.

Other people aren't the only ones we try to fool. We also attempt to fool God by only including Him in the traditionally "spiritual" parts of our lives, like church or a monthly prayer meeting. In our daily tasks and challenges, the places we face our internal struggle the most, we often convince ourselves He can't see or won't know and attempt to handle it all on our own instead. We recognize on some level that with God actively involved in every area of our lives, we can't pretend our selfishness is acceptable. We know that one day He'll require us to change. And, well, we just don't want to have to deal with that.[1]

---

1   This concept is also essential to the topic of sexual integrity. You can find *All Man*, my book on sexuality for men, at liveupresources.com.

However, trying to simply ignore the struggle between your-self and your sin will eventually destroy you (James 1:14-15). You may be able to convince yourself for a little while that you can get away with indulging your sin nature occasionally or that it's not really hurting anyone. But as the saying goes, sin begets sin, and it always affects those you care for—including your child. They are watching and learning from your every move, which means that no matter how you instruct and direct them, it's what you do (or don't do) that will really teach them about life (James 1:22). Even when you don't indulge your sin nature in front of your child, they will still sense your inconsistent way of living. Over time, your un-checked sin nature will fuel theirs, creating a perfect storm. And if left unaddressed, that storm will eventually consume both of you.

So rather than trying to run from the struggle between who you are and who you want to be, you must engage with it directly. By actively participating in this battle, you affirm your deepest spiritual desire—to do fathering God's way. As you look at the parts of yourself that need to change, you will find yourself moving closer and closer to achieving that goal. After all, it's only in the recognition of how we're not living up to our potential that we can discover our mistakes, learn from them, and become the fathers and men God wants us to be.

A HUMAN SOLUTION

So far, I've focused on the struggle against our sin nature as it applies to our overall ability to father our children well. But if we aren't careful, it can also have an impact on how we directly treat our children. As fathers, we all have a natural desire for our chil-dren to do better than we ever could, not just with their goals and relationships but also with their sin nature. We know where we've faced the most temptation and where we've failed to resist it, and we have faith that if we teach our children well now, we can help them avoid those same pitfalls.

When we focus on God's standards and rely on His guidance, we can certainly achieve this goal. But when we're instead motivated by a desire to cover up the inadequacies or shame we feel about our own sinful behaviors, we can instill within our children something just as damaging—an unachievable sense of perfectionism.

God is the only truly perfect being in the universe, and though He wants us to strive to live up to that same standard, we all inevitably fall short simply because of our human nature (Matthew 5:48; Romans 3:23). Our children can also never achieve that level of perfection, and when we expect them to, we only set them up for failure. That's because we don't just give them an impossible standard to live up to. We also teach them to emphasize following the "law," or doing everything completely right, which limits their abilities in multiple ways. For one, it shifts their reliance off of God and onto their own willpower, which simply isn't enough. But even as they fail more and more, they will continue to push God away, convinced they can handle it but becoming increasingly less likely to ever accomplish anything.

Furthermore, perfectionism causes our children to doubt their own value. In trying to be perfect, they attempt to do more than is possible and then get angry at themselves when they fail, which inevitably leads to shame. Shame is actually a form of pride where we're so focused on our own worth (or lack of it) that we see ourselves as beyond God's help and incapable of redemption. With such a negative self-focus, it's no wonder these children fail. They've blocked themselves off from the encouragement and love they need to make positive changes in their lives.

Needless to say, a child who is pushed to strive for perfection often winds up being anything but perfect. But instead of accepting their natural imperfections and helping them work through their failures, we often end up attempting to control the uncontrollable. When our children follow their God-given direction to be independent, or when they choose to respond in sinful rebellion, we're meant to react with the grace and guidance God would give us in the same situation. But when our focus is on perfectionism, we often overlook our children's individual value and try to bend their will to ours or push them too far. Such dominance is not fatherhood—it's abuse. And that, from a manhood perspective, is weak.

Our children are reflections of us, but they are not an extension of us, which means we can't control their decision-making no matter how much we think it's for their own good. The goal of fatherhood is to help your child grow into the potential God gave them, but despite your best efforts, you ultimately can't make them be or do anything. You can't dictate their behaviors, interests, or beliefs. Your child gets to decide for themselves what they will or will not become.

However, that doesn't mean you're completely powerless. There's so much you *can* accomplish as a father, but it starts with ditching the idea that your child should be perfect. Fatherhood is a role of influence, which means your main approach should be guiding and teaching through actions, such as establishing consequences, communicating intentions, and affirming good decisions, all of which we'll talk about more later on in this book. And while such an approach may not always go smoothly, I can tell you one thing—it'll go a lot better than trying to make them perfect.

IMPERFECTLY PERFECT

Of course, our children aren't the only ones we can put pressure on to be perfect. As men, we all have a desire to appear unflappable, like we're on top of everything at all times. And the more aware we become of our sin nature, the stronger this desire grows, especially when it comes to our fatherhood. We desperately don't want to let our children down or fail them in any way, so we push ourselves to be the best fathers in the world—and beat ourselves up when we aren't.

Not only is it exhausting to attempt to meet such a high standard, but it's actually unnecessary. In the early 1950s, D. W. Winnicott, a pediatrician who extensively studied child development, came to a rather interesting conclusion on parenthood. He found that to help a child develop well, a parent doesn't have to be perfect. They just have to be good enough.[2]

Now, I know the phrase "good enough" isn't one we typically like to hear applied to ourselves. After all, it most often means someone isn't totally happy with a result but doesn't feel like trying anymore. But in terms of fatherhood, "good enough" emphasizes that you *are* trying. An action's outcome is somewhat dependent on the motivations behind it. So when you put yourself aside, allow God to work through you, and focus on just trying to get it right, your child will feel the full extent of your love. And sensing that support and value from their father is often, well, "good enough" to help them trust themselves to accomplish all God has in store for them.

The most important factor of succeeding at this "good enough" goal is simply to be present. Just look at how God fathers us. Due to His omnipresent spiritual state, He is always there for us. He's constantly cheering us toward all of our accomplishments and triumphs, and He's continually loving us by empowering, confronting, and guiding us through our daily lives.

Of course, we don't always recognize or accept His presence—but that doesn't mean He isn't there. Sometimes it's actually when we fight against Him that we can feel His presence the most. Going up against His will, struggling against His strength, and feeling temporarily abandoned by Him helps us come to the conclusion that God is in fact with us. Through moving away from Him and

---

2   D. W. Winnicott, *Home Is Where We Start From: Essays by a Psychoanalyst* (New York: W. W. Norton & Company, 1970).

seeking our own independence, we discover that He knows who we are and what's best for us, even when we don't. And when we finally come to that realization and turn back toward Him, instead of rejecting us for our wandering ways, He rejoices in our return (Luke 15:20-22).

As fathers, we should treat our children the same. Being unconditionally present is the best gift we could ever give them. When you're emotionally, mentally, physically, and relationally available for your child, you can become the steady, reliable resource they can rely on as they learn to navigate life. They'll know that no matter what, you will always have their back. As a result, they'll gain the confidence not just to take risks and try new things, but also to learn from failure and seek forgiveness when necessary.

When it comes to being present, consistency is key. You must learn to be present, like God is, during both the good *and* the bad times. When your child makes poor decisions or struggles with a challenge, don't use your moodiness, critical judgment, dominating personality, or controlling actions to get them to do what you think is right. Instead, drop the rope, avoid a power struggle, and respond in a way that reflects both God's and your love for them. That's the only way you can break down the human barriers that exist between you as a result of your sin nature. When you create a loving image of your presence deep within your child, they will know that they can always return to you for support no matter the circumstances.

However, learning to be present and love your child as God does doesn't mean you'll never screw up again. That's just the way life is. You will continually experience the struggle between giving in to your sin nature and being the father God created you to be, which is why you must learn to rely on Him at all times. True change is only possible when you seek out God. You need His influence in all areas of your life, which means turning your will over to Him regarding both your sinful struggle and your fatherhood.

When you do that, He will give you the guidance and empowerment not only to know what you should do in any situation but also to have the strength to follow through on it.

When you decide to be a father, your destiny is on your knees. Because of your sin nature, you will need to constantly seek forgiveness for your negative choices, ask for empowerment, and learn to start again. As long as you do that and always keep God involved, you will build a loving, trusting, and supportive relationship with your precious child. And you know what? That's good enough.

 ROBERT'S STORY

Besides my wonderful eldest daughter, Sophia, I have a younger, smaller princess who's just as dear to my heart—a tiny firecracker named Angelina, or Angie for short. People say all the time, "She looks just like you," and for the most part, it's true. She has eyes like me, facial expressions like me, and she also sins—like me.

Awhile back, I was upset over a missed flight. It was completely my fault, but I was furious. I found ways to blame my alarm for being too quiet, a thunderstorm for being too loud, and even my wife for not helping me go to bed early enough. Ridiculous, I know.

Later that evening, stuck in the airport until the next morning, I was on a video chat with my wife when a tsunami of toddler emotions swept across the room behind her. It appeared that Angie and her sister had been playing a game when she accidentally spilled her glass of water over Sophia's iPad. Rather than apologize, Angie immediately began to blame her sister for putting the glass on the table. She kept repeating, "It's not my fault! It's not my fault!"

I almost couldn't believe what I was seeing. The accident was clearly caused by Angie, and yet she was not interested in know-ing or accepting this truth, instead deflecting responsibility so she wouldn't have to face the guilt of being at fault. Strip away the devilishly cute face, the long hair, and the adorably tiny voice, and you'd be looking at me. In fact, it was so much like the ridiculous tantrum I had thrown just hours earlier that I could only imagine God looking down via His video chat the way I was with Angie, watching me regress to a four-year-old with a better vocabulary.

In that moment, I realized the true impact of my sin on my children. Whether Angie picked it up from my actions or inherited it through my genes, she had still gotten the behavior from me. And that meant I needed to wrestle harder with the impulses of my sin nature. More importantly, I needed to step up as a father and help my daughter learn to do the same

So I asked Angie to sit and listen to me as I told her about my attitude earlier. Using words she could understand, I told her that sin will always come easy to us. It's what we do next that makes all the difference. After a couple minutes of discussing and navigating through our emotions, Angie and I could both easily see the error of our ways. We prayed together to ask God to forgive us and help us manage our mistakes in better ways.

Looking back, I'm not sure who the teacher really was that day, but in the end it didn't matter. We both learned a valuable les-son, and we both grew. And that's what fatherhood is really about.

💬 DISCUSSION QUESTIONS

1   How have you experienced the struggle between who you are and who you want to be? How might deliberately engaging in that battle help you become a better father?

2   What role does perfectionism play in your life? How has it negatively impacted your ability to accomplish your goals? How can a mindset of being "good enough" help you keep a proper perspective on your expectations?

3   In what ways do you feel God's presence in your life? What are some of the benefits you receive from it? How can you give your child this same gift of being present for them?

4   Discuss what Psalm 139:7 says about God's presence. How does it relate to your own role as a father?

How can I get away from your Spirit?
    Where can I go to escape from you?

03

WINNING THE BATTLE

At this point, I wouldn't blame you if you were a little bummed out. I know I can't help getting slightly discouraged whenever I think about my sin nature. But as we discussed in the last chapter, just because your sin nature exists doesn't mean it has to take over your life. It all depends on how willing you are to engage in the battle against it—and how much you include God in that battle.

The reality is that your own willpower isn't enough to successfully manage this deep internal struggle. If you want to be able to fight off your negative impulses and instead behave according to God's standards, you must rely on Him to strengthen you. That begins by working on your own internal development, building up where you're already strong and cutting out what holds you back. And there's no better place to start than with your spirituality.

Spirituality is perhaps the most important element of our identity, and yet it's also the one we tend to misunderstand the most. Given that we each have separate and distinct physical, mental, emotional, and relational parts of ourselves, it's only logical that there'd be a "spirituality" category too, right? However, because of God's all-knowing power and omnipotence, *everything* you are and do is within the realm of spirituality. And that means that your spirituality should be present in every area of your identity—including your fatherhood.

When it comes down to it, your ability to succeed in your

struggle with sin, or even to put into action any of the practical requirements of fatherhood, all depends solely on the strength of your spiritual foundation. Just as you were made for fatherhood, you were made for an intimate, transparent, moment-by-moment relationship with God. And to have any hope of handling the many trials you'll face on your journey through life as a father, you'll have to rely on Him much more than ever before. In this chapter, we'll discuss the importance of God's presence and how tuning in to it can help you take on His characteristics in the everyday moments of life, drawing you closer to Him and, in turn, closer to becoming the father you're meant to be.

A SPIRITUAL FOUNDATION

If I had to guess, I'd say you probably take God for granted sometimes. Now, I'm not trying to cast judgment on you or your faith in Him. I'm guilty of this too, after all. I simply want to highlight the fact that as we work on our spirituality, we don't always fully appreciate just how much God cares for and does for us.

As we touched on in the last chapter, it's often easier to try to keep God out of the picture than invite Him into our lives. Our sin nature would rather have us be in charge so we can do as we please and ignore the implications of our negative behaviors. But even without our sin nature, we can still subconsciously leave God out of certain areas of our lives. It can be easy to fall into the pattern of thinking about God only when we're at church or talking to Him only when we say grace before dinner due to the obvious spiritual context. Such a mindset leads us to create a neat box to put God in that doesn't intertwine with the other areas of our daily lives. As a result, we begin to automatically ignore His presence in many of the areas we need Him the most.

However, whether you hide from God's presence or are simply unaware of it, the result is still the same. God designed us to be His whether or not we choose to take advantage of this special spiritual state. This means that if you're not inviting Him into every area of your life, you are actively rejecting Him. You're telling Him that you don't need Him. You're saying that your willpower is good enough.

But let me tell you a little secret—it's not. Anyone who works in the self-help field will tell you that willpower is definitely not enough to achieve what we want, and deep down we all know this. The law written on our hearts, described in Romans 2:15, points us toward what is right and godly even when we don't acknowledge it. It's only by recognizing that we are failing to live up to this law that we can finally understand the truth we've been avoiding—that to effectively manage our sin nature and combat our many challenges, we need a spiritual framework grounded in God's love, wisdom, and guidance. And that means we must fully relate to God.

Thankfully, all we need to do is accept His presence in every area of our lives. You can never truly keep anything from God, because God is everywhere. Even if you choose not to tell Him about something, He still knows what's in your heart (1 Kings 8:39). However, it doesn't change His love for you. Nothing you could ever feel, think, or do could prevent Him from wanting to be a part of every area of your life. That means the moment you decide to open your heart to Him, He will be there waiting with open arms.

Accepting the reality of God's presence will help you prepare for fatherhood in a number of ways, such as by teaching you how to be present for your child, as we discussed in the last chapter. Beyond that, God's presence can also show you how to stay in the present to fully experience life and its many blessings. God is with you right now, just as He is with your child, and He knows what they need from you in this very moment. When you focus on Him, He will help you release your worry about a largely uncontrollable future and stop defining your child based on their past successes or failures. Instead, you can celebrate who they are in the present

regardless of what has happened or what may happen, fully trusting in His plan for their future.

Above all, God's presence can help you develop into the man
you need to become in order to be a good father. Through your relationship with Him, He will teach you to filter your natural responses through His Word and experience His love, guidance, and
empowerment in your conversations with Him. In this process, He
will purify your character and actions and cleanse you of all your
sins (Leviticus 16:30). Then you can make the changes necessary
to avoid repeating the mistakes of your past and continue moving
forward, becoming an example to your child of how to follow God's
guidance in the process.

Part of why it's important to find out who you are through
God is because the better you know yourself, the better you can
help your child. By accepting the fact that God made you to be
amazing and wonderful, you can in turn understand the complexity of your child's development and learn to be open to really hearing what they need and expect from you. As you allow God to help
you take that step of growth and put aside your self-centered perspective, you will engage more fully as a cocreator with Him to help
your child become their very best (2 Peter 1:3-4). Even further, you
will begin to do something that will strengthen your fatherhood
tenfold—become more like Him.

BEING LIKE GOD

As part of my lifelong mission to help all men uncover their
God-given potential, I've built a film studio in Lebanon, Pennsylva-
nia, along with Robert Amaya, who is also the executive director of
LiveUp Resources.[1] Our first big project at the studio was to film a

---

1   LiveUp Resources creates programs for men, women, and youth to help them de-
     velop their full, God-given potential. For more information on these resourc-
     es, visit liveupresources.com. For more information on the film studio, email
     info@liveupresources.com.

sixteen-lesson video series on manhood, called *Identity*. As Robert and I planned out the general concepts and goals for the series, we wrestled with what direction God was calling us to go with it. We discussed many different spiritual topics, including one that made us both feel uncomfortable, threatened, and yet inspired at the same time—that God created us to be like Him.

Why was this mandate so intimidating? Well, because being like God doesn't just seem impossible. It's also very easy to misconstrue. There's a fine line between trying to be *like* God and trying to *be* God. Being like God isn't about trying to seize His power or elevate yourself above Him. It simply requires modeling your life after Jesus's and working to live up to His standards. In fact, the more you participate in meeting this challenge, the more you will recognize how much you *aren't* God and never will be. Such a realization will result in a natural humility that won't just make you a better man. It will also make you a gentler, more loving, and more forgiving father.

Unfortunately, our sin nature likes to get in the way of this mindset, convincing us instead to focus on ourselves and what we want to get or do. Like Adam and Eve, we can become discontent in our relationship with God and compelled to know what He knows (Genesis 3:5-7). As a result, we try to wrestle control from Him and make everything all about us. In our pride, we convince ourselves that we are outside of God's control and that we have no use for Him whatsoever.

There are multiple reasons why we try to resist being like God, many of which we've already touched on in both this chapter and the last. One of the biggest of these reasons is shame. When we slow down and think about what it really means to be like God, the reality can be overwhelming. It doesn't always feel natural or realistic to respond the way He wants us to. But instead of trying anyway, we convince ourselves we're just not good enough. We use our sense of shame as an excuse, claiming that we're so worthless there's no point in even bothering to try.

Another reason we avoid being like God is that doing so causes us to become accountable for actions we don't actually want to change (James 3:1). Trust me, I get it. Just acknowledging that God wanted and expected me to write this book made my life a lot harder. It's definitely much easier to ignore or dumb down what God expects of us. Then we can get away with doing what He wants only when it's aligned with our own selfish desires.

However, no matter the excuses you make or how inadequate you feel, you're already more than good enough in God's eyes. As a result of Jesus's sacrifice, God sees us as perfectly able to meet His standard of holiness (2 Corinthians 5:21). After all, He created us in His image to bring glory to Him (Genesis 1:27; Isaiah 43:7). And He will be there every step of the way to help you achieve that high standard regardless of your failures or shortcomings. You just need to accept His constant presence and power. Through His instantaneous forgiveness, He will help you break down your narcissism and your shame, build up your confidence, and begin the process of living a godlier life.

Once you commit to being like God, He will step in to help you develop strengths in every area of your life, including in fatherhood. You won't have to rely on your own willpower or wisdom to know how to guide your child. Instead, you'll continually ask yourself how God would respond in certain situations and then seek His help to do just that. As long you involve Him, even when you're confused or unsure of the best course of action, your child will experience God through your responses. And that's ultimately what matters most.

CLOSER TO GOD

I'm sure this will shock you, but being like God and guiding your child like He would are only possible through first being close to Him. This begins by answering His question: "Do you accept what my Son, Jesus, has done for you on the cross?" Your response will determine whether you're willing to give up control as Jesus did to follow God's plan for your life. Once you demonstrate that you are, you can give up trying to be God for the nobler quest of being like Him.

Of course, answering that question is only the first step. Just like fatherhood itself, being like God is an ongoing process that will look different for everyone and will never be truly complete. Throughout your life, you will need to continually engage in the following key processes that will help you grow closer to God. Only then can you truly commit to accomplishing such a supernatural feat.

1   Accept God's presence.

As I've indicated throughout this chapter, the main reason you can become like God is because He is constantly showing you how to do so. When you accept His presence, the pressure of perfection is lifted off your shoulders, helping you take your mind off yourself and instead focus on letting God infiltrate every aspect of your life. You must become fully attuned to the Holy Spirit working within you and strengthening your identity. When you do, you will learn to express the fruit of the Spirit to your child in the same way God would.

2   Read God's Word.

Although God is present at all times, it isn't always easy to know what He's trying to teach you. Regularly reading His Word allows you to grow in your ability to recognize and understand His messages. It also makes it easier to internalize His standards, which in turn provides the structure necessary for you to apply those standards to every choice you make as a father.

3   Follow Jesus's example.

Not only did God create you to be His representative on this earth, but He also shows you how to succeed in doing so through the example of His Son, Jesus. Just as Jesus responded to His Father's presence and will for His life, you must do the same. The more you read about Christ's life in the Bible and walk daily with Him, the more you will begin to take on His characteristics and continue becoming who God created you to be.

4   Label what's going on within you.

In Genesis 2:19, God instructed Adam to give names to his surroundings, and He expects the same of us. When you learn to accurately label what's going on both outside and inside of you, you will gain the ability to include God in your daily experiences. And the better you can talk to God about these issues, the more He can guide you in managing them. This process is especially important in parenting, where you have to understand not only your own emotions, ideas, and processes but also your child's. By strengthening your ability to label them, it will become easier to react in godly ways.

5   Go outside your comfort zone.

While God does follow certain spiritual patterns, He also isn't afraid to move in unexpected, spontaneous, and miraculous ways. In the same way, you must always be willing to adjust your responses based on your circumstances, your child's needs, and God's plans for both them and you. There are some benefits to routine, but not if you're doing it because you'd rather remain in your comfort zone. You can't always do what's easy or what you want. Instead, you must learn to live by faith and not by sight (2 Corinthians 5:7 NIV).

It's not easy to give up the desire to be God. But when we cling to a false sense of control, we ignore the resources God has given us through the example of His Son's life on earth, the inspired Word of the Bible, and the Holy Spirit living within us. If you truly want to be who God created you to be, you must learn to seek His assistance and commit to being like Him in every area of your life. When you do that, you'll find that success in fatherhood will follow.

 ROBERT'S STORY

Here's a secret I rarely share: I'm terrible at accents. I mean, embarrassingly terrible. To hear me speak in an accent is to subject yourself to strange, contorted noises that barely sound like words. To the world at large, that's not a concern. But to me, as a professional actor, it can be a big problem.

In 2010, I was offered my first contract for the movie *Courageous*, for which I was to play a Latino immigrant husband and father... with an accent. Have I mentioned my problem with accents yet?

I still remember the anxiety and cold sweat of internal despair I experienced. I felt so much pressure to perform this role correctly that I convinced myself I would get fired on day one. That's when my dad said the perfect words at the perfect time: "Hijo, Dios está en control." Son, God is in control.

While the message of his words was powerful, it was the *sound* of those words that really comforted me. See, my dad is a Latino immigrant from Central America. Like many others, He came to this country to make a better life for himself and to grow a family. He knew he could accomplish this goal by learning the language and working hard. Thankfully, my dad never lost that work ethic, and though he did learn English well, he also never lost his beautifully thick accent.

The moment he spoke to comfort me, just like he had done so many times before, he brought unexpected hope to my seemingly impossible dilemma. I asked my dad to read a few lines from my script out loud. When he did, it felt like a grand piano had been lifted off of my back. All the pressure I had felt immediately disappeared. And why? His accent was *perfect*.

Over the course of a few days, my dad read all my lines to me as I took phonetic notes. Day and night I spent time with him, paying close attention to every word and phrase. It was a strange feeling. I had grown up with my dad, but I had never spent so much time deliberately attempting to be more like him. The more hours I spent with him, the more I began to mimic not only his accent, but also his style and mannerisms. Eventually, I didn't just perform my role—I lived it internally as my father. I embodied every action as if I were him.

The thing is, I would have never been able to sound like a Latino father unless I spent time with one. Just hanging out with my dad helped me accomplish something I thought I was incapable of doing.

That's how it works with our heavenly Father too. The more time we spend with Him, listening to Him and watching Him at work, the more we end up being like Him. It doesn't require special skills, merely interest and focus. Imagine what we could accomplish if we just hung out with God! Imagine the ways He could influence our behaviors and our choices!

Ultimately, I dedicated my role in *Courageous* to my dad as thanks for all of his help and influence. Maybe if we'd spend more time with God, we'd find it easier to dedicate our lives to Him for the same reasons.

💬 DISCUSSION QUESTIONS

1   When and where did you make a commitment to God through Christ? If you haven't, is this a decision you're ready to make today?[2] How much do you include God in your life? In which areas are you currently ignoring His presence?

2   Write down some of the goals you have for your child's development in each of the following categories. How can your relationship with God help you and your child achieve them?

Physical: _____

_____

Mental: _____

_____

Emotional: _____

_____

Relational: _____

_____

3   How do you respond to God's call to be like Him? Does it make you feel uncomfortable? Why or why not? What are some steps you can take today to become more like Him?

---

2   We'd love to hear about your faith walk. Email us at info@liveupresources.com to share your experience.

4   Discuss what 2 Peter 1:3-4 says about the purpose God has for each and every one of us. How can this passage motivate you to father your child as God would?

God's power has given us everything we need to lead a godly life. All of this has come to us because we know the God who chose us. He chose us because of his own glory and goodness. He has also given us his very great and valuable promises. He did it so you could share in his nature. You can share in it because you've escaped from the evil in the world. This evil is caused by sinful desires.

04

THE ULTIMATE FATHER

In the last chapter, I gave you an important assignment—try to be more like God. It's not an easy task, but it's certainly a doable one, as long as you tune in to His presence. As you spend time with Him, you'll see how He fathers you and how you can father your own child like He would. The spiritual framework of God's presence will combine with His efforts to make you like Him, creating an important spiritual foundation you can then build on and use to adapt to any challenge you face in your fatherhood.

In other words, it's your awareness of and response to God's leadership that defines the type of father you will be, which brings us to a question—*how* does God guide us as our Father? It isn't a secret. God isn't trying to hide from us. But in the busyness of life, we can lose sight of the specific leadership principles that characterize who He is, which means we must be deliberate about examining the example He sets for us in our own fatherhood. The more you recognize and live by these principles, the better you can understand how to become more like God, and the more equipped you'll be to achieve that goal.

GOD THE FATHER

Before we unpack the various aspects of God's fatherhood, it's important to first consider why we define God as our Father. A big reason, of course, is that Jesus called Him "Father" repeatedly during His time on earth. But Jesus also claimed that He and God are one and the same, which is definitely not possible the way we think of a father-son relationship (John 10:30). So if Jesus is actually God Himself, why did He refer to God as His Father?

Well, I believe He did it as a gift to us, to help us connect with God more easily. If you've ever been in a position of authority, then you've seen how people can struggle to relax and be themselves with someone who has command over them. They simply find that person's status and power too intimidating. They know that with a single decision, that person could alter their day or even their entire lives.

Given that we can feel this way about our bosses, it's no surprise that many find the God of the universe to be absolutely terrifying. The power of His presence can be awesome and intense. When God shows up, bushes burn, the earth shakes, and shoes come off (Exodus 3:1-5; 1 Kings 19:11-13). That's enough to make anyone feel like this loving resource is simply inaccessible.

And that's why I think Jesus called God His Father. Everyone innately knows what a father is and does, or at least what a father should be and do. For those whose fathers were positive authority figures who loved them, thinking of God as a Father makes Him seem very approachable. And for those who *didn't* have great fathers, imagining God as their Father provides hope that they can make up for all they've missed out on.

This is why your role as a father is so important. Because a child's mind is still developing, they often look for concrete explanations for the more abstract parts of life. They do this with everything from death to love to, yes, even God. I remember once driving up a deserted mountain on a four-wheeler holding my six-year-old daughter, Kim, on the seat in front of me. When we stopped at the top, I asked her what she thought God was like. She quickly replied, "That's easy, Dad. He's like Aslan from *The Chronicles of Narnia*."

Children will associate God will all kinds of images, whether it's Aslan, a king, or an old man in the sky. But the most common image they compare Him to is their father. If you ask a child to describe their father, hopefully they might say he's strong, smart, loves them a lot, and does all kinds of things with them. Then if you ask that child to describe God, they would use pretty much the same attributes they'd just used for their father.

Of course, this association isn't always quite so positive. I've had many clients in counseling over the years who had a negative experience with their fathers and, as a result, preferred that I didn't refer to God as our Father. Even though they longed deep down for the love God could give them, they found it too difficult to trust in it as a result of how badly their earthly father had failed them.

As your child's father, you are a physical frame of reference for them of how Jesus wants them to grow spiritually in all the different possible ways. This means that your actions can impact not only their ability to become the person God created them to be but also their very relationship with Him. It's your combination of loving support and firm authority that will prepare them to accept their need for greater guidance in their life.

Are you feeling the weighty responsibility that comes with being a father? It's hard to comprehend the full impact that you will have on your child, but it's important to recognize the power you have. Many people enter into parenthood almost with a shrug, as if they assume everything will work out fine in the end—and with that attitude, it often doesn't. You can't assume that your influence is going to be positive just because you trust in God. God wants to help you help your child. And that means you need to make sure you are continually making choices that leave them with a positive image they can rely on.

LEAD TO SERVE

In nearly forty years as a counselor, I have had countless married couples come into my office looking for help. And most of them had a similar problem—the husband had no idea what it meant to be a leader. They all knew Ephesians 5:22 (NIV), which says, "Wives, submit yourselves to your own husbands as you do to the Lord," and they all assumed it meant they were the head honcho, completely in control of their wives. They believed that their wives weren't allowed to have any voice in the relationship and were supposed to simply comply with whatever their husbands wanted. Unsurprisingly, these women turned out to be much less compliant than their husbands had hoped.

Usually when I had a couple like this in a counseling session, the husband would look at me expectantly, waiting for me to say there was something wrong with his wife, that she had to listen to him more and obey his every command. Instead, I would turn to the wife and ask, "Would you be okay with your husband leading you if he consistently put aside his needs in order to meet yours?"

"Yes," she'd reply without missing a beat.

"And as long as he did that, would it be okay if he sometimes disagreed with what you felt you needed, but only if he had a biblical reason to justify his stance?"

"Yes," she'd say again.

I have offered this deal to more women than I care to count, and not one has turned it down. That's because the scenario I lay out for these women is exactly how God wants us to lead as men. If you read further in Ephesians 5, you'll see that Paul also gives a command to men: "Husbands, love your wives. Love them just as Christ loved the church" (Ephesians 5:25). And how did Jesus love the church? The answer is right there in the rest of the verse: "He gave himself up for her."

Throughout His life on earth, Jesus consistently gave up His needs for the sake of serving others. He washed the feet of His disciples, removing His own outer clothing in order to do so (John 13:3-5). He spent time with those who needed Him most, even at the cost of His reputation (Matthew 9:9-13). And then He made the ultimate sacrifice—giving His life as the price for setting others free (Mark 10:45).

God continues to love us through this same type of servant-hood. He doesn't just want to be listened to and obeyed. He wants an honest, relational connection with us, which is why He's willing to meet us where we're at and repeatedly forgive us for the many offenses we commit against Him. It's why He actively pursues us when we reject Him and empowers us to succeed even though we're often ungrateful. His patience with us is unbelievable, but that just shows how much He cares. No matter what we do, no matter how far we drift from Him, He is always there, waiting and willing to serve us.

God wants us to love not just our wives but also our children in the same sacrificial way. While servant-leadership is important in a marriage, it is absolutely essential to a successful fatherhood. For much of their young life, your child simply isn't capable of taking care of themselves. They rely on you for everything, from food and shelter to love and comfort. And that means that no matter how tired, grumpy, or hungry you are, when your child is sad, hurt, or even just excited to share their passion, you must put your needs aside, get a bowl of water, and start washing some feet.

GODLY LEADERSHIP

One of the biggest ways God expresses His love within us is through exhibiting the fruit of the Spirit—love, joy, peace, patience, kindness, goodness, faithfulness, gentleness, and self-control—all of which are actions that directly benefit others (Galatians 5:22-23).

And if we're willing, He gives us the same ability to serve. When you let the omnipotent, all-powerful, and awesome God lead the way, you will embody the following godly characteristics, allowing you to father your child just like He would.

1   Be relational.

As our leader, God is more concerned with our relationships than with what we accomplish with Him. While He does want to help us do what's right, He's mainly interested in being with us and being included in our experiences. When we talk with Him, the actual content of the conversation matters less than the fact that we're taking the time to get to know Him. As long as we relate to others and to God, all of the good actions and behaviors He wants us to exhibit will naturally fall into place.

In this same way, you must focus more on the relational aspect of fathering when engaging with your child. When they help you with a project around the house, or when you work with them on their homework, the success of the interaction isn't determined by how much you accomplished. What matters is that you spent time with your child, helped them develop new strengths, and grew closer as a result.

Besides focusing on your relationship with your child, following God's lead also requires learning to accept the numerous conflicts that will arise when your child's choices don't align with what you want for them. Because both of you feel like you're right in these moments, your emotions can become heightened, making it easy to fall into the trap of what therapists call transference and countertransference. This is when either party redirects their unprocessed feelings about a situation onto the other person, which distorts their view of who the other really is. Your child may do this by transferring their anger about an experience onto you or by blaming you for what happened. And you may respond just as unproductively by offering unwarranted advice or making the conversation about you instead of about your child's feelings.

If not resolved properly, transference can create relational barriers between you and your child that can limit your relationship in the long run—especially when you transfer your own feelings back onto them. This only makes you less present for them. When they are making negative choices, there's often a deeper issue influencing them, which you won't be able to recognize if you get caught up in the conflict. You may be able to win that momentary battle through domination, but in the process you lose the ability to help your child through the war of whatever's lurking underneath.

A father is more prone to react to his child negatively when his own identity is incomplete, because it's more likely that his worth will be tied up in the choices his child makes. When you see your child as an extension of yourself, you lose sight of their individuality and instead attempt to push them down the path you choose for them. Your inability to control them in this way will cause you to feel anxious when they make different decisions. And in your panic, you may end up pushing them even further away.

This is one of the many reasons why personal growth is so important to fatherhood. God knows who He is, and He isn't intimidated by the ways we're different from Him. In fact, He created us with the ability to choose our own path (Matthew 7:13). To fulfill God's desire for you to become like Him, you must strengthen your identity so you can become more secure in who you are. When that happens, you can accept your child's differences, adopt God's relational emphasis, and focus on being an ever-present, consistent resource for your child, just as God is for you.

2   Be involved.

As God builds up your identity in Him, you will become more and more equipped to help your child build their own identity that will empower them to thrive, adapt, contribute, and love well. But your efforts shouldn't stop with ensuring your personal growth. To have the fullest impact on your child, you must also live life with them just as God does with you—by being there to provide support and love in every way.

This is often easy to do during the biggest and best experiences of your child's life, but those aren't the ones that matter most. It's in the seemingly insignificant events and in their struggles where you will truly apply God's loving presence. Your child needs to know that you want to be with them through *everything*, not just the happy times. When you prove that you're willing to get down and dirty in the rough and uncomfortable parts of life, you will become a place of refuge for your child. And then when life beats them up, they'll know you'll be there to help them recover and prepare for their next step.

The main goal of fatherhood is to help your child grow and develop into fulfilling God's design for them, but you can only do that when you're active in their life. It's when you consistently apply God's truth to your relationship that your child will grow beyond your wildest dreams. They will learn to be self-aware and to listen when life points out that their narcissistic belief in themselves is false and that they do need to improve. In turn, they will figure out how to apply who they are to the situation at hand and discover what they are yet unprepared for. With your guiding hand, your child will blossom physically, emotionally, mentally, and relationally, becoming more and more confident in their ability to successfully meet any challenge life sends their way.

3   Set standards.

As important as it is to be involved in your child's life, it isn't enough simply to be present. You must also be *active*, which means not just engaging with your child but also setting standards, confronting them when necessary, and enforcing consequences. After all, God does this with us. In the Bible, He shares clear standards regarding what He expects from us, along with His expectations for how we should both internalize and follow through on them.

Of course, we don't always follow those standards, and when that happens, we must face God's confrontation. Sometimes He does this directly, as in the story of Jonah and the fish (Jonah 1:1-17). Jesus also engaged in direct confrontation, clearly calling out those who were doing wrong and warning them of the consequences (Matthew 23:29-33). He even made a whip and confronted evil and spiritual immaturity when it presented itself (John 2:13-16).

However, God's primary style of confrontation is to allow the consequences of our choices to be fully experienced. Life often adheres to cause-and-effect principles. If you don't work, you won't eat. If you don't try, you'll never succeed. If you treat others poorly, people won't support you. There's always a link of some kind between our actions and our present circumstances. So if life is going well for you, it's likely because you've made some good choices that led to your success. And if you're miserable, your past actions probably played some role in it, either directly or indirectly. When that happens, God won't step in and fix everything for you. Instead, He'll let you experience the consequences as a way to help you learn from your mistakes and know how to do better the next time.

Just as God does with you, you must clearly state to your child your standards for them. They won't always be happy with those standards, which isn't surprising given that we don't always want to follow God's standards either. But no matter how much your child whines or complains, you can't give in just to make them happy. You want to give them a good life, but that doesn't mean always trying to please them. Most of the time, it means helping them learn how to build that good life for themselves. And that requires teaching them to accept and follow a standard of right and wrong that is not solely dependent on what they feel in the moment.

If you want your child to follow your standards for them,

there must be consequences when they don't. Since these standards should reflect God's, those consequences will typically come naturally, and like God, you simply need to allow your child to experience them. Sometimes, though, you will have to add further consequences to ensure they understand the importance of the standards you set. Keep in mind that these consequences are not necessarily about punishing your child. If your focus is on punishment alone, it's less likely that they will take in the lesson or feel your motivation of love. No matter the consequence, always be sure to explain the purpose of it and, if necessary, guide them through processing their mistake to ensure they learn from it.

Unfortunately, your child won't always like you for enforcing these consequences. In fact, you'll probably hear them scream at least once, "I hate you!" But like Jesus, you must not be intimidated by their response (Matthew 26:50-53). Their imperfections are not an excuse for you to meet them at a similarly immature level. Instead, show them love whether they want or like it. Then, as hard as it is, you can be like God by having the strength to allow life's many consequences to happen and help your child grow through them.

4   Respect their independence.

As involved as you must be with your child in the ways described above, you must also recognize and respect their independent nature. Like we do with God, every child struggles with wanting to be independent while actually being dependent. Even at a young age, children yearn to prove themselves despite not really being ready to, like when they insist on getting dressed without their parents' help or carrying their own cup to the table. And this only gets exacerbated as they grow up. Even as a teenager embraces dependence when it comes to using their parents' money or car, they still fight against every other restriction placed on them.

To know how to manage this struggle, as always, you need to look to God. As I noted in the last chapter, we all want more control over our lives, sometimes to the point of attempting to be our own God. But no matter how much we try to do things our own way, God is not threatened by our independence. In fact, He wants to help us deserve it. He is excited about us one day walking with Him through our garden, intimately and confidently relating to Him daily (Genesis 3:8).

That's why God lovingly empowers us to continually grow and develop ourselves. As you begin to regularly put into practice the holistic spiritual emphasis God is working to instill within you, you will grow in your overall development. God will then use this spiritual process of dependence to help you internalize the next standard and the next, until you reach spiritual maturity (John 13:34-35).

This doesn't mean you will no longer need God, because you always will. Rather, it means that you've reached a point in some areas of life where you've become so like God that how you feel and act is fully congruent with who He is. Then you can begin to hear from Him more easily about the choices He wants you to make, because how you think is founded on His identity in the first place (Ephesians 5:1-2).

In the same way, you should want your child to one day stand on their own two feet and experience life on their own. You should want to see them live in a way that shows you they understand and practice the basic messages you were trying to share with them. Ironically, though, this is actually the same reason why many fathers find themselves resisting their child's independence so much. While a father may freely give his child independence to complete certain responsibilities around the house, he may limit their independence when it comes to freedom outside of the home, either because he's unsure that they're fully prepared for what may happen, worried he won't be right beside them if they need help, or even afraid that they may succeed in an area that's different from his definition of them.

That's where trust comes in. One of the most important elements of any relationship is trust, and at some point, all parents need to trust that their children can handle life well. And the only way to build trust is to put in the work to help your child internalize the standards of behavior they need to navigate all of life's twists and turns. When those standards have become so ingrained within your child that to act differently would be to violate who they are, you can be confident they have fully taken in your perspective and made it their own. And when you can trust them to consistently make good decisions, well, their freedom won't seem quite so threatening.

KEEP IT SIMPLE

God knows that becoming like Him is not a once-and-done accomplishment. Life is simply too complex for it to be that easy. The reality is that we will never fully arrive, which can make it difficult to navigate our own complexity. And when you add the responsibility of helping your child develop their complexity while trying to relate to a challenging world, it's easy to feel completely overwhelmed and discouraged.

In order to manage the nuances of life, you need to establish a firm belief in something greater than yourself. It's our spiritual connection with God that helps us know when to meet our needs and when to put them aside to take care of others. With His loving guidance and supportive presence, we can both develop ourselves internally and know how to father our children well, no matter how complicated the world gets.

When confused by the unknown, all you need is to come back to this simple truth. It's easy to lose focus when you forget the underlying principles of God's reality. But keeping your gaze on who He is allows you to refuel and prepare for the difficulties ahead (Colossians 3:2). As you take on the challenging task of fatherhood, hold firm to the following foundational beliefs to help you keep a proper perspective on both God and your role as a father:

- Salvation is a gift from God, and our forgiveness is its result.

- God has given you the ability to have a relationship with Him.

- God celebrates your successes, comforts you when you fail, and confronts you when you act self-destructively.

- God empowers you to do what's hard, which helps you apply the truth of His Word to your decision-making.

- The existence of your sin nature causes you to need to examine yourself, ask for forgiveness, and praise God for His mercy.

- God is our Father, and you are the father figure in your child's life.

- God loves you, and you love your child.

- God created you to be a vital resource in your child's identity development.

- As God's representative in your child's life, you empower them to do what's right through your guidance, encouragement, and confrontation.

When you hold firm to these simple truths, you will be amazed by what you can accomplish during even your greatest challenges. God will fill you with the fruit of the Spirit, which you can then pass on to your child. You will love them unconditionally and exhibit joy about all they can become. You'll experience a peace that will provide a sense of stability for your child and a patience that will help you guide them through their mistakes. You'll reach out in kindness to understand and encourage them. You'll display goodness that serves as a positive example for them. You'll be faithful to your child no matter how much they may push you away, and you'll be gentle to them when they come to you in pain. Above all, you'll be able to control yourself so they know that they always come first. As long as you stay true to each of these characteristics, you'll lead your child to develop into all of who God created them to be.

 ROBERT'S STORY

We were just about to start a new episode. Last time, we saw Luke lose a hand, and the Empire was becoming stronger than ever. The familiar, glorious scent of warm chocolate chip cookies had taken over our home, and our anticipation for delicious gooeyness was in overdrive. My wife brought a plateful to the couch, and we settled into the cushions, eager and ready.

But before I could hit play, Angelina asked us to wait. Into the kitchen she ran. She opened the refrigerator door and reached for a nearly full carton of milk. The parental alarms inside Colleen and me immediately shot from zero to DEFCON 1. However, I grabbed her arm just before she could get up. I told her that spilled milk could be cleaned, but this was a big moment for our little five-year-old. She agreed, and we sat watching our daughter, ready to run in at a moment's notice.

Angelina definitely struggled. First it was picking up the heavy carton of milk and putting it on the counter. Then it was climbing onto the counter and grabbing a cup from the top cabinet. Finally, the moment came that had us all in anxious suspense—Angelina opened the carton and began to pour. To our relief, she didn't spill a drop (at least not any we could see from our seats). She closed the carton, put it back in the refrigerator, carefully picked up the cup, and walked into the family room.

That's when she did something completely unexpected. Instead of going back to her seat, Angelina walked straight toward me. She put the cup of milk down on my TV table and said, "This is for your cookies, Daddy!"

If my heart had tear ducts, I would have been drowning inside. I was so touched by my little girl's actions. Her desire to accomplish something new was ultimately meant to love me and make me proud. This showed me that I was doing my job as her father by representing God well to her. And if I continued to do so, she may also seek to please Him in the same way.

Sometimes God stands back and helps us develop ourselves by letting us take a risk or try something new. He is always there, ready to run in when we need Him. The key is motivation. Just like Angelina was motivated to face a challenge simply to please her dad, God gives us the freedom to find our own ways to be motivated to seek and please Him. And when we help our children gain the confidence to do the same, they'll be able to achieve anything, no matter what the future holds.

DISCUSSION QUESTIONS

1   Have you ever struggled to refer to God as your Father? What does God being the ultimate Father mean to you? How does it relate to your own fatherhood?

2   How do you express your servanthood within the home? How easy or difficult is it for you to sacrifice your needs in order to meet the needs of others?

3   Which of the characteristics of godly leadership do you already practice well, and which do you need to work on? What are some other ways God leads us? How are these leadership principles connected to your foundational beliefs?

4   Discuss what Proverbs 1:7-9 says about a father's role in his child's life. How does it relate to the concept of servant-leadership?

> *If you really want to gain knowledge, you must begin by having respect for the LORD.*
>   *But foolish people hate wisdom and instruction.*
> *My son, listen to your father's advice.*
>   *Don't turn away from your mother's teaching.*
> *What they teach you will be like a beautiful crown on your head.*
>   *It will be like a chain to decorate your neck.*

05

A GREAT RISK

Paul says it best in 1 Corinthians 13:2: "Suppose I can understand all the secret things of God and know everything about him. And suppose I have enough faith to move mountains. If I don't have love, I am nothing at all."

Let me put it this way. Suppose you tune in to God's presence and strive every day to be more like Him. Suppose you fully understand how He fathers you and leads you through service. And suppose you dedicate your full efforts to putting that knowledge into practice. All of this may make you a good dad in theory. But unless it's done with love, none of it really means anything.

Just as you strive to lead your child through serving them as God would, you must also must love them the same way He does—unconditionally, sacrificially, and without expectation. This type of love isn't easy, but it is possible as long as you stay continually connected to God's love. He will help you keep your motivations pure so your child can always trust that you have their best interests in mind. And He will help you keep your sin nature at bay so you can show your child that no matter what happens, you will be there for them. They won't have a perfect life as a result, but as long as they have a father who loves them, they'll feel empowered to take on the whole world.

WHAT IS LOVE?

Love is one of the most misunderstood words in the human language. We tend to think of it solely as an emotion, only existing somewhere deep within us. We believe that as long as our relationship is strong enough, or we're compatible enough, or the other person is agreeable enough, love will just... happen.

This mentality makes love seem pretty easy, doesn't it? After all, if love is something that's out of our hands, then it's not our responsibility to work hard at it. We can live "happily" ever after with the assumption that we're perfectly capable of loving well with no effort on our part. That attitude may work fine for a while—as long as your love is never tested. But I can guarantee you, it will be.

The truth is, love is much more than just a feeling. The flutter in your chest when you see your wife or the pride that surges through you when your child walks for the first time are *indications* of love, but they do not make up love itself. Real love is a choice to commit to another person. In other words, it *isn't* based on your feelings. After all, we don't always feel loving when it's inconvenient or when we think the other person doesn't deserve it. The decision to love them anyway is what defines the difference between a relationship that fades along with the initial wild passion and one that endures even through the arguments and conflict.

Just as love isn't a feeling, it also isn't a statement. Many people who say they love don't actually love in reality. In my years as a therapist, I've had dozens of men struggling with addiction tell me over and over again how much they loved their families. I had to look them in the eye and tell them that simply wasn't true. They might've *wanted* to love others, and they certainly seemed to want others to believe they loved them. But their history of abandoning their families and selfishly prioritizing their addictive behaviors demonstrated the opposite. Despite their claims, these men simply did not yet have the ability to follow through on their desire to love.

This isn't to say that telling your child you love them isn't important. It just shouldn't be the *only* way you convey your love to them. Once you make a verbal commitment to love, you must follow it up with consistent action (1 John 3:18). During their younger years, your child will give you the benefit of the doubt regarding your love, and at first your words will be enough. But if you don't consistently prove your love through your actions, they will begin to distrust it. As they mature, they will begin to sense the inconsistency between what you say and how you actually treat them. Over time, they will slowly pull away from you, dismissing any of your attempts at fathering because they feel they simply can't trust your motivations.

Knowing how to put love into action doesn't always feel intuitive, especially if your own father didn't demonstrate real love to you. But we've already covered two of the best ways to do it so far in this book—be present, and be active. You show your love when you leave work early to go to your child's science fair, or when you willingly spend hours of your evening helping them practice throwing a baseball. Love really isn't all that complicated. It doesn't matter if you're complimenting, soothing, comforting, helping, encouraging, collaborating, forgiving, or confronting. These are all acts of love—and they're ones your child can trust.

NO RISK, NO REWARD

Most people like the general idea of love. After all, with love comes consistent support, soothing comfort, and a mutual enjoyment of life, all of which sound pretty nice. More than any of that, though, we're drawn to the affirmation of love. While many of us try to change ourselves to get others to like us, deep down we yearn for the complete acceptance that comes with real love. We want to be valued for who we really are, imperfections and all, and not who we pretend to be (1 Samuel 16:17).

However, when it really comes down to it, many people are too afraid of love to ever build such an honest relationship. That's because love isn't a one-way street. If someone loves you, they expect love in return and, well, that's just way too risky. You can't touch someone on an emotion level without letting yourself be touched in return. And that means that the minute you lower those walls between you and another, the minute you let yourself be vulnerable, you make it that much more likely that you could be hurt.

Unfortunately, these fears aren't unfounded. Love does come with many potential costs, the most debilitating of which is rejection. No matter how valuable and important you treat someone, they may not reciprocate. Sometimes this rejection is blatant, like when someone outright ignores you or tells you they don't want a relationship with you. And while someone may not directly reject the relationship, they may still lie to you or behave inconsistently. In this way, they reject your value, implying that you aren't worth their authenticity and respect.

Even if another person doesn't reject you, loving others can still bring disappointment. When you choose to love someone, you want the best for them, which makes it painful to see them make negative choices that gradually pull them away from what you know they can be. But you can't determine what they become, and trying to do so often only drives them further away. It can feel easier to simply withdraw your love completely. If you don't care, it won't hurt when they go astray.

So yes, it's true. To love your child is to take a risk—but there's no reward if you always play it safe. When you open yourself up to your child, you will get back more than you ever thought possible. And that's true even if they *do* reject you or don't always do what you wish they would. That's because love is a connecting rope between two people, and the rope is still a rope even if both people aren't holding their end. If your child drops theirs, you can still be there holding yours, loving them no matter how far they walk away.

MAKE THE SACRIFICE

When Kim was five years old, she and I were sitting at the kitchen table when she started misbehaving. I told her to go to her bedroom for a ten-minute time-out so she could settle down. Unsurprisingly, she did not take that very well. Glaring at me with as much anger as she could muster, Kim told me defiantly, "If you make me go to my room, I will never be your friend."

The threat was meant to be cutting, but I couldn't help stifling a smile. I knew that in her fiery five-year-old way Kim wasn't really trying to insult me—she was testing my love for her. Her statement was actually a question. Could I love and value her for who she is, not what she could do for me? Could she rely on me to do what was right for her even when I got nothing but criticism in return? In other words, underneath the anger, she was trying to see if my love for her was dependent on her love for me.

So I looked at Kim and told her, "Kim, it makes me sad that you don't want to be my friend. I take your decision very seriously. But you know, the neat thing about friendship is that even when you choose not to be my friend, I can still choose to be yours. And I want you to know that I will *always* be your friend, no matter what. Now go to your room."

Kim stomped off to her room in a huff, but when she returned, our friendship was quickly reestablished. I had proven to her that my love was something she could trust. By wanting to still be her friend, I'd indicated that I *did* care about what she thought and felt about me. But at the same time, I wasn't going to let that get in the way of doing what was right for her. Because I took care to meet my own needs outside of our relationship and had a strong understanding of who I was, I could love her without strings attached. And that meant sacrificing my desire for her to be happy with me in a moment where fathering her was more important.

In other books I've written, I use this story to demonstrate how love is unconditional. It didn't matter what Kim did or what she said to me—I was going to love her no matter what. But this story is also an example of how love is sacrificial. Your child needs you to do right by them, which means giving them your full attention, effort, and prioritization regardless of the circumstances. Sometimes what you sacrifice in the process is your child's happiness with you, and other times it's your own serenity. Either way, you must continuously choose between two options—doing what feels good or easy, and doing what's right for your child.

The thing is, you can't love like this with a weak identity. The level of security and confidence you have in who you are is what will determine how well you can put your love into action. If there are any lapses in your maturity, your ability to love will be lessened, and you'll be more likely to try to find your value in your child's return of that love (1 Corinthians 14:20). But as you become more secure in your identity, you will finally begin to love your child as God does—without expecting anything in return.

BOUNTIFUL RETURN

When a father chooses to love his child, he's choosing to enter into the unknown. You can never know for certain what the relationship will become or what the outcome of fatherhood will be. But when you choose to love sacrificially, you make it much more likely that the process itself will be filled with happiness, hope, and excitement, even in the low moments—and not just for your child. As the bond between you strengthens, the sacrifices you make will reap the gifts outlined below. These gifts will do more than just help you develop all of your capabilities. They'll also show you how to be an even better father and man along the way.

1   Reflection and feedback

We are all aware on some level of our weaknesses, but it's easy to shrug them off when they don't have obvious consequences. Fatherhood, however, shines a bright light on these deficits, and when they cause you to struggle to father well, you're forced to reflect on how you need to change. Your child also won't be shy about letting you know when they're upset with you. Although their feedback won't always be based on reality—such as when they just don't want a time-out—listening to their perspective will help you better understand the situation and recognize how to achieve a more positive outcome the next time (Proverbs 19:20).

2   Hope

Sometimes all the difficulties life brings can cause us to feel stuck or like our circumstances will never improve. Your child doesn't yet have that viewpoint, however, and their relentless joy will provide you with a sense of hope and inspiration. Seeing how they push themselves (and how they push you as a father) will show you that your present patterns don't have to limit you but can instead motivate you. Then you can once more reach for something extraordinary.

3   Timely escape

Because of the sin nature within each of us, we often overvalue ourselves or get caught up in our impulses. While this self-centeredness may feel good in the moment, it will eventually take its toll on you. Love, however, reminds you that everything isn't all about you. It shows you that giving is more important and rewarding than receiving. When you focus on loving your child, you will be more able to resist your ignorance, your narcissism, and your desire for self-comfort. Instead, you will find the pleasure you seek through the love you give, which is far more fulfilling and enduring than any-thing you could give to yourself.

4   Inspiration

Children are true gifts for a number of reasons, but es-pecially for the wonder they can create within us. It's inspir-ing to see your child learn to face their challenges and discover the world for the very first time. Sometimes that inspiration can motivate you to find new ways to adjust your own plans and increase the likelihood of your success, and sometimes it simply drives you to improve in your fathering. Either way, living life with your child is refreshing, and no matter the in-spiration, it can help breathe new life into you.

5   Appreciation

Part of putting love into action is demonstrating appre-ciation for others by letting them know the value you see in them and affirming what they add to your life. As a father, you will naturally do this for your child, and without expect-ing the same appreciation in return. But that doesn't mean your child won't give it to you in less direct ways. Whether they ask you for help in areas they know you excel in or sim-ply want to spend time with you, they will continually convey that they understand, celebrate, and rely on who you are. This recognition of how you make a difference in their life will in turn enhance your sense of meaning, allowing you to become more confident in your purpose and more dedicated to work-ing toward it.

6   God's guidance

Interacting with and relating to others is a primary way we hear God speak and learn to understand how He is work-ing in and through us. And it's no different with your child.

As you watch them develop, you will gain a new appreciation for how God works in their life and thus in your own. And as you father them, you will learn to be more accountable for your actions not only as a father but also as a man. God expects you to continue growing and improving, and by speaking through your child, He will show you how to do exactly that.

As you can see, loving others is good for us on several levels, and it doesn't stop with the short list above. When you choose to love others as God does, you will experience a sense of connection that helps you stay grounded in an often disconnected world. As your relationships grows, that connection will deepen and enhance your life in ways you never could've imagined. Life's meaning will become less mechanical and more personal. You can stop just surviving in a world full of chaos, destruction, and negativity. With a life filled with love, you can finally begin to really *live*.

 ROY'S STORY

For much of her young-adult life, my daughter didn't have what I would call the best choice in boyfriends. However, Jan and I both felt it would be counterproductive to complain or try to lecture her. So any time Kim introduced us to someone new, we did our best to treat him as part of the family. Our goal was to subtly help him become what God created him to be. At the very least, we wanted to show Kim through our actions the difference between our love for her and his. Let me tell you, we spent *a lot* of prayer time trying to figure out how to respond positively to some very... interesting young men.

After a particularly bad year with a boyfriend who seemed to be the worst of them all, I finally initiated a conversation with Kim about the issue. I told her that I loved her very, very much. In fact, I could love her better than any of the men she'd dated with both hands tied behind my back. That was why she could take riskier choices with her love life—because she knew I was there for her to depend on if she needed to. But I wouldn't always be able to be present for her like this. She needed to find a man who was "in the zone," which was a label I came up with to describe the kind of guy who could love Kim better than I could, support her for life, and help her develop the kind of future she was dreaming of.

Shortly after our talk, she found a nice guy while going to grad school in Texas. After meeting him at her graduation, I quietly pulled her to the side and said, "He may not be the one, but I'm telling you, he's in the zone."

Well, that "nice guy" turned into a nice husband, and then a nice father. And let me tell you, I'm so glad that Texan has become a permanent part of my life. I can see that he loves Kim in all the ways she needs and all the ways she deserves, even if it means challenging her at times. And I know that it was all possible because of the way God as our Father loved us first. Thanks to His empowerment, I was able to love Kim exactly as He does—unconditionally, sacrificially, and with every ounce of my being.

💬 DISCUSSION QUESTIONS

1   How do you define love? What are some ways you demonstrate love to the most important people in your life? How can you love them better?

2   What are some risks associated with loving your child? How can you learn to love them sacrificially anyway?

3   Pick two of the gifts you've received from your child and describe how those gifts have made a difference in your life.

4   Discuss what lessons Luke 15:18-20 teaches about sacrificial fathering. What are some similar ways you can demonstrate love for your child?

> *"I will get up and go back to my father. I will say to him, 'Father, I have sinned against heaven. And I have sinned against you. I am no longer fit to be called your son. Make me like one of your hired servants.'" So he got up and went to his father.*
>
> *While the son was still a long way off, his father saw him. He was filled with tender love for his son. He ran to him. He threw his arms around him and kissed him.*

06

WHAT TYPE ARE YOU?

As we discussed in the last chapter, there's a difference between saying you love your child and actually putting in the work to truly love them. Love requires action and commitment, which to some fathers can seem pretty easy. They say to themselves, "I've already got this. I go to work so my child can eat, I provide them with a house to keep them safe and warm, and I make sure nothing bad happens to them." However, while physical care is necessary and good, it's also not the full picture—to love your child well, you must equally provide for them emotionally.

From the beginning, your child has an instinctual desire to attach to you. No matter how much you give them or protect them, what they will care about most is the intimate connection you create together. When they grow up and think back on your time together, they won't recall many of the specifics of what you did, said, or provided for them. What they'll vividly remember is how safe they felt in your arms, how much fun you were to be around, and how good you made them feel. If you want to create such enduring memories for your own child, you must find a way to connect with them. And that starts by establishing a secure, loving, and emotional attachment with them.

IN THE BEGINNING

When a child is born, their immediate experience is a world of chaos. The womb they lived in for the first nine months of their life was tranquil and comforting, and the environment they emerge into is loud, unfamiliar, and confusing. They are so lost and undeveloped that they can't even tell the difference between you and themselves, unable to realize that the hand feeding them isn't their own.

However, it doesn't take long for them to get used to their new environment, and pretty soon they begin to understand some of how it works, if only subconsciously. They learn that others are different from them and that they have to depend on these people to meet their needs. As their bonding instincts kick in, they begin making an effort to be interesting and respond pleasantly to their caregivers as a means of ensuring their own survival. And when their needs aren't fulfilled, they make loud, rigorous demands in order to get what they want.

Even as infants, however, children need much more than just food, shelter, and sleep. In the 1940s, psychoanalyst and physician René Spitz observed the first year of life of two groups of babies—one raised in a penal institution, and one raised in a foundling home for babies who'd been abandoned.[1] For some reason, more than a third of the babies in the foundling home had died by the end of the year, and the ones who did survive were scrawny and had developmental issues. In comparison, the babies in the penal institution not only did not die but were also stronger both physically and mentally.

The confusing thing was, there were no major differences between the two institutions in regard to medical care, housing conditions, or the quality of the clothing and food. So what was the

---

1   René A. Spitz, "Hospitalism: An Inquiry into the Genesis of Psychiatric Conditions in Early Childhood," *Psychoanalytic Study of the Child* 1 (1945) and 2 (1946).

problem? Well, in the foundling home, there were only six nurses in charge of the forty-five babies in their care, which meant that those babies lacked human contact for most of the day. But the babies in the penal institution were under the full-time care of their own mothers. In other words, they were raised with the love and attention of a devoted parent.

As Spitz's study suggests, your child can only truly thrive when they can depend on you emotionally. God called you to be a father, and with that role comes the responsibility of working with Him to provide a relational environment that encourages your child to grow. That begins by simply spending time with them, even when they're too young to really know who you are. The affirmation, appreciation, and interest you demonstrate will show them that there is at least one person in their corner. That feeling of support will empower them as they sort through their various impulses, biological processes, emotional responses, physical awareness, and complex thoughts and attempt to organize it all into a solid identity. It won't even feel too scary or overwhelming to them, because through your connection they learn not only how to do it but also that it's possible.

Besides enhancing the development of your child, building an intimate attachment early in your relationship will also make fathering your child later in life much easier and more effective. This is true whether you're a biological father who witnessed your child's very first breath or an adoptive father or stepfather who met your child when they were already well on their way to independence. The more trust you build early on, the more influence you will have in the future. When you've already proven that they can rely on you, they'll be more willing to listen to you during new experiences and challenges, from learning to drive to folding their own laundry. Even if they don't always like your guidance, they'll know you've got their back.

A HEALTHY ATTACHMENT

To start building into your child emotionally, you must begin with your relationship as a whole by making sure it's founded on a strong and healthy attachment. However, such a task won't be easy, because you aren't starting with a blank slate. Most people tend to follow a single attachment style in all of their relationships, a style that they likely developed at a young age. We internalize the idea that how our parents related to us is how we're supposed to relate to everyone—including our children.

This concept is especially important to understand if you're fathering an older child, because you won't be the only one in the relationship who's been impacted by early attachments. Whether they learned it from you or from previous father figures, by a relatively young age your child will have already formed a specific style of attachment. And depending on what that style is, it can put even further limitations on your attachment with them.

As I've already mentioned, however, you can't change your child. You can only change yourself. As their father, you are in charge of deciding what type of bond you want to form with them. That means you must evaluate your current and past relationships to determine your attachment style (Lamentations 3:40). Then you can know which changes you need to make to become fully present and engaged in your fatherhood. And through these changes, you will also encourage your child to change their attachment style. As you demonstrate your willingness to love them openly and honestly, over time they will learn to trust you and open up at an emotional level, strengthening your relationship into what it needs to be.

There are four main attachment styles we can adopt, three of which are unhealthy and limit our relational development. Though I explain them primarily from the father's point of view, many of these characteristics show up in children in similar ways.

Understanding how to recognize these characteristics will help you identify them both in yourself and in your child, allowing you to make adjustments in your emotional connection and create a stronger, more impactful bond.

1   Anxious attachment

A man with an anxious attachment style has little faith in any relationship he forms. Instead of developing trust in the other person, he obsessively questions their commitment. In his fear of losing them, he attempts to control them by violating their boundaries and personal space, only making it more likely that he *will* lose them in the end.

For a father, this may mean setting dominating rules for his child and always trying to dictate their choices and actions. He may force physical affection on them as a way to prove his love, even if the child rejects it, or he may struggle to let them go anywhere without him. The insecurities of an anxious father make him feel that if he isn't continually active in the relationship, it will fall apart. Not only does this limit his child's individuality, but it also restricts his own need to risk and pursue personal goals, because his mind is always on his child.

2   Avoidant attachment

This attachment style is similar to an anxious attachment in that it is founded on a sense of distrust. However, instead of trying to control the other person, an avoidant man puts as much distance between them as he can. He knows that the closer he gets to someone, the likelier he is to get hurt, so he does whatever he can to make sure he never has to be dependent in this way.

In fatherhood, this attachment style usually shows up in the emotional distance a father creates between himself and his child. Since he can't really avoid his child in his own home, he does what he can to keep their relationship shallow. He avoids spending quality time with them and having deeper discussions, especially about topics related to their relationship. Instead, he lets his wife do the hard work of providing for their child's emotional needs. But as a result of the father's extreme independence, his child will never receive the complete nurturing they need.

3   Disorganized attachment

A man with a disorganized attachment style exhibits behaviors similar to both the avoidant style and the anxious style. Although he wants to be close to others, he's also afraid of the vulnerability of such intimacy, and so he bounces back and forth emotionally between the two extremes. Such instability creates a volatile relationship between him and his child. His child never knows if he'll be playful with them or will ignore them completely. There is never enough balance for trust to form, which consequently causes the child to feel both afraid of their father and dependent on him, creating a constant sense of uncertainty and insecurity.

4   Secure attachment

In contrast to the other three attachment styles, a man who builds secure attachments isn't afraid of intimacy and willingly engages in his relationships at a deep, emotional level. He is confident in his identity and knows that while relationships benefit his life, they do not define his value, which allows him to love others, follow through on his promises, and always do what's right.

A father with a secure attachment style commits himself to fatherhood completely and doesn't back down from its challenges. He encourages honest and realistic communication between him and his child so that when there is a threat to the relationship, they can work together to minimize it before it strikes. He also never takes his child for granted and consistently demonstrates through words and actions his appreciation for them. He does whatever it takes to maintain the relationship, because he knows it's his fatherhood that will help his child achieve all God has in store for them.

CHOOSE YOUR STYLE

God created us to be social creatures, which means we can survive longer, accomplish more, and enjoy life better when we're around others (Hebrews 10:24). Not only do our interpersonal interactions serve to sharpen our mental, physical, and emotional capabilities, but they can also compensate for our shortcomings. In an area where you feel like you can't measure up, someone else will flourish, and together your separate gifts can enhance one another's lives in ways you could never hope to achieve on your own.

These same benefits are available to both you and your child, but only after you establish a secure emotional bond. The more emotionally connected you are with your child, the more you will be able to guide them toward God's will for their life. Your viewpoints, interactions, beliefs, guidance, responses, and ideas are effective resources for your child—but only when they feel secure and cared for. Effective fatherhood is only possible with such a bond. And that means you must make the continual commitment to minimize any emotional distance between you and your child.

Unfortunately, emotional bonding doesn't come naturally to most males. You may already be squirming in your chair at the thought of talking to your child about your feelings. As I've touched on in earlier chapters, we tend to shy away from emotional connection, preferring instead a life of isolation. It feels safer and more comfortable to form shallow relationships that never discuss serious issues. After all, the more superficial we keep things, the less likely we are to get hurt.

However, when you put emotional distance between you and your child, you don't just deprive yourself of the blessings that come with intimate relationships—you also hurt your child. They rely on you to show them how to develop themselves, navigate the world, and build a relationship with God (Psalm 78:5-7). When you choose not to lead them in this way, you turn their future over to chance. They're forced to find other resources to try to figure out what to do or who they're supposed to be, and they usually don't pick the best ones. And even when they do, they don't know how to connect with them, because they've learned an unhealthy attachment style from you that will limit their ability to form an intimate bond with anyone they meet.

The only way to ensure a better future for your child is to actively choose a secure relationship. The emotional attachment between a father and his child is a God-given gift they give to one another. When you embrace this gift and nurture it, you create an opportunity for both of you to encourage and challenge each other to be your best. Whether through constructive feedback or discussing new ideas, you can both discover ways to increase your knowledge and strengthen your identity. And in the process, you'll create the right environment for your child to develop the relationship skills that will help them continue to grow once they finally leave the nest.

As with any other fatherhood topic, building a secure attachment with your child begins with God. Through securely attaching to Him first, you can experience His relational healing, which will greatly increase your ability to connect with your child. But as we discussed in Chapter 3, the only way to create such an attachment with God is to turn everything over to Him. The good news is, He's already everywhere working to do His good will (Philippians 2:13). All you have to do is willingly and completely let Him in.

In addition to attaching to God, you must also put in the effort to form long-term relationships with other men, such as through a church men's group. A common problem I've seen in struggling marriages is that the husband relies on his wife to fulfill all of his relational needs, which creates an imbalanced dependence on her and unrealistic expectations that she can never achieve. And unfortunately, the same relational dependence can happen with fathers and their children.

Establishing strong, deep relationships with other men—and especially other fathers—will help prevent this issue for multiple reasons. For one, these men will fill some of the emotional needs you have so you don't subconsciously put them on your child. They will also give you an opportunity to develop relational skills you can then take home and practice with your child. Even better, they will give you a place to share not only your struggles and worries in fatherhood but also your triumphs. As a result, you'll receive advice, celebration, and support that will reenergize you to continue becoming an even better father.

As a father, you are creating an intellectual, emotional, and relational legacy for your child, which can feel like a huge responsibility for one man. But if you learn to practice good relationship skills consistently in all of your relationships, you'll find that a strong, secure attachment with your child comes naturally. And as that love and emotional bond deepens, together you will honor and glorify God exactly as He created you to do.

 ROY'S STORY

One of my biggest struggles as a father was trying to *do* for my daughter rather than just *be* with her. Now, I wasn't a totally absent father. I attended many of her events, certainly more than my father attended of mine (which was none). I took her on plenty of vacations. Once I even built a pond with her by our house. Though I did the heavy lifting, Kim helped me design, construct, and stock the pond, picking out all the fish, crayfish, freshwater clams, and bullfrogs she wanted to let loose in it. I'll never forget the sense of satisfaction we both felt as we sat by the pond watching it fill up with water.

However, in day-to-day life, I often failed to prioritize what really mattered. I became so focused on building my counseling company that I let the duty of nurturing Kim fall mostly on my wife. I'd make up excuses for not being around or would show up physically but let my mind or attention be on my work.

In her adulthood, Kim and I have had several cleansing conversations about the ways I failed her, and our relationship couldn't be any better now. But I'll always be astutely aware of what I missed, of how I didn't give her all she deserved.

I can't change the past, though. So instead I focus every day on trying to answer an important question: what am I going to do today that's more godlike than the day before?

DISCUSSION QUESTIONS

1   What kind of relationship do you want to have with your child? What do you need to do to create such a relationship? What might get in your way?

2   Which of the attachment styles applies most to how you form relationships? Which of your early relationships taught you to attach in this way? How easy or difficult is it for you to express yourself emotionally and be vulnerable with others?

3   What is your current attachment to God like? What can you do this week to strengthen that relationship? How will it in turn benefit your relationship with your child?

4   Discuss how Colossians 3:21 instructs fathers to relate to their children. How can you apply this guidance to your attachment with your own child?

Fathers, don't make your children bitter. If you do, they will lose hope.

07

EXPANDING THE DREAM

You've done a lot of work so far thinking about some tough aspects of fatherhood, and I have to say, I'm proud of you! You've learned to develop a strong and solid foundation you can build your fathering on, which means you're ready for the piece of fatherhood I may love the most—your vision for who your child will become.

Along with the uncertainty of becoming a father comes an amazing surge of excitement for what the future holds. For me, being a dad was something I've always wanted to do. Even as a young man I'd dream about taking my future son fishing or teaching my daughter to ride a bike. I actually had my daughter's name picked out long before I was even married.

But a father's vision is about so much more than what you wish for them. It's about what God designed them for and the plans He has in store for them. As their father, it's your duty not just to teach them all that you know but also to help them develop their unique God-given gifts. And your ability to do that is directly affected by how well you practice each aspect of fatherhood we've talked about so far—committing to your role, embracing your sinful struggle, accepting God's presence, following His example, opening yourself up to love, and building a secure emotional attachment. Now that you've laid that foundation, you're ready to take that step and delve deeper into the vision every father should have for his child.

THE VISION

Simply put, a father's vision for his child should be to see them develop into all of who God created them to be. This vision is built from the dreams, passion, and hope a father has for his child. It's what underlies all that he does for them and is the driving force behind his unconditional love.

What is less simple, however, are the individual steps required to move toward this vision. Understanding how each of the following steps relates to the vision of fatherhood will help keep your perspective congruent with God's, allowing Him to work through you to develop your child into all they can be.

1   Grow yourself first.

While every father's dream is to provide an even better life for his child than the one he had, doing so isn't always within our power. Ultimately, only God can bless our children further than we can take them ourselves. However, that doesn't mean we're completely powerless. When you put your faith in Him, He won't just enter into your child's life as He has in yours. He will also show you how to maximize the influence you *do* have to help them achieve His plan for them.

As you draw closer to God, He will work in you to strengthen your identity and develop your abilities, which will have two positive effects on your relationship with your child. For one, the stronger you become on the inside, the more equipped you will be to guide them through the hardships and challenges of life. But more importantly, the more assured you become in your identity, the more accepting you will be of the idea that your child may surpass you.

If we're honest, our natural competitiveness as males can actually make us jealous of our children's success. Sometimes we get so caught up in encouraging them toward our plan for their life that we forget God has something even greater in store. But when you find your true value in God, you won't feel threatened by their achievements, no matter how different they are from what you envisioned. After all, as their father, your child's success *is* your success—and their growth reflects the depths of yours.

2   Follow God's standards.

As you develop your relationship with God, your vision will naturally begin to align with His, and you will gain a better understanding of what exactly your child's successful future should look like. Our dreams often tend to focus on worldly success, defining it in terms of skill, money, popularity, status, or career achievement. But as God reminds us in the Bible, true success is measured by how well we honor Him (Romans 12:1).

Because God defines success differently than the world, your focus in fathering should also be different. Your goal should be to guide your child to achieve success by godly standards, which means that in fathering you must concentrate more on who they are meant to be than on what they will do. No matter what you do with your child, your focus should always be on making them strong on the inside so they can experience the fruit of the Spirit. When they are filled with love, joy, peace, patience, kindness, goodness, faithfulness, gentleness, and self-control, they will gain the spiritual maturity and confidence to act as Jesus would. And when you see your child fully free to be themselves as they serve others and live with honesty and integrity, you'll know you did your job as a father.

3   Trust the process.

While your initial dreams for your child may involve field trips, board games, laughing, or roughhousing, I'm sure you already know that's not really the full picture of fatherhood. It also involves conflicts, arguments, and disappointments, such as seeing your child get cut from the team or flunk out of college. Life isn't easy. It puts each of us through a forging process we'd all rather avoid. But as metal is heated to become stronger, we must experience all of the hardships, challenges, and discomfort of life that will strengthen us into who God created us to be.

Sometimes this process will make you feel like you're being smashed down in a grinder, especially when it involves seeing your child struggle. But that's part of God's plan. God intentionally lets us experience pain to remind us of His presence and show us how to be more like Him (2 Corinthians 1:3-4). It is these painful experiences that will bend your will to His, which will allow Him to shape both you and your child into His diamonds, cutting away the unhealthy parts of you to discover the beauty underneath.

You must also be an active part of your child's forging process by using your own internal strength to help them face the hardships of life (Proverbs 27:17). While discipline, support, encouragement, and guidance are all useful tools to achieve this, often the most effective way to help your child build such internal strength is through example. Children pay far more attention to what we do than what we say, and by observing our emotional responses, behavioral patterns, and relational skills, they will internalize how they should respond to life. This is the only way you can truly pass your vision onto your child. And as your strength becomes their strength, know that God will take them farther than you ever thought possible.

THE FEAR

One thing these three steps toward your vision have in common is that they all depend directly on what you do or don't do in your everyday life. The idea that you can influence your child this much without even realizing it can be a scary thought. Even something you say offhandedly or to someone else in the room can be accepted by your child with no questions asked. While this does mean you can teach them responsibility and integrity simply by doing your housework or treating their mom well, it also means they can internalize the sarcastic comments you make, the unhealthy relationship you form, and the ways you express (or don't express) your emotions.

In addition to being scary, the responsibilities that come with being a dad aren't always fun, especially when it comes to your need to let your child make their own decisions. Watching someone you care about struggle and experience pain is tough, and as a father, your first instinct is probably to try to fix everything. Sometimes this may cause you to rush your child through an experience that they should be processing slowly in order to internalize its lessons. Other times you may step in to solve an issue yourself instead of letting your child work through it. While this will momentarily stop their pain, it will also create a dependence on you, which will only increase their struggles in the future as they'll never learn how to handle them on their own.

Though the responsibilities that fall on your shoulders are heavy, the reality is that they're most likely not on your shoulders alone. Because this book focuses specifically on a father's relationship with his child, I haven't talked much about the fact that your child also has a mother who is building her own unique bond with them. Regardless of what your relationship with her is like, you can be united in your love and concern for your child, sharing the responsibility of working toward their future success. Together you can provide for your child both physically and emotionally and encourage them to grow. Creating such a mutually supportive force will allow you each to stay steadfast in always doing what's best for your child, no matter how difficult it may feel at times.

Of course, your child's mother isn't your only partner in fatherhood. Whenever you start to feel panicked and overwhelmed by the pressure of your need to grow, the difficulty of following godly standards, or the pain of the process, pause, take a deep breath, and reach out to God (1 Chronicles 16:11). As we discussed with the first step of a father's vision, God is the one ultimately in charge. He is always watching out for your child, even when you feel most unsure. As long as you constantly keep your faith in Him, you can know that no matter what happens, His vision will work out for your child's best.

THE DIFFERENCE

Putting a father's vision into three neat steps may make it seem pretty straightforward, but there's one fact of fatherhood that throws a giant wrench in the process—your child is different from you. When your child is young, it's easy to keep a proper perspective on the vision of fatherhood, because everything is possible at that point. You don't know enough about who they will become to be able to worry about what might hold them back. So as your baby grows into a child, you eagerly encourage their self-discovery, trying to figure out their interests, emotional development, thought processes, and basic temperament. Are they quick or slow to respond? Do they act boldly and confidently or with fear and reticence?

However, the more involved you are in their growth process, the quicker you'll become aware of all the ways they're different from you—and they won't always be differences you'll feel okay with. Suddenly the superstar athlete you dreamed of wants to play the violin instead, or your future Harvard graduate seems more interested in making pottery. These discoveries will force you to confront your own self-centeredness and make a significant choice. Will you adjust your vision in order to work with the interests and tendencies God gave your child? Or will you demand that they fulfill your expectations and follow your dreams for who they become?

Fathers who choose the second option may tell themselves they're acting in their child's best interest, but they're really acting in their own. They don't want to have to change their mindset, so instead they try to change their child. Other immature fathers simply choose not to answer the question at all and instead walk away in defeat, assuming that either they or the child will inevitably fail. But avoidance is not acceptance. No matter how much a father pretends, his child will sense his displeasure over their natural differences, leading them to suppress their gifts so as not to disappoint him.

Let me give you an example of how I approached this question. I've had to answer it many times on my own journey as a father, but there was one instance that was especially difficult for me. When Kim was in kindergarten, I discovered that she had a serious psychological problem—she loved cats.

I was devastated. I didn't want a cat running around my house! But despite my displeasure, I knew I needed to be like God, which meant making a sacrifice so she could experience her greatest wish. However, in my quest to see her happy, I made the mistake of not setting any ground rules. As a result, I had to call the cat the very unmacho name of Priscilla for the rest of its life. Worst of all, when Kim went to college, she left the cat behind!

Now, this was a relatively minor situation, but in regard to my relationship with Kim, it still played a vital role. Besides showing her that I valued her more than I disliked cats, fulfilling her wish gave me the opportunity to teach her an important lesson. I told her that there are differences between us, some of which are okay and can even be celebrated, like our differing opinion on cats. But when our differences lead to unhealthy, harmful choices, I was not going to tolerate it. That didn't mean I wasn't going to respect her independence or would love her any less, but I *would* step in and do what was right for her, because I loved her that much.

Accepting and appreciating your child's differences is a godly act, but that doesn't mean it's an easy one. When you find yourselves at odds with your child, even over a minor issue like the one I had with Kim, you must enter into a heart-to-heart conversation with God. God knew your child and made plans for them even before He formed them in the womb (Jeremiah 1:5). Nothing they do or say is a surprise to Him. In His eyes, they are simply expressing who He created them to be.

Since God accepts your child's design as they are, you must do the same. Just tolerating the differences is not enough—you must get over yourself and learn to appreciate them as well. God wants you to give your child the freedom to develop within themselves the very thing that rankles your feathers. But to do so, you'll need to put your trust in Him. And just plan a little better than I did with Kim's cat. Then things will work out just fine.

THE WAY FORWARD

As you execute your vision and accept the differences in your child, it's important to remember that your success should not be dependent on their acceptance. Just as God has a plan for you that you don't always follow, you can't control the results of your fathering. For this reason, you must measure your efforts by your ongoing attempts to be like God to your child, not by how your child responds.

This can be a difficult concept to accept. It's frustrating to work so hard on being present only to have your child subtly or blatantly reject your spiritual vision. It's easy to sink into despair, get angry, give up, or become distant. You may even try to enter into a power struggle with your child. But the more you get into a battle of wills, the more resistant your child will be, and their self-destructive tendencies will only increase as a result.

That brings us back to step one and the concept of taking charge of the one thing you *can* control—your own development. Your child's negative behaviors didn't come out of thin air. The physical, emotional, mental, or relational deficits that you see in them were most likely internalized as a result of viewing how *you* interact with the world. If you look closely enough at their behavior, you'll probably find something strangely familiar.

This realization should serve as a wakeup call. As I've already stated numerous times, a father cannot develop his child beyond what he himself has already achieved. And if what he's achieved isn't good enough, then that means he is obligated to learn, grow, adapt, and yes, change. It is only by overcoming our own challenges and negative behaviors that we can gain the ability to help our children move past those same negative attributes we instilled in them.

God created you to pass on your identity to your child, which means He wants to help you achieve this developmental growth. As you learn to apply biblical principles to your life, so will your child. As you create structures within yourself to gain control over your biological and emotional impulses, so will your child. And as you lead them as God would, His empowerment will help your child understand their need for Him, allowing Him to show them all they can become.

In the next section of this book, we'll delve into some of the specific developmental processes you need to go through in order to prepare yourself to father your child well. They will be challenging, but your willingness to engage with them will prepare you to tackle the specific fatherly duties outlined in Part III. These chapters were designed to test you and push you to your limits. As you go through them, continue to rely on God. With Him walking beside you on this journey, you will make it through, no matter how difficult it may seem.

 ROY'S STORY

Many years ago while Kim was finishing up her doctorate degree, we took a twenty-hour drive from Pennsylvania to Disney

World in Florida. Jan and I had one goal on that drive—to make sure Kim knew she could go out on her own and do whatever she wanted.

See, Kim had just spent the past few years studying to become a psychologist, just like her parents. And given that I had founded a counseling company that literally grew out of her childhood home, we were afraid she might feel obligated to go work there once she graduated. It was important to Jan and me to establish that as much as we would love it if she became a part of our professional lives, we accepted the reality that she might not.

However, we'd barely made it two minutes into the conversation before Kim piped up from the backseat. "Listen, you guys," she told us. "I know I can do whatever I want. But I know your company's mission, and I want to be a part of it. I'm already planning on coming back and leading it when I'm done with my education. So why don't we wrap this up so we can just enjoy the trip?"

Tears of pride streamed down my cheeks as we continued driving south. It was amazing to know that Kim wanted to come to the company I had invested so much of myself in. But more than that, I was proud of the strength of her identity. Even though she made the decision I wanted, I knew she didn't make it for me—she made it for herself. And that's all a dad can really hope for.

💬 DISCUSSION QUESTIONS

1   Review the three steps toward the vision of fatherhood. Which feels the most natural to you? Which do you struggle with? How can you begin taking these steps in your fatherhood?

2   Name some ways your child has defined themselves differently from you. How open are you to accepting these differences? How can you respond well even when they make choices that you don't agree with? How can God help you accomplish this acceptance?

3   What difficult life experiences have helped forge you into a stronger and more adaptable man? What are some areas you still need to grow in? How can you involve God more fully in this forging process?

4   Discuss how Proverbs 22:6 relates to the vision of fatherhood. How can it help you keep a healthy perspective on your goals for your child?

Start children off on the right path.
    And even when they are old, they will not turn away from it.

part II

A LOOK
INSIDE

"When he has tested me, I'll come out as pure as gold."
—*Job 23:10*

08

CHOOSE YOUR OWN ADVENTURE

Back when I was a young father, we'd all carry around printed photographs of our kids in our wallets. And the moment someone would ask about them, we'd proudly pull out our photos to show off those angelic faces, smiling like the little cherubs they were. Although it's a different forum now with smartphones and social media, the concept is essentially the same. Our love and pride for our children is so big that we just have to show them off to the world, using a picture of perfection to do so. The problem is, that picture is usually not even close to the reality of our daily lives.

Now, it's not like we're deliberately trying to fool everyone. Most of the time, we actually view our children in that same static snapshot way. You can see this with the father who's completely unprepared for his daughter to start dating, because in his mind she is and always will be his little girl. Or look at the father who can't understand why his son suddenly doesn't want to be seen with him, when not all that long ago his dad was nothing less than a superhero.

Unfortunately, life is much more complicated than we wish it were, especially when it comes to our children. Nothing lasts forever, not even the image we have of our children or the expectations we have for our relationship with them. Eventually, the intricate, God-given complexities of a child force all of us to do the one thing we've spent our lives trying to avoid—change.

THE MOVIE OF LIFE

Life is constantly moving, and as a result each of us is continually changing, whether we recognize it or not. This means that who your child was yesterday might be different today, and your view of them should reflect that. When you hold on to that still picture, clinging to a snapshot of who your child was in a single moment in time, you prevent yourself from seeing the true depth of who they are and who they can become. Instead, allow yourself to have a constantly developing perspective of them, more like a scene in a movie. When you do, you'll become more present with them through each step of their development, allowing you to continually encourage their growth and keep your focus on your greater vision for them.

However, seeing your child as capable of change and growth directly depends on how you view yourself. For many of us, once we leave school and the mandatory learning that comes with it, we lose sight of our own growth and settle into a life of comfort, routine, and stagnation. Then a child comes along whose natural curiosity and learning spirit unexpectedly shakes up that life of comfort. But instead of embracing such an opportunity for growth, we often cling to our passivity, unknowingly limiting our children in order to protect ourselves.

There are many ways your child's growth can make you uncomfortable. By acknowledging them, you can learn instead to embrace and encourage the wondrousness of their curious spirit. It's only with this change in perspective that you can truly become open to God's work within you, allowing you to both help yourself grow into the father He wants you to be and help your child reach the depths of their own potential.

A CHALLENGER APPEARS

Right from the start, your child's very existence is an inconvenience. Even in the womb, they take your wife's attention away from you. And then once they're born, they begin pushing all of your boundaries. They don't always follow the rules you establish, especially when they're too young to have the cognitive ability to follow them. They constantly want your attention, even when you're clearly unable to give it. They bring a random, chaotic attitude to your household that undermines any structure or habits you've worked hard to create for yourself. And to make it all even worse, you can't even get the sleep you need to handle it all with grace and patience.

In their youthful innocence, our children have a natural positive energy we often both envy and resist. While we may have stopped dreaming long ago, life for them still feels like an adventure. They want to be a hero who uses their superpowers to contribute to the world. Unlike us, they're less focused on defending their own comfort than on achieving this dream. They don't hesitate to take risks, make discoveries, try new skills, and test their strength.

While such unabashed excitement for life can make us chuckle at times, there can also be something threatening about it, especially because our children are often eager to take us along for the ride. Their curious minds send them into places we have learned to block out. Their "why" questions stretch our minds beyond our accepted patterns of thought. And their attempts to understand life force us to question our own beliefs.

Most of all, your child's development naturally challenges your accepted status quo. To be truly engaged in their growth, you must continually focus on the present, which means you can no longer rely on the behaviors and responses you've become so comfortable with. Not only does being present in this way make it harder to cling to a static view of your child, but it also makes it harder to cling to the one you have of yourself. In every interaction with your child exists an opportunity for you to transform part of yourself. As they grow and stretch, they will remind you of the areas in which you need to grow and stretch as well, areas you long ago turned a blind eye to.

The reality is that your child is going to keep changing, and they are going to keep asking you to be with them as they discover and navigate their internal processes. They will assert themselves into your life by trying to get their way or demanding your attention. And that means that one way or another, you're going to have to decide: will you step toward the challenge, or will you stay right where you are?

CREATURES OF HABIT

One of the biggest ways your child will challenge your comfort is by resisting your routines. As we age, we all develop little patterns we rely on to help get us through the day, many of which have become completely unconscious behaviors. Some of those routines may be obvious, like how you brush your teeth before you wash your face every morning, and some are harder to identify as routines, like how you say, "Good, and you?" every time someone asks you how you're doing.

Either way, many of these routines are useful for helping us manage life effectively. They save us time and reduce the energy we spend on meaningless tasks or responses. Besides allowing us to focus on more important endeavors, this frees us up to be open to God's spontaneous work in our lives. In this way, our routines can make us feel safe enough to go after the new, the risky, and the miraculous.

Unfortunately, not all of our routines are quite so useful. Just as our children dream of being heroes, we also have a God-given heroic nature meant to push us to go after our dreams and accomplish

His plan for our lives. However, as a result of our unresolved losses, past defeats, lack of supportive encouragement, or long list of obligations, we have repressed our heroism and given up on our goals. Over the years, the weight of life's many challenges can cause us to exchange our drive to discover life for a desire for comfort and safety. As a result, we become passive, submit to the monotony of routine, and commit to the status quo.

Of course, most men don't consciously decide, "I'm going to stop dreaming and quit trying!" In fact, you may not even be aware you've done it at all. That's because the life challenges that beat down our heroic nature aren't always something concrete, such as being rejected by a girlfriend or getting fired from a job. More often it's the accumulation of small disappointments and failures that lead to that nagging thought of "maybe I'll never measure up." As a result, we quit dreaming altogether, not because we want to, but because it just seems safer that way.

When we replace our heroic nature with a life of routine, we begin to organize our environments to make them as predictable as possible. Not only do we attempt to make every day the same, leaving no room for the spontaneity and creativity needed to fully develop our potential, but we also try to organize our relationships in the same patterns of routine. In order to make sense out of life, we oversimplify the sophisticated complexity God created within each individual and instead create those immovable, deceptively perfect pictures of our lives.

At the same time, though, we still want to have that great vision for our children. We dream of who they will become and what they will accomplish. We want them to grow and change. And yet because of our desire for routine, we treat them like they can't. This mixed message both confuses them and instills a sense of doubt within them. How can they expect themselves to grow when we don't seem to believe they ever will?

The worst part is, we're often blind to what we're doing. By getting so caught up in our mindless routines, we lose the ability to be fully present in our children's lives. Instead of living with them and experiencing God's miraculous presence together, we live at a distance, giving the same automatic responses day in and day out. As a result, we don't just lose sight of how God is working in us and in our children. We also become unable to recognize that we've created that distance at all.

This is exactly why some parents end up looking back over their child's life and exclaiming to themselves, "Where did the time go?" Life does move quickly, especially as we get older, but it moves even faster when we aren't paying attention. As easy as it may be to rely on your routines and hope for the best, your child will challenge you to do more. You just have to be willing to step toward them with that old heroic vigor God created you with and rediscover your excitement for life.

THE CHOICE IS YOURS

Whenever a father's life of routine is threatened by his child, he typically reacts in one of two ways. The first, as mentioned above, is to distance himself from his child and put them in a box. The other, unfortunately, is to repress his child's independence and individuality through setting strict rules and enforcing harsh consequences.

Like Peter, your child dreams of getting out of the boat and walking on water (Matthew 14:25-29). When you overload them with rules or fail to be present for them, you are inadvertently telling them to stay in the boat. Through your choices, you say to them, "I want you to change, but not in a way that forces me to change." In clinging to your insecurities, you snuff out their passion and make them doubt their dreams.

Such a reaction to your child's excitement for life primarily comes out of fear. Deep down, you like that part of them and want to experience it yourself. That's because the heroic spirit you repressed long ago is still there underneath all your comfortable routines and easy habits. You still want to feel and express your passion for life. You still want to be a hero for your family. You still want to connect up with God and experience His awesomeness daily.

And God desires this for you as well! That's why He wants you to embrace your child's willingness to throw off the status quo and allow yourself to experience the world through them. Jesus had a strong appreciation for how children threaten an adult's routine. He even proclaimed that those who don't receive God's kingdom like a child will not enter it (Mark 10:13-16). Of course, He doesn't mean we should be immature and naive. He's saying that we are to be hopeful, open-minded, and honest, just as all children are when they're young and inexperienced, before the world teaches them otherwise.

When you embrace your child's perspective in this way, you will benefit both yourself and them. Their unpredictability will teach you how to let go once in a while and be spontaneous with them, and their natural curiosity and creativity will drive you to make new discoveries about yourself and the world. And from these adventures and discoveries, you will learn exactly where you still need to grow in order to maximize your influence as a father.

This is one area my own father did exceptionally well in. Throughout my childhood, he continually encouraged my learning spirit and my questioning of life. I remember many nights where he'd read me stories before bed as I'd imagine far-off lands and amazing adventures. As I grew older, the bedtime stories stopped, but he continued to foster that learning spirit. From an early age, I was very interested in the field of apologetics and exploring Christianity from a philosophical, historical, archaeological, scientific, and biblical perspective. As a pastor, my father would continually ask me spiritual questions that drove that natural curiosity within me. He didn't demand that I confine myself to his answers but truly wanted me to discover my own conclusions. It was these stimulating conversations that caused me to think about the importance of biblical principles being at the foundation of every decision, like a series of steps, one building on the next.

In the same way, your journey with God and His transforming power can help you embrace your heroic spirit so you can enter your child's world of possibilities. As you engage in their imagination, goal setting, and dream fulfillment, you will be able to guide them as they explore the world and model for them the best way to do so. Rather than being intimidated by their lack of structure, you can be their supportive coach, cheering loudly for their slightest success and standing by them during every stumble.

As you engage in fatherhood at this level, God will be cheering for you in return. You will feel His grace, love, and acceptance in each spontaneous moment, allowing you to fulfill His law and love your child like He does. In response to the risks you take together, God will bless even the most ordinary of moments and turn them into growth. Through this gift, He will ensure that the mutual give-and-take cycle between you and your child continues to spin in the years to come.

THE NEXT STEP

Now, I know that letting go of your routines, stepping into the unknown, and committing to your own growth is much easier said than done. But thankfully, we have the perfect example of how to take the first step. In Jesus's interactions with others, He shows us how to break out of our routines and accepted ways of thinking. He defined the woman caught in adultery not as she was but as what she could be, even when others tried to limit her (John 8:1-11). He appreciated the Roman commander's faith in Him, even when most people denied who He was (Matthew 8:5-13). And He made

His Spirit available to us to make our miraculous development more possible, even though He saw all the evil within the world (Matthew 7:7).

But Jesus didn't stop there. He shows us not only how to stop our routines but also how to initiate life-altering change through our faith in Him. He led the first disciples to leave their comfortable careers as fishermen and enter an unpredictable life of servanthood (Luke 5:1-11). He healed deep-rooted wounds and empowered people to walk into the unknown future (John 9:1-7). He even changed how the whole culture defined the church, which at the time enforced routines through its emphasis on the law (Luke 11:37-54).

The best way to break free of your routines and change your life's direction is to do exactly as Jesus suggests—strengthen your relationship with God and fully tune in to His presence (Luke 10:42). As you do, you will hear Him talking to you constantly. When you feel uncomfortable by how your child's independence takes them outside of your grasp, He will say, "Trust me. I will take care of them." When you become too passive, He will command, "Get up, and become more involved with your child." And when you feel uncertain of what the future holds, He will repeat, "I am in charge of tomorrow. Simply walk by faith and trust in who we are together today."

Thankfully, God doesn't just speak to us—He also coaches and supports us as we attempt to rise to His challenges. He provides unwavering guidance through the scars we experience, the mistakes we make, and the many times we have to restart. More amazingly, He forgives us for all of it and doesn't use those experiences to define our value. Just like you must view your child through their unimaginable potential, God sees you as the father you are becoming, not the father you are today. When you rely on His presence, He will help you stay in the present without getting too caught up in the past or becoming too stressed about the future. Instead, you will maintain hope in all the possibilities that surround both you and your child.

To cheer for your child, be creative, and love them despite your differences, you must experience your heavenly Father doing the same for you. Heroes who attempt the extraordinary need an extraordinary God. With Him, you can fly with your child into an amazingly unknown world—even if you have to build it out of cardboard boxes and blankets yourselves.

A MOMENT OF CREATIVITY

I spent a lot of time deliberating on the title of this chapter. Part of the reason was because there are so many different themes to take away from it, and part of it was that it was just fun. I crossed out quite a few titles I particularly enjoyed, like "Ramblings with Roy" and "No More Routines!" before I finally decided on "Choose Your Own Adventure." After all, fatherhood *is* an adventure, and ultimately, it's up to you to decide the direction that adventure will take. No one else's child is the same as yours, which means what's best for one might be completely wrong for another. You must forge your own path with God to figure out the unique lessons you need to learn and the specific steps you need to take to become the father your child needs.

However, another title I think might've worked just as well is "A Child's Gift." As this chapter shows, it's much too easy to become complacent with ourselves and life without even realizing it. Our children's very presence alters that mindset. Their excitement for life confronts our self-focus, causes us to recognize our need for God, inspires us to become more than we thought possible, and teaches us to live in the present with them. In other words, their change stimulates our change, naturally pushing us toward the path God set out for us.

Such a gift should never be overlooked, but it isn't always clear what we should do with it. That's why the rest of Part II will continue in this chapter's footsteps, challenging you to understand and work through certain processes that will strengthen you as both a father and a man. The topics we'll discuss are ones that may apply to both you and your child, as are some of the ones in Part III, which focuses more directly on how to guide your child. But the topics in this section are especially important to consider from a father's perspective, as your ability to handle them well will directly influence how you lead your child.

Adventures aren't easy. This journey will dig up some tough questions and will require you to do a lot of deep thinking. Just remember not only that were you made for this adventure but also that your child deserves your full participation in it. By doing the hard work of looking at yourself and growing in the present, you will secure success for them now, in the future, and long, long after you're gone.

 ROBERT'S STORY

In her twelve short years of life, Sophia has already earned herself numerous regional and national championship titles as a dancer. These accomplishments have come from hundreds of hours of practices, rehearsals, and performances. Her grace in fluid motion is matched only by her beauty standing still. To say I'm proud of her is a massive understatement.

I'd like to tell you that all of Sophia's triumphs have come from my unending determination to see her become the best of the best—but they don't. Unfortunately, I am often guilty of focusing too much on practicality and asking if the monetary cost of dancing is really worth it. (Dance dads, you can feel me, right?) After all, shouldn't kids be spending their time with toys and playing on playgrounds? Why is Sophia so different? Why can't she just be "normal"?

The truth is, it takes only one glimpse of her arabesque to melt my logic into awestruck tears. It always has. Even when she was first starting out and her most eloquent move was "march in place and don't pick your nose," her dolled-up makeup and lollipop dress still left me speechless. Why? Because although I want to be responsible and reasonable, I also crave the excitement of adventure and the joys of experiencing something new.

Growing up, I convinced myself that I had to fit a mold that showed others I was a "real" adult. I thought that paying the bills and getting amazing acting roles would lead to success. But Sophia's dancing helped me discover that success is actually determined by how much I enjoy my daughter, her sister, and their mom. It's about how much I'm present for them through their triumphs and failures.

I haven't stopped being responsible, but I have started intentionally enjoying the fruit of that responsibility. I started enjoying being a dad. And suddenly, without warning, I found myself on the adventure of a lifetime.

💬 DISCUSSION QUESTIONS

1   What are some routines and habits in your life? Which are useful? Which might limit you in ways that could negatively impact your child?

2   What are some ways your child challenges you? How easy or difficult is it to engage with and encourage their curiosity and creativity?

3   What are some benefits of embracing all of who your child is? What could you learn from them? How can relying on God help you deepen your relationship with them?

4   What does Matthew 19:14 show us about how Jesus viewed children? How can you apply this lesson to your view of your own child and your vision for them?

Jesus said, "Let the little children come to me. Don't keep them away. The kingdom of heaven belongs to people like them."

09

AN HONEST LOOK

One thing about my life that I've alluded to but haven't fully addressed in this book is the truth about my childhood. I grew up in a tiny town in central Pennsylvania with my mom, dad, and three siblings, right beside the mighty Susquehanna River. At first glance, such a childhood back in the '50s and '60s might seem pretty close to the American ideal—a husband and wife working together to raise a band of unruly, happy children out in the open air of rural life. A family that could stick together no matter what, knowing they'd always have each other's backs.

But if you looked closer, you'd see a little boy holding a pillow over his head as his parents scream at each other downstairs for the hundredth time that week. You'd see a father spending long hours at work just to avoid the family he often wished he didn't have. You'd see a mother drowning in severe mental health issues and coping by taking her children down with her.

We all have our issues, whether or not they're as obvious or intense, and many of them originate during childhood. Just as the influence you have on your child makes a lifelong impact on who they become, the influence your own parents, particularly your father, had on you helped shape you into the man you are today. Though you may not recognize it, what you learned from your father through both his direct guidance and his indirect influence continues to affect your decisions and behaviors today in both good and bad ways.

Whether that influence was largely positive or inherently negative, you must evaluate it if you want to be an intentional father to your own child. It's only by facing it head-on that you can build on the positive lessons your father gave you—and finally process and move on from any purposeful or unintentional pain he left behind.

A MOST POWERFUL INFLUENCE

Several years ago, I was walking around my pond feeding the trout when I accidentally disturbed a family of geese. Since I was obviously a threat, the parents immediately began speeding away in a zigzag formation, honking to their goslings as they did so. To my amazement, those goslings fell perfectly in line behind their parents. Despite how ragged and complicated the path to escape was, they followed it exactly and without hesitation.

What I observed is an instinctual process called *imprinting*. Many animals are wired to automatically identify and bond with their parents, usually by following their movements. Not only does this dependency ensure their survival at an age when they're too young to take care of themselves, but it also teaches them important lessons on how to find food and shelter and how to avoid danger. It's these lessons that ensure that when they're old enough to separate from their parents, they can do so with confidence in their own ability to care for themselves (Hebrews 5:13-14).

Unfortunately, it's pretty easy for this instinct to backfire. I once saw a nature show where a duckling hatched from its egg just as an alligator chased its mother away from the nest. As a result, the alligator was the first thing the duckling saw, causing it to imprint on the deadly predator instead of on its mother. Operating purely on instinct, the duckling compliantly followed the alligator, right to its unpleasant end.

God has created each of us with a similar imprinting instinct. It's part of why we yearn for the attachment described in Chapter 6 and why we stay so close to our parents when we're young, just as those goslings did to theirs. We sense that they're supposed to teach us how to navigate life, and as a result, we trust everything they do or say, often without question (Deuteronomy 6:1). When our parents are like the geese by my pond, this means we learn godly principles that help us develop mature structures and prepare us to face the world. But when our parents are alligators, we wind up with internal chaos, never developing the self-control, strengths, or skills we need to achieve our full, God-given potential.

In reality, most parents aren't all goose or all alligator. Typically they're some combination of the two. My own father certainly was. As I said in the last chapter, my father was a pastor and a follower of the Bible, and as a result, he instilled in me a deep love for God and His Word. Because of his work in the community, I learned at an early age the importance of serving others, and I've dedicated much of my life to helping them just as he did.

However, my father was certainly far from a perfect man. He had plenty of his own unresolved issues that hurt both him and his family. Besides having a father who was in prison, he also had an unloving mother who told him when he was just five years old that she'd wanted to abort him but couldn't find anyone to do it. Because he never dealt with this pain, he ended up marrying a woman who was just like his mother in her resentment and abuse toward him. Then, instead of committing to the children who needed him, he abandoned us by escaping into ministry. And in his later years, he made choices that destroyed his reputation and betrayed those he'd helped in the past.

Part of why it's important to understand the power of your parents' impact is because their influence doesn't end with you. Our natural instinct for early dependence on our parents, and specifically on our fathers, gives them considerable power in determining the people we become. And since we have the same influence on our own children, this means that our fathers inadvertently have some power over who they become as well.

When we brought my baby daughter home for the first time, I found myself singing her a song that I hadn't heard in over twenty years—the same song my dad sang to my younger sisters when they were babies. It made me wonder: if I could remember a song from that long ago without even thinking, what else would I unknowingly pass on to my children from my father?

I quickly realized that I needed to take a deep look into my past and ask myself the questions I'd been avoiding in order to resolve the pain I didn't even know was there. See, the ideas and beliefs you internalized as a child will be passed along to your own children, even when you don't intend to do so (Exodus 34:7). It's simply a fact. For this reason, you must be willing to shine a light on the past to directly examine the example your father set for you. It's only by sorting through the good and bad of his influence that you can process his legacy and ensure the one you pass on to your child is better than the one you received.

Working with God to finally process our past memories and experiences helps you become a better father in multiple ways. For one, it increases your ability to be fully present for your child. But just as important, directly examining your past experiences with your father allows you to identify the specific aspects of his fathering that you may have overlooked or were ignorant of altogether.

It's only by determining all of the positive and negative aspects of the lessons he taught you that you can determine which ones you should build on and which you need to unlearn. When you do that, you will finally be able to choose a better path, one that allows you to more intimately engage with your wife and child and truly become a positive resource for their spiritual development.

UNPACKING THE PAST

No one escapes the influence of their father, whether he was a goose, an alligator, or simply absent. Ignoring this legacy won't make it go away or reduce its impact on you. In fact, doing nothing is actually what causes your past to become your present, because it allows your past to influence you at a deeper level that's much harder to recognize and control.

This is especially dangerous with men, who already naturally struggle with experiencing their emotions in positive ways. It doesn't matter if we're scared, sad, or simply annoyed—our favorite response is anger. And that anger and emotional repression will be magnified tenfold when you don't understand what's causing it (Proverbs 14:29). When left unresolved, those past experiences will pop up in your memories at unexpected and inconvenient times. While you may not know why you're remembering something you thought you got over long ago, the old emotion will still be there—as strong and unmanageable as it ever was.

You can't change the fact that your father was never there for you, expected too much from you, or actively insulted you. However, you *can* control how you respond to that pain. Being a father requires taking responsibility for your life, which means unpacking and learning from your story so you can stop its unseen influence on you and your child. Understanding how your father handled certain issues such as finances, work, or relationships will shed some light on the reasons behind your approach to those same issues, whether it's similar or different from his. The stronger this understanding is, the easier it will be to slow down, evaluate your approach, and act responsibly instead of simply responding impulsively.

Every choice you make has consequences, and part of being a responsible father is understanding how your choices are affected by your past. When you tune in to God's strength to help you do this, He will help you both heal the hurt you endured and change the negative habits it left behind (Psalm 71:20) . He will show you the strengths you gained as a result so you can build on them and develop new ones in order to be a good father. Part of this process will include directly facing some unpleasant memories, but when you rely on God through faith, He will get you through to the other side so they no longer have to pull you down.

The following survey will help you begin this process of discovery by assessing your father in various areas of fatherhood. You can also evaluate any other significant father figures whose influence you want to understand better. Some of the items on the list may not be as relevant to your father or your unique relationship with him, but thinking through them will still help you gain a more rounded view of the example he set for you, which is the first step in unpacking his influence. Then you'll be ready for the next chapter, where we'll build off of what you discover by discussing the implications of the survey's results and how exactly you can redefine your father's influence.

Because the reason we should evaluate our fathers is to know ourselves better and recognize how we can improve, I recommend going through the survey twice, once to evaluate your father and once to evaluate yourself as a father. Seeing how your ratings compare to his will provide an even better understanding of his impact on your current beliefs, tendencies, and behaviors. In turn, you can further engage in the growth process and transform these early life lessons into future strengths in your own journey as a father.

A PRAYER OF STRENGTH

God, help me take the following survey mindfully. Give me the courage to face my past, however painful it may be. Show me new reasons behind why I respond the way I do, and encourage me to talk with you about what I discover. Give me the wisdom, grace, and humility to

*understand how to reframe or build on my early life experiences so I can
respect myself and love others better. I praise and thank you for all the
ways you intervene in my life, even when I'm not aware of it. Amen.*

THE SURVEY[1]

Rate your father on a scale of 1 to 5, where 1 indicates that
he has not modeled this attribute well and 5 indicates that he has.
Then go back and rate yourself as a father on the same scale.

_____	1	Dad took care of himself physically.
_____	2	Dad controlled his anger.
_____	3	Dad guided his sexuality well.
_____	4	Dad was responsible, and he was willing to face life's challenges.
_____	5	Dad maintained a positive attitude.
_____	6	Dad was able to grieve through life's losses.
_____	7	Dad courageously faced his fears and was willing to change.
_____	8	Dad had a positive and realistic view of himself.
_____	9	Dad willingly gave of himself and made sacrifices for others.
_____	10	Dad had a supportive team of trustworthy friends.
_____	11	Dad maintained a balance between work and casual fun.
_____	12	Dad faced the pain of life directly.
_____	13	Dad chose his life principles well and lived by them.

---

1   For a printable version of this survey, visit liveupresources.com/fatherhood. A
version of this survey that you can take with your child to evaluate your own effect on them can be found in our mentoring resources *Bull* and *Pass It On* at
liveupresources.com.

_____ 14   Dad protected every member of our family.

_____ 15   Dad was good at listening, communicating, and show-ing that he valued others.

_____ 16   Dad expressed himself emotionally in healthy ways.

_____ 17   Dad handled decision-making well.

_____ 18   Dad had a strong relationship with God and inspired others to do the same.

_____ 19   Dad was aware of his sin nature and worked to control it.

_____ 20   Dad did what was required to correct his mistakes.

_____ 21   Dad forgave others when they hurt him.

_____ 22   Dad learned from his past and exhibited healthy growth.

_____ 23   Dad acted confidently and without unnecessary defensiveness.

_____ 24   Dad spent productive and positive time with me.

_____ 25   Dad often told and showed me that he loved me.

_____ 26   Dad demonstrated a healthy marriage by how he treated his wife.

_____ 27   Dad lived with integrity and good character.

_____ 28   Dad disciplined me fairly and controlled his anger while doing so.

_____ 29   Dad listened to me and complimented me.

_____ 30   Dad drank appropriately, if he drank at all.

_____ 31   Dad taught me new skills and encouraged me to learn.

Doing the hard work of evaluating your father's influence takes courage and resiliency, so I applaud you for doing it! And now I want you to take it one step further to truly drive home the changes you need to make—discuss your survey answers with a trusted friend or your men's group.

It isn't easy being that vulnerable, but the benefits far outweigh any potential costs. When you open up to other men, they will provide you with the strength and support that will help fortify you to keep going. They will hold you accountable for your growth, reminding you that it isn't something you can run from. In this way, engaging with a band of brothers you can trust will reinforce your decision to become your own man and decide for yourself the type of father you will become.

So look back over your survey and think about what you could share. Which areas did your dad get a low score? How have those insufficiencies affected your own responses and expectations? How can you overcome those negative lessons so you can raise your child in a better way?

The more effort you put into assessing these questions, the more present you'll be for your child, loving and serving them as God would. And the more time you spend challenging, growing, and changing yourself, the more naturally fatherhood will come to you. And I don't mean the fatherhood your own father modeled or some unattainable ideal described in parenting books. I mean your unique, God-inspired, personal fatherhood, the kind that only fits the individual needs of the one person who will benefit from your influence the most—your child.

 ROY'S STORY

When I was young, my mom would occasionally leave town to visit her parents. Now, knowing what you know about my mother, you'll understand what a relief this was for me and my siblings.

We'd finally have a break from her constant criticism, abuse, and inconsistencies, if only for a few days.

It was also a relief for my dad, who got a much-needed respite from his wife and their constant conflicts. With less of a reason to avoid his home life, he would suddenly become more active in parenting us. He'd come home early to make us dinner, and even though my mom usually left us food to eat, my dad preferred to make what he called "mystery soup." Basically, he would throw every type of leftover imaginable into a pot and hope for the best. Sometimes it was pretty tasty, and sometimes it was really, *really* not. But either way, we always ate it and laughed together, because it just felt good to spend time with our dad.

I thought of our mystery soup nights quite frequently while I wrote this book. As a result of being without my wife and children, unable to go anywhere or do anything, and surrounded by the distressing news of the COVID-19 pandemic, I had been feeling a little depressed. But then one night, I decided to throw together a hodgepodge meal not unlike my father's mystery soup. As I ate, I smiled. More than fifty years later, those memorable evenings with my father and siblings still brought me comfort, even during as dark a time as this.

Looking back, I can see that my dad taught me a lot with his mystery soup, though I had no way of realizing it when I was young. I learned that no matter how hard life can be, you can always find moments of laughter with others. I learned how to be resourceful in ways I could apply to areas beyond my next meal. And I learned to see the value of being present with the ones you love, even during something as silly as a dinner of absolutely disgusting soup.

As a therapist, I've gotten pretty good at identifying the ways my father influenced me, both in the big moments of our relationship and in the seemingly insignificant ones. But I've also come to realize that a father's influence extends beyond just the lessons he teaches. The positive experiences we have with our dads turn into memories that can serve as guiding lights in moments of darkness. Whether those memories simply give us comfort when we're feeling low or reveal to us a lesson we hadn't realized we needed to learned, they serve as proof that even after a father is long gone, he's never done fathering.

💬 DISCUSSION QUESTIONS

1 Discuss what you discovered from the survey. What did you realize about your father that you hadn't considered before? In what ways are you similar or different from him?

2 Describe a positive memory of your dad. How did that experience influence you as a child? How do you feel thinking about it now?

3 What experiences did you have with your father that you don't want to repeat with your child? How can you learn from those moments to influence your child in a more positive way?

4 Discuss the example of fathering shown in Luke 11:11-12. What does it teach us about what fathers can give to their children?

   Fathers, suppose your son asks for a fish. Which of you will give him a snake instead? Or suppose he asks for an egg. Which of you will give him a scorpion?

10

FACING FACTS

Before taking the survey in the last chapter, I'm guessing you had certain expectations for how it would go. But what you probably found was that there were some areas where your father excelled in his fatherhood and others where he floundered. That's how it is with all fathers. Even the ones who seem absolutely perfect and the ones who are downright evil will have both positive and negative aspects to their influence, if only to a small degree.

It's through recognizing and understanding these nuances of your father's influence that you will discover how to become the best father to your own child. You probably already know not to adopt your father's most obvious shortcomings, like his alcoholism or the degrading way he talked to your mom. But in between those blatant deficits may be smaller or even unknown issues you subconsciously internalized and may be passing on to your child.

Likewise, some of the most valuable lessons don't come from your dad sitting down and having a deep conversation with you. Rather, they're more often found in the seemingly inconsequential moments. A positive lesson you learned without even realizing it might be the one that will help you finally relate to your child the way you've always wanted to.

Even if you don't feel like you learned anything new from the survey, it's still valuable for what it might have highlighted or reminded you of in your father's example. It can be easy to take his positive influence for granted, especially as, over time, that influence becomes simply part of who you are. And it can be even easier to block out the ways he hurt you so you never have to feel that pain again.

In either case, you must consciously recognize every aspect of how your father impacted you so you can turn those experiences over to God. With His guidance, you can take your father's positive lessons even further and grow stronger in your skills and abilities. And with His gentle love, you can reconcile the negative parts of your past and finally take hold of your future, once and for all.

A CHIP OFF THE OLD BLOCK

In the last chapter, I discussed the concept of imprinting, the survival instinct all babies have to bond with their parents. Now I want to look at it from the other side to examine the role a parent plays in this imprinting process. In counseling, I often refer to it as *computer chipping*. Just as a computer tech installs chips that tell a computer how to run properly and process information, parents install similar "chips" in their children that help them know how to manage their emotions, relate to others, rely on God, and simply survive in a chaotic world.

These chips are invaluable to our ability to react well to the challenges of life, because as with computers, they allow us to process a situation and respond without having to spend too much time thinking about it. By having predetermined principles, foundational knowledge, or baseline abilities, you can be thrown into almost any circumstance and be able to sort out the best way to react fairly easily. Then you can focus on putting your energy into finding the next step or tackling a more challenging endeavor.

However, unlike computers, we can have a chip installed completely unintentionally. The ways we experience our parents handling life from an emotional, mental, or physical perspective inadvertently plant chips within us that become just as essential to our internal operating system as the ones they plant deliberately. The closer the emotional bond we have with our fathers, or the greater the dependence, the more they unconsciously install chips based on their patterns of behavior, and the easier we accept them without question. If it's good enough for dad, we think, it's good enough for us.

As we discussed in Part I, children learn best by example, which means that even while your father may have tried to teach you good values and principles, you probably also internalized bad ones simply as a result of witnessing his natural shortcomings. Just look at the story of Abraham and Isaac. I think we'd all agree that Abraham, the father of nations, was nothing short of a biblical hero (Genesis 17:4-7). His relationship with God was a model of intimacy, and his dedication to his faith led him to succeed in many areas of life (Hebrews 11:8-10).

But even with such a positive legacy to pass on to his son, Isaac, he also unintentionally passed on his weaknesses. Upon finding himself in a new city, Abraham told a lie to protect himself, saying his wife was actually his sister. Although Isaac wasn't even born at that time, years later he told the same exact lie about his wife for the same exact reason (Genesis 20:1-2; 26:7).

However, whatever your father's imperfections were, they don't negate the positive ways he impacted you. For some of you reading this, your father might have been a good role model overall. Because he was mature, internally strong, and confident in his identity, he passed on a godly legacy to you both through the secure attachment he formed with you and the example of godly leadership he modeled. As a result, you gained not only the chips that will help you live by the same principles and values but also the confidence that comes from doing what's good and right. Your father's example has shown you that when you live like him, life will continually reward you. You will find success simply because you aren't afraid to fully engage all of who you are in achieving your goals.

When we receive such positive chips from our father, we must be careful not to squander our good fortune and instead refine and develop those lessons even further. One of the best ways to do this is to pass along your father's legacy to your own child. When your child expresses passion for life, foster it as your own dad did with you. When they struggle to label what's going on within them, use your father's response to your similar struggles to help guide them through it. Continue your father's legacy, and instill within your child the same chips that will lead them to the same good future your father led you to.

ALLIGATOR FATHERS

During the Iran hostage crisis of 1979, a group of Americans were taken captive by Iranian rebels for 444 days. When they were finally released, however, they weren't immediately sent back to their families. Instead, they were taken to a hospital in Germany to be medically cleared. Besides their physical well-being, the US government was concerned about their mental health after being held in captivity for over a year by a group of Iranians who directly opposed America. The US wanted to make sure the former hostages were properly deprogrammed before they returned to the country and began expressing any anti-American sentiments.[1]

You may be asking why in the world people who were threatened and abused would in any way accept the beliefs and viewpoints of their captors. Well, it's a strange phenomenon that researchers have termed *Stockholm syndrome*, which causes a person held captive to display loyalty to or even affection for their captor. When you're completely at the mercy of another individual, you'll often say or do whatever you can to make them like you. Your instincts tell you that the less you anger them and the less you appear to be different from them, the better they'll treat you. The problem

---

1   Jack Lesar, "Stockholm Syndrome in Tehran" (*United Press International*, January 16, 1981), https://www.upi.com/Archives/1981/01/16/Stockholm-Syndrome-in -Tehran/8870348469200/.

is, the longer you engage with these thoughts and behaviors, the more you start to actually believe them, and the likelier they are to become ingrained in the very fabric of your identity.

Though it may not be such a life-and-death situation, those of us who had verbally or physically abusive fathers likely reacted in a very similar way as those American hostages. We quickly learned what we needed to say or do to avoid our fathers' anger or abuse, learning behaviors that still linger with us to this day. For instance, maybe your embarrassment of your father's actions kept you from inviting friends over, stunting your relational development. Or maybe you repressed your own feelings and opinions as you tried to guess how he wanted you to respond, leaving you with little understanding of or confidence in your internal processes.

Those whose fathers weren't directly abusive but were rather absent or neglectful likely also bear scars of survival, though they look a little different. For one, it's not unusual for a child to personalize their father's behavior. They can't help but think it must be their fault he's not around much, or at all, and that if they were better somehow, he'd be more interested in them. As a result, they develop a negative definition of their capabilities and value that lasts with them as they grow up, limiting what they can achieve.

Additionally, when a father isn't present, his child simply can't imprint on him, and so they have to learn for themselves how to survive in the world. When it comes to the practical aspects of life, this often means figuring it out by trial and error and clumsily piecing together their own computer chips to fill the void. But rather than creating a strong identity, such self-exploration often leads us to become dependent either on others or on unhealthy coping mechanisms. And unfortunately, we end up taking those ineffective chips with us into adulthood, stunting our growth and limiting our ability to relate to others on an intimate, emotional level.

While it may be easy to pinpoint the alligator parts of your father, it can be much harder to know what to do about it. When those negative lessons linger, some people end up getting stuck in what is known in psychology as *repetition compulsion*, unconsciously making decisions that recreate their past trauma or negative experiences in hopes that they can achieve a different outcome. This can come in the form of repeating behaviors you internalized even though you know how unhelpful they are, returning to harmful relationships, or moving toward an obviously negative event instead of away from it. In other words, if you don't expend effort to change yourself and learn to follow God's guidance, you will continue to fail and get hurt again, and again, and again.

So what can you do with your father's alligator parts, whether they were intentionally installed within you or not? Do those negative chips destine you to feel beaten down and defeated your whole life? Are you doomed to live out his legacy by becoming an alligator to others? Or might there just be a better solution?

FORGING A NEW PATH

The answers to the questions above ultimately depend on whether you believe in the transforming power of God. Your sin nature wants you to live with the assumption that you're incapable of being wrong. Even worse, it tricks you into viewing life in black and white, making you avoid emotionally evaluating any gray areas. It encourages you to believe it just isn't worth the effort to face the nuances that make you who you are. But ignoring our full potential doesn't make life easier. It just leaves us with an emptiness, one we wind up filling with false gods that bring temporary pleasure, such as drugs, alcohol, gambling, pornography, food, or even work.

Instead, we need to choose to live by faith. When you walk with God through each moment, you will no longer be weighed down by your past. He will show you what you need to do to resolve your old wounds and even embrace them so you can turn your weaknesses into strengths (2 Corinthians 12:9). In this way, you can break free from the tyranny of a negative legacy, allowing you to truly be like God with your child and gain control over the influence you have on them.

The first step in this process is understanding that God doesn't view human suffering like we do. He understands that the only way to change the negative patterns we're so used to relying on is to create tension that breaks up our routine, and He will give us the challenges to help us do just that. It won't always be fun, but remember that God doesn't waste pain. There is always a purpose in every challenge. As long as you hold sight of that purpose, you will come out the other side even stronger than before.

And God will go after more than just your behaviors—He'll also attack your negative internal habits, including how you think about yourself. My childhood home life was defeating and confusing, but it helped me learn that who I am is more important than what I do. I believe God cares far more about strengthening our identity than about giving us rules. That's because He knows that the closer we are to being who He wants us to be on the *inside*, the more equipped we'll be to honor Him on the *outside*.

So if you want to truly change and go further than the legacy your father gave you, you must commit to your own recovery. Recovery is often narrowly applied only to people struggling with addiction, but I believe everyone has something in their life to recover from, whether it's a parent who put them down or a self-inflicted failure that made them question their own worth. And just like in addiction counseling, recovery must be approached two ways at the same time, which I call Recovery 1 and Recovery 2.

To understand these approaches, let's use the example of an adult son struggling in his relationship with his abusive father. Recovery 1 focuses on stopping the behavior, which for this son could mean limiting his interactions with his father or perhaps, if necessary, ending the relationship entirely. However, it also requires the son to stop participating in behaviors that are abusive to himself or others. Any negative coping mechanism he's developed as a result of his relationship with his father would need to be confronted and changed in order for him to reframe his past and move on.

To truly reconcile his father's legacy, though, the son would need to take charge of his life and actively meet the needs his father failed to. And that means engaging in Recovery 2, which focuses on accepting some responsibility for your responses to the negative situation and healing the needs, motivations, traumas, and habits that may have contributed to it. For the son, this could mean recognizing his tendency to people please, learning to stand up for himself, and setting healthy boundaries to limit the abuse he will tolerate from his father.

The only way to unlearn the negative behaviors we got from our fathers is to enter into recovery and process the experiences, insecurities, and emotions that initiated those behaviors in the first place. Regardless of how severe your father's alligator tendencies were, what happens from this point forward is entirely up to you. The sin that passes from one generation to the next can stop with you, and God is standing by ready to help (Deuteronomy 5:8-10). As Jesus said, "Come to me, all you who are tired and are carrying heavy loads. I will give you rest" (Matthew 11:28). When you rely on Him, He will not only ease your burden but will also help you turn those challenges into strengths. As a result, your past circumstances and relationships no longer have to define you. Instead, you can take charge of your destiny and create the kind of legacy for your child that will carry them through the rest of their life.

 ROBERT'S STORY

Growing up, my father was the patriarch in charge, and no one ever questioned him. Although he was a wonderful father and encourager in my formative years, he wasn't always the best husband. His culture had taught him that strength meant being the decision maker and always having the answers. As a result, he believed that allowing my mother to influence major decisions (particularly financial ones) was a sign of weakness or insecurity. Especially in front other men, asking to confer with a wife or family members would provoke demeaning comments and instill shame.

This is the baggage I brought into the beginning of my marriage. Thank God that He joined me to a woman made strong in Christ.

It didn't take long for Colleen to express displeasure toward my learned attitude. But rather than argue or emotionally push back (which is what I was used to), she dismantled my logic and exposed the biblical deficiency of my belief. How? By simply making me explain my viewpoint as thoroughly as I could. And in my attempt to do so, I inadvertently discovered the danger in it and its incompatibility with God's views.

As we journeyed through the Scriptures together, I learned that the head of the household was supposed to be a spiritual, emotional, organizational, and strategic leader. It meant that I was to follow Christ's example and put my wife before myself. It meant that my presence should strengthen, encourage, and protect every aspect of her life. I'm not weak because I go to my wife. I'm strong because I'm defined by who Christ says I am, and that means recognizing who Christ says she is too. We are strong together because we are one in Him.

I'm so grateful God used my wife to help me redefine what being "the man of the house" is, according to Scripture, because it means I won't pass unbiblical beliefs onto my daughters. Instead, I'll model how they should be loved and respected through how I love and respect my wife. They'll learn that their dignity does not come from a man but rather from God.

I'm also grateful my enlightenment has reached my dad and

the baggage he carried as well. Through God's mercy, we have both set aside these views and have discovered the joys of loving our wives as Christ loved the church. So yes, thank God for strong women like Colleen. She helps make me a better dad each and every day.

💬 DISCUSSION QUESTIONS

1   What positive computer chips did your father install in you growing up? How can you build on them to become even stronger in your own fatherhood?

2   What parts of your father were more like an alligator? How can you learn to respond to life differently than he did? How can you rely on God to emotionally process his influence so you can be more present in all of your relationships?

3   Think about some of your most painful early experiences. How can God use them for your good? What skills and abilities came out of them that you can further develop?

4   Discuss how Philippians 3:13 relates to a father's relationship with his own father. How does it guide us in accepting God's influence?

Brothers and sisters, I don't consider that I have taken hold of it yet. But here is the one thing I do. I forget what is behind me. I push hard toward what is ahead of me.

11

OWNING YOUR SCARS

Thankfully for some of us, the last chapter wrapped up our discussion on assessing and resolving the lessons we've learned from our fathers, both positive and negative. But even though we're done talking about our fathers, we're not done talking about recovering from our past. After all, although he's the one who has a more direct, obvious impact on the way you father now, your father isn't the only thing capable of hurting you.

Whether it's our father, mother, a peer, our own failures, or even the culture, we all experience pain in our lives, long before we ever meet our wives or have children. And just as with our father's influence, when we don't process and work through this pain, we allow it to continue influencing our lives, limiting our ability to be emotionally available for the people we love most. But when you let God help you do the hard, often heart-wrenching work of reassessing those past wounds and turning them into strengths, not only will you feel lighter and freer, but you'll also become truly engaged in fatherhood, able to guide your child through their highest joys and their lowest sorrows.

THE PAIN OF LIFE

As men, we like to think we're pretty good at handling pain. Sure, it hurts to slice your leg on a rock while cliff-diving into a lake or to wipe out on concrete trying to execute a bike trick. But who cares if it hurts as long as you looked brave and cool doing it? Besides, all you have to do is rub some dirt on it and everything will be fine. And when the stiches come out or the scab comes off, you'll have a pretty awesome scar to show for it—and women *love* scars.

But what about emotional pain? Are you as willing to admit your greatest secrets and weaknesses to a friend, or to pour your heart out to the woman you love when you have no idea how she'll respond? Instances like these also require a certain amount of bravery, and yet we avoid them like the plague. That's because emotional pain is much more complicated than physical pain, and it can't be resolved simply through stitches, antibiotics, or even "taking it like a man."

When someone you love dies, or you're socially rejected, or you fail at achieving a goal you really wanted, you don't just feel hurt and angry—you also feel confused, upset, embarrassed, frustrated, anxious, and a whole range of other emotions that can be hard to recognize and understand. While thoughts are easy to organize into neat categories and examine with logic, emotions can't be cleanly sorted and processed by the same mental guidance system. They're messy and free floating, blending into each other in inexplicable ways and making it feel impossible to know how to begin to work through them, let alone explain them.

So instead, we shrug them off or push them down, telling ourselves we're fine. However, ignoring your negative feelings won't make them go away. It will just limit your ability to experience any feelings at all, including the good ones, like happiness, tenderness, love, or optimism. Whether you're aware of it or not, the pain that results from emotionally intense experiences tears into you like an open wound. And when you refuse to treat it, it will continue to fester to the point of infection, spreading into every other area of your life.

So what *is* the treatment? Well, there's a pretty simple term for it—grief work. However, the process itself isn't quite so simple. It involves grieving your losses and hurts so you can redefine how those experiences affect you in the future and free yourself from the weight of your past. Once you start to understand and take ownership of the pain you need to resolve, the process of healing can begin. But if you instead ignore your need to grieve, that open wound will just grow bigger and bigger until eventually it destroys your whole life.

AVOIDING GRIEF

Because of the fluid nature of emotions, any unresolved grief always inevitably infiltrates other thoughts, feelings, and even physical responses, no matter how unrelated they may seem to the original pain. As a result, your reactions to even the most harmless experience can become unnecessarily intensified or personalized. You may feel enraged after hearing about a close friend's disappointment because it reminds you of your own pain, or you may overreact when receiving negative feedback because similar criticism in the past led to you getting fired from your job. This type of disconnected response can happen even as a result of hearing good news from others. Instead of being happy for them, all you can focus on is how unfair it is that they're succeeding and you're not.

Such emotional disconnect is often a direct contributor to a lifestyle of passivity, as we discussed in Chapter 8. Unresolved grief leads to a sad heart, which produces a broken spirit, which causes us to give up on our dreams (Proverbs 15:13). When you don't process your pain, it can eat away at you, making you start to think that there's nothing good about life at all. Even worse, you begin to believe there's nothing good about *you*. In turn, you become blind to the ways you could change and make your life better, instead choosing the comfort and safety of your unhelpful routines.

The most important part of grief you need to understand is

that, just like the other areas of life we've discussed in this book, not taking a deeper look and resolving your pain harms more than just you—it also harms your child. Like you, your child will experience their own pain through rejections, accidents, losses, or self-inflicted emotional, mental, or physical injuries. When they're young, the emotional intensity of these experiences is often beyond what they are capable of digesting, even when it comes to something as minor as the death of their pet goldfish. They aren't yet developed enough to really understand what happened or why, which means they don't have the ability to put what they're feeling into words or to process what happened.

That's where you come in as a father. It's your job to help your child mitigate and manage their pain so that it doesn't negatively change how they view themselves, others, and life. But if you're unable to work through your own grief experiences, you will also be unable to help your child through theirs. Their grief will remind you of your own failures and unresolved pain, which can overwhelm and distract you from being fully present for your child. While you may reach out to help them through their pain, you do so by providing simplistic answers meant to "fix" your child without having to connect with them emotionally and feel their hurt with them. Furthermore, because of how your own unresolved grief can make you feel like life is harsh and unchangeable, you may actually have trouble intervening at all in your child's struggle. If you can't face and resolve your own issues, how can you tell your child that things will be any different for them?

The only way to truly be present to help your child through their moments of pain is to stop denying your own need to do your grief work. You must face your grief head-on so you can come to terms with what happened and forge those experiences into strengths. You may never be able to forget the pain, but when you label, understand, and learn from it, it will lose the power it wielded over you for too long.

Finally free from your past, you can then be present with your child in their grief. Instead of confusing your own pain with theirs, you will use your experiences to guide them through what they're feeling. And through the intimate connection you build, you will find more opportunities to encourage your child and help them find a positive perspective, allowing you to step into a more hopeful future together.

TRACED TO THE SOURCE

So how exactly can you process and resolve the pain that has lingered within you for so long? Well, the first step is pretty straightforward—recognize the exact circumstances, relationships, or events that you need to grieve. Of course, it isn't always easy to pinpoint the original source of your pain, especially when that pain happened a long time ago. That's why, like we did with our fathers, we must take a hard look at our past, no matter how difficult it may be, so we can finally begin to identify and reconcile with our deepest traumas.[1]

Part of this difficulty is that you've likely been taught to think of grief solely in terms of loss, such as with a devastating injury or the death of a loved one. But there are plenty of smaller moments that can also cause lasting pain. Although there are far more examples than we can discuss here, understanding some of the most common ones will help you be better able to recognize your sources of grief so you can begin the process of unpacking and working through them.

To start, the simple act of growing from a child into an adult produces grief. We have to say many goodbyes as we age, to our kindergarten teachers when we graduate to first grade, to friends who move away, or to pets or family members who pass on. In the

---

1   For further understanding of different types of trauma, how they're created, and how they affect us, check out *The Deepest Well: Healing the Long-Term Effects of Childhood Adversity* by Nadine Burke Harris.

transition from elementary school to junior high, we grieve not being in class all day with the best friends we grew up with. In high school, we grieve growing apart from those friends even further as we develop different interests or create new relationships, leaving behind the old. And once we graduate and move out of our childhood home, we grieve the simplicity of life before adulthood and the carefree dependence we once had on our parents.

This type of grief can be particularly difficult to identify and process because the experiences that cause it are often inherently positive. Maturing means changing more and more into who you're meant to be, gaining bigger responsibilities, and accomplishing even greater tasks. But in the process of discovering those skills, going after those goals, and learning to relate to others, you will also experience failure, rejection, and the harsh realization that you aren't perfect.

In truth, very few experiences, even the happy ones, are completely without some level of pain. For example, getting a better, higher-paying job may also mean saying goodbye to your favorite coworkers or moving away from the place you called home. Even something as exciting as getting a new puppy often has a tinge of grief associated with it, because you know that at some point you'll have to say goodbye to it as well.

In this way, grief is simply the cost of engaging fully in life. And the more you engage, the more you open yourself up for disappointment. When you first imagined what you could do with your life, you created the possibility of never fulfilling that dream. Any time you put effort into achieving a goal, you make it more likely that you will experience the pain of failure along the way. Any time you try to develop an aspect of yourself, you are forced to recognize how far you have to go to achieve it. And any time you learn something new, there's that subliminal realization that what you knew before was somehow inadequate.

The grief of engaging in life shows up in our relationships as well. By choosing to intimately attach to others, you open yourself up to experience pain at their hands. Your empathy for them allows you to deeply feel their hurt, and your love for them causes you to mourn their potential if they choose self-destructive behaviors. You experience the pain of rejection when they let you down, dismiss your ideas or feelings, or ignore you entirely. And when they take advantage of your loving generosity without even a thank-you, you feel the sting of having your value overlooked.

On top of all of that, we can even experience grief as a result of practicing our faith. When you choose to submit to God, you become vulnerable to the reality that sometimes God doesn't do or allow what you would want. And though you know He's ultimately right, coming to that conclusion often takes a period of grieving. Additionally, sharing your faith with others can also lead to grief. In being open with them, you create the possibility of seeing them actively reject their spiritual needs, just as Jesus saw with the people of Jerusalem (Matthew 23:37).

All of the above situations and events can cause pain and influence your emotional responses in the present, no matter how much time has passed since the original experience. However, your trauma does not excuse your actions. It is your responsibility both as a man of God and as a father to do whatever it takes to gain control of your behaviors and emotional responses. And as much as you may not like it, that means you must find your pain and face it directly.

A SPECIAL KIND OF LOVE

Generally speaking, most of our sources of grief are singular events or brief experiences, which can make it easier to put them behind us completely once we process them. Others, however, carry lifelong consequences that we can never fully overcome. Losses like a physical disability or the death of a loved one make huge, fundamental changes to a person's life, and even as we work through our initial feelings of grief, we will face continual reminders of what we've lost. In those moments, our grief will resurge, and we will have to reconcile with it once more so we can keep moving forward.

One major lifelong loss that relates directly to fatherhood is having a child with a mental, emotional, or physical disability. Before your child was even born, I'm sure you had dreams about what they would become and all they could achieve. Consequently, it's devastating to learn that their limitations will prevent them from ever realizing those dreams. Not only will the life you imagined for your child be completely different, but your relationship with them will change as well. Although your love for them will always be the same, your life with them will not.

While Kim's birth filled my life with unimaginable happiness, I'd always dreamed of having a son as well, someone I could teach everything I knew about life, God, and manhood. And nearly three years after Kim was born, I got that wish—though its results were much different than I'd anticipated.

Immediately after my son, Nick, was born, Jan and I knew something wasn't right. The doctor and nurses in the delivery room stood in silence for a moment before breaking the news that Nick had Downs syndrome. If that weren't devastating enough, at the age of two, he was diagnosed with severe autism, and we realized he would likely never speak a word. Due to his disabilities, someone would have to constantly care for him and watch his every move to make sure he didn't hurt himself. As my son, I loved Nick with all my heart, but this was certainly not the journey I desired for him, myself, or our family.

I travel frequently to speak at conferences across the country, and whenever I talk about Nick, I usually have a few men come up to me afterward to share their own journey. With mutually wet eyes, we acknowledge the grief we've both gone through.

Sometimes these fathers are well into their grief-work process and tell me how their pain has made them stronger and closer to their child. But other times they still feel lost. In their grief, they are searching for some explanation for that haunting, unanswerable question: "Why?"

This type of challenge is something we can either run from or choose to regularly grieve through. And unfortunately, many men choose to run. Either because they simply don't want to put in the work to meet the special needs of their child or because they're afraid they couldn't even if they tried, men often choose to ignore the problem altogether, leaving their child's care up to their wives and focusing on getting on with their lives.

The one thing that has aided my own questioning and grief process is relying on God's plan. We all cry out to God at some point searching for answers, but it can be especially difficult to see His purpose in the limitations of our children. After Nick was born and Jan and I were still deep in our grief, my brother-in-law came to visit us. What he said stuck with me: "I don't know why this has happened, but I can tell you, God takes responsibility for it." And then he shared Exodus 4:11 with us: "Who makes human beings able to talk? Who makes them unable to hear or speak? Who makes them able to see? Who makes them blind? It is I, the LORD."

In this verse, God is replying to Moses, who had just claimed he couldn't do what God called him to do because of a physical limitation. But God doesn't see human struggles the same way we do. He creates each of us with a specific purpose, and He gives us the resources we need to fulfill it. We may never fully understand our children's disabilities, but if we can learn to let go of our anger and dissatisfaction and instead trust in God's plan, we can learn to see our children like God does—fearfully and wonderfully made, and with extraordinary value (Psalm 139:14 NIV).

As part of this process, we must courageously and continuously come to terms with any losses connected to our expectations for our children. We must accept that our original dreams for them will not be achieved and that we can never make their lives "normal," despite our best efforts. And we must repeatedly do this throughout our children's lives. Each stage they reach will remind us that things will be different for them than we imagined, causing us to grieve all over again the loss of what might have been.

That may sound like a lot of grief to go through, but out of this grief will come new strength, love, and appreciation. The truth is, God's plan for your child will never be what you imagined, regardless of what challenges or disabilities that journey holds. But once you let go of what might have been, you can be fully present and able to focus on who God created your child to be.

Whether or not you have a child with special needs, they will require the same special love from you as their father. No child is perfect, which means you will need to let go of the image and expectations you had for them in order to love them as God does. When you pinpoint the areas you need to grieve, whether they're related to your child's life journey or are from somewhere deep in your past, you'll be able to take a vital step toward your grief work process. Then you'll be ready for what comes next: the five stages of grief and six key strategies for processing your pain.

Always remember that God is with you in every moment of hurt and disappointment. As you grieve life's many losses, He will help you recognize the good in them. Once you do, you can become the man He's called you to be and, most importantly, love and lead your child like they deserve.

 ROY'S STORY

In the midst of writing this book, I had to go through the hardest grief experience a parent can imagine—saying goodbye to

my child. At thirty-two years old, Nick had already had a number of health issues, and after suffering a bad bout of pneumonia, his lungs were failing. After being rushed to the hospital, he was completely intubated and, unfortunately, medically sedated. We've always said Nick had superhuman strength, and if he'd been at all alert, it would've been impossible to keep him in his bed, let alone attached to any machinery.

After six weeks of being unable to breathe on his own, Nick's lungs had weakened considerably. Jan and I had to make a tough decision. We could keep him alive, but because of his lung issues, he would have to have a tube in his trachea for the rest of his life. But we knew that if that happened, he would be unable to resume the good life he had. He would just be constantly tearing at the tube, uncomfortable, miserable, and a constant threat to himself.

So on a Saturday in September of 2020, we went into the hospital to turn off the machine, begin our grief process, and accept that Nick would now be with Jesus. As I thought about Nick's life, I realized that although he would never have the life I imagined for him before he was born, I'd come to appreciate the life he did have. The caretakers in his group home truly loved and supported him, becoming the friends I never knew he'd make, and he taught many people how to find joy even in the smallest areas of life. (He especially enjoyed his ketchup and French fries.)[2]

Nick never said a word to me, but he still taught me so much about God and about life. In fact, one of the nicknames I gave him was the Professor. As hard as it was to say goodbye, I felt some gladness thinking about Nick's entrance into heaven and his very first words, which would have been spoken to none other than Jesus Himself. And even in his death, the Professor still reminded me of an important lesson—we don't always know God's why.

My, I miss him.

---

2   To watch a seminar I presented about Nick in our *Real Men* video series, visit liveupresources.com/fatherhood.

💬 DISCUSSION QUESTIONS

1   Describe two experiences in your life that created lasting pain. Have you fully grieved those experiences? If so, what did you learn from them? If not, how can you start the grief process today?

2   How can working through your own grief allow you to guide your child through theirs? What areas of life have you seen and experienced your child grieving through?

3   What grief goes along with loving a child with special needs? What are some of the benefits? How must you similarly grieve a child's limitations, imperfections, and negative choices in order to love them well?

4   Discuss how Psalm 34:18 can help you begin the grief process. How can it show you how to be there for your child's pain as well?

The LORD is close to those whose hearts have been broken.
He saves those whose spirits have been crushed.

12

SCARS TO STRENGTHS

When Nick died, Jan and I were both understandably devastated by the loss of our child. But what was interesting was that although we were experiencing the same grief, we handled it in completely different ways. While I wanted to sit quietly in my room and spend my time writing, praying, and thinking over my many memories of my son, Jan wanted us to watch videos of Nick together, laugh about his lovable quirks, and cry over the lost hopes and dreams we had for him. We both wanted to honor his memory. But while I wanted to do so by moving on with my life and incorporating all the lessons he'd taught me, Jan wanted to take her time with her sadness so she could really internalize her memories of our son.

And neither of our grief journeys were wrong! Grief looks different for everyone, especially as time passes and you get further away from the original experience that caused it. That's why it's important to understand the various aspects of grief, which we started to unpack in the previous chapter, whether or not they relate to you in this moment. Doing so will not only help you identify how you're presently responding to your grief but will also give you insight into and compassion for the grief of others. The better you understand how grief works, the stronger you'll be at processing your own grief, and the more you'll become the supportive, loving resource your child needs to do the same.

STAGES OF GRIEF

After you recognize the areas of life you need to grieve, the next step is to recognize where you are in the grief process. There are five well-known stages that mark this process—denial, anger, depression, bargaining, and acceptance. Though most of these stages may sound like something you *don't* want to do, they are essential for ensuring that you keep moving forward in your pain instead of remaining stuck.

Understanding them can be especially useful for you as a father, since gaining the ability to look for those stages in your child's responses can alert you to the fact that they're experiencing grief in the first place. They may feel hurt or disappointed at times by things you wouldn't expect, and by learning to recognize those feelings, you can be better equipped to help them work through them rather than try to dictate the grief process for them. After all, it's *their* grief, which means they get to decide what's worth grieving, not you. Your job is just to help them do so.

As you look over these stages of grief, keep in mind that they're in no way definitive, and not everyone will experience them the same way or in the same order. In fact, a person may not experience certain stages at all. The important part is to make sure both you and your child continue moving forward, not allowing your pain to hold you back in any one stage but instead always working toward true peace.

1   Denial

In the denial stage, you attempt to ignore the reality of your circumstances. While you may not be able to deny what happened, you do whatever you can to pretend life hasn't changed as a result. Say you're grieving a job you were laid off from. You drive home feeling numb, trying to think of a way to break it to your wife. Then suddenly, you think, "Maybe they got it wrong... maybe they meant to fire someone else! I should call my boss and try to fix this."

Your denial may not always be so obvious, though, instead coming out in different "why" questions that start running through your head, distracting you from the reality of the situation. Why did this have to happen? Why can't I catch a break? Why doesn't anyone see my potential? Denial can be an incredibly useful stage of grief, because it can help ease you into the harsh reality of your pain. Just be careful. If you get caught in an endless loop of those "why" questions, it can easily tempt you into trying to run away from the pain forever.

2   Anger

Grief brings a lot of emotional pain that's confusing and overwhelming, and it can be easier to try to funnel it all down into one simple emotion—anger. It's natural to be angry over the loss, over how things have changed, and over the fact that you even have to experience grief at all. But anger is only one tiny piece of the enormous picture. Focusing on that piece can help you take the first steps in your grief work, but make sure it doesn't block out all the other elements and emotions that will help you move toward a resolution.

3   Depression

Unlike the denial and anger stages, which are ways we avoid our pain, the depression stage occurs when we fully recognize what happened and succumb to our sadness. You've given up trying to fight against reality and turn your focus on the pain you feel. As with denial and anger, however, depression can be useful too. As long as you don't let it drag you down too far, your sadness can help you finally begin the process of recognizing, working through, and ultimately resolving your hurt.

4   Bargaining

The bargaining stage comes as a way to regain control, especially in situations where your pain was the result of your own choices. As with the "why" questions in the denial stage, you get lost in a loop of "if only" statements. If only I hadn't skipped work, or if only I were more like my coworkers, things would be different. You may even try to make a deal with God, promising to change your behavior or finally accept a task in exchange for a different outcome or relief from your pain. Bargaining may give you hope for a moment, and it may even give you a sense of control. But ultimately, it's just another way to avoid facing your grief directly.

5   Acceptance

Regardless of what your individual grief process looks like and which stages you do or don't encounter, we all must reach the final stage of acceptance. Acceptance doesn't necessarily mean being free of the pain, but it does mean coming to terms with it and understanding how your life will be different going forward. In this way, you can finally learn to live with what happened and go on with your life free from the heavy weight of your grief.

DO THE WORK

Now that you understand what you need to grieve and where you are in the process, you're ready to take control of actively working through your grief. To help you do so, I've put together a short list of strategies for processing pain. These strategies are useful not just for your own grief work but also for helping your child navigate their grief experiences. As you review them, think about what areas in your own life you could apply them to so you can finally move forward, and think about how you can help your child do the same.

1   Don't make your pain worse.

No matter what the source is, all people who are in pain wind up with a single dominant desire—to make that pain go away. As we've been discussing, the only way we can really do that is to face it head-on and process it emotionally. Unfortunately, however, it's often much easier to try to take a shortcut. Whether it's substance abuse or overworking ourselves, we engage with some kind of demeaning, ritualistic, or compulsive action as a way to numb our feelings and avoid the pain we can't seem to escape from.

But while these behaviors may temporarily pull you out of your grief, you will only find yourself sinking further down into it once the distraction ends. Even worse, the behaviors you engage with may lead to further physical or emotional pain, such as when you push away supportive relationships in favor of your addiction. As you work through your grief, always keep in mind the potential consequences of any coping mechanism and stay away from the ones that could make your pain worse. And just as importantly, you must do the same for your child. Be cognizant of any ways they may be trying to numb themselves, and redirect them toward more helpful grieving strategies. When you do, they'll be able to work through their pain honestly and gain new strengths in the process.

2   Talk with God.

1 Peter 5:7 tells us, "Turn all your worries over to him. He cares about you." God stood by Jesus through each of His ups and downs, and He stands by ready to do the same for you. However, God isn't always our go-to in moments of pain. More often, we try to take the wheel by deliberately distracting ourselves from our grief or heroically trying to move on. But these methods will only elongate the pain further, causing you to bottle up emotions and create even more stress and discomfort for yourself. We all need quieter moments simply to reflect on our grief and turn it over to

God. Taking time just to be with Him will help orient you, allowing you to tackle your grief with a much clearer perspective.

Quiet time is also important for your child. When they are young and learning to develop their emotional capabilities, they're often more likely to become agitated or disruptive in their grief. Pulling them out of the situation and away from external stimuli can help them calm down, focus on what they're feeling, and limit its control over them. Just be careful to assure them that quiet time is not a punishment. One way to do this is to sit quietly with them. Besides showing them how to be still and talk to God, your presence can give them a sense of comfort and support, which will make them feel safe enough to tackle their grief work.

3 **Share with others.**

As we discussed in Chapter 9, it's important to talk with other men about what's going on inside you. Besides providing you with acceptance and support, these men can also serve as mirrors. Hearing them repeat back to you what they think you're saying will allow you to get an outside perspective on your grief, which will help you recognize your own flawed thinking or misinterpretations. In turn, you will increase your ability to label what happened and the emotions you feel, making it easier to redefine and let go of what haunts you.

As a father, you must act as this same mirror for your child. But in order to do so, you must learn to listen with your heart, not just your head. While it's hard to experience the pain of someone you love, it's essential for helping them get through it. Jesus cried at Lazareth's death, both for His own loss and for the loss Lazareth's sisters felt (John 11:17-35). So instead of trying to fix your child's pain, simply listen and feel. With your support, they can begin their own process of understanding and releasing their grief.

4   Practice forgiveness.

In your grief process, you'll come to a point where you have to decide whether or not you'll forgive whoever had a hand in your pain. However, forgiveness doesn't mean you have to reconnect with that person or even tell them you forgive them. Instead, it can mean learning to forgive for your own sake. In addiction recovery, there's a saying that tells us "those who anger us control us." As long as you're waiting for someone to make amends or pay for the pain they caused you, you'll be emotionally held hostage by them. By forgiving them, you're not saying that what they did was okay. You're simply recognizing what occurred as a result of their actions, trusting God to help you emotionally process it, and finding a way to move on.

Forgiveness isn't just something to give to others—it's also something you need to give yourself. Some of what you need to grieve likely came from your own negative choices, and it can be easy to beat yourself up over it, making those "if only" statements. But the amazing truth is that God has already forgiven you (1 John 1:9). Rather than devaluing yourself by sinking into shame, you must turn over your pain to Him and seek His forgiveness. And when He grants it, you must accept it, forgive yourself, and use His strength to start again.

Forgiveness is especially important to teach to your child, because hurt and anger internalized at a young age can disrupt their development and have a lifelong impact. When they make mistakes, encourage them to forgive themselves, and show them your unconditional love. And when someone else hurts them, encourage them to forgive that person and reconcile when possible. Just be careful never to attempt to force them to do so. True forgiveness can only happen on their own terms.[1]

---

1   For more on the process of forgiveness and letting go, check out our manhood resource *Being God's Man* at liveupresources.com.

5   Redefine the experience

The main goal of grief work is not to dwell on a painful experience but instead to find a way to redefine it. Nothing is ever completely bad, no matter how much it seems so at the time. Think about it this way. God could have stopped the pain from happening. Because He didn't, that means there's something for you to appreciate about it or a lesson to learn from it (Genesis 50:20). As you do your own grief work and guide your child through theirs, always keep your focus on the strengths that can come out of it. This is not to ignore the pain or to attempt to rewrite history but simply to change your perspective. It's a reminder that no matter what happened in the past, it no longer has to determine the future.

6   Leave some questions unanswered.

Sometimes we hold on to grief too long because we're searching for answers to explain what happened. Why did they have to die? Why did that person hurt me? Why didn't my parents love me? Unfortunately, the reality is that some experiences can never be fully explained or justified. Rather than driving yourself crazy trying to understand what happened, sometimes the best way forward is simply to accept that it did. When you focus on forgiveness and on putting your faith in God, you won't just let go of your own past. You will also guide your child toward a better future.

7   If necessary, seek counseling.

As daunting or uncomfortable as the idea of seeing a therapist may be, the trauma you experience in life can sometimes be too difficult to process on your own. If you find yourself struggling with your grief for weeks or months without any apparent progress, it may be helpful to seek a professional who is trained to help people work through pain just like yours. Besides being an objective viewpoint, they can also help walk you through the stages of grief or give you concrete tasks that can move you forward in processing your pain more productively. They can even help you determine if the emotional shock of the trauma has interrupted your normal biological processes and whether medication can be useful in your healing.

Counseling may also be necessary for your child at times. A younger child often tends to be hypersensitive to pain and disappointment, taking rejection harder or blaming themselves. Their lack of development and understanding might lead them to respond chaotically and self-destructively or by seeking immediate pleasure no matter the long-term consequences. And unfortunately, in these times you may simply not know how to guide your child the way they need.

As fathers, we all want to be enough for our children, but that doesn't mean doing it all on our own. Sometimes it includes finding the resources that will allow us to help our children as best we can. Whether you see a counselor yourself to learn how to father them better or find one to work directly with your child, their expertise can help show you the best way to move forward again.

As you go through your grief work and help your child through theirs, it's important to remember that no one other than the person experiencing grief can ultimately accept and resolve it. This means that you must not become dependent on someone else to overcome your grief for you, nor must you attempt to fix everything in your child's life. As much as you may at times wish otherwise, you can't heal their wounds for them. However, you can heal yourself, be their supportive pillar to lean on, and trust that God will do the rest.

THROUGH THE TUNNEL

Whatever type of pain you experience in life, whether it's a single moment of failure or an ongoing experience like a disability, you will have to repeatedly engage in grief work. That's not an easy undertaking. Sometimes the pain will feel relentless, and it can be hard to tell if you're making any progress at all. But growth doesn't always come as a big, resounding breakthrough. Instead, it's often found in the small victories.

The following points are some easy ways to know you're progressing in your grief. This isn't a checklist, but rather some examples that can give you hope. When you realize one of these circumstances has happened, you'll know you or your child are on your way toward resolving your grief for good.

- You accept your responsibility to resolve your grief instead of waiting for someone else to fix it.

- You can recall the painful event without becoming overly angry, depressed, or agitated about it.

- You are willing to face periodic moments of grief directly rather than trying to ignore them or will them away.

- You are willing to process your grief with those who were part of the experience that caused it.

- You can talk about your grief with others without becoming overly defensive or upset.

- You are willing to grant forgiveness, either to the person who hurt you or to yourself for how you contributed to the problem.

- You can recognize the strengths and growth you gained from the experience.

- You set boundaries within your relationships based on the lessons you learned.

- You can experience fun with others and develop secure attachments.

Grief is one of the trickiest parts of life because it never fully goes away, even when you've done your grief work well and turned it over to God. Just as all wounds do, your grief will leave scars deep within you that may throb at times when you're reminded of that painful part of your past. But that pain doesn't mean the wound hasn't healed. It's simply a reminder of all you have survived and how much you've grown.

Knowing that it's okay to hurt and to grieve is the most important step. Once you let down your barriers and admit to God your deepest pain and failures, He'll hold your burden and walk with you the whole way through the fire (Daniel 3:19-29). And in return, He'll give you the strength to do the same for your child in the moments they need you the most.

 ROBERT'S STORY

Beaches, sun, culture, food. For many, Miami is a vacation destination of endless fun and activity. For most of my life, it was also the place I called home. It's where Colleen and I grew up, where our friends and family lived. It's where our church and ministry were based. But eventually, it became a place that was too cramped for our growing family. It became a place where having to drive anywhere was a traffic-ridden chore. And finally, Miami became the place we moved away from.

Following a series of opportunities and lots of prayer, my friend (and, coincidentally, coauthor of this book) Roy called me up and asked, "How would you like to move to Pennsylvania?" I think I laughed at the time. But the more I heard him speak about what he was planning and what God was preparing him to build, the more obvious it became that this opportunity was certainly no joke.

I remember going to my wife about it with little hope she'd

respond with excitement. But to my surprise, she didn't hate the idea. In fact, the more we talked and prayed about it, the more God made it clear. In record time, we turned our entire lives upside down, completely uprooted, and made Pennsylvania our new state. A year later, we purchased a house, larger than what we ever had in Miami, and officially finished our move.

It was a dream come true. We'd left the stressful hustle and bustle of a big city and stepped into the tranquility of a small town. My daughters finally had their own rooms, we had the perfect amount of closet space, and we even had a guest bedroom. Better yet, we had clear, God-given opportunities to further the Gospel to many more areas around the world. My brain wanted to shout "Hallelujah!" For some reason, though, my spirit could not.

One cold evening, as the four of us sat by our new fireplace, I looked around and realized no one was smiling. In fact, no one seemed happy at all. Although we had every reason in the world to be ecstatic, our hearts could not follow suit. My wife and I truly missed our families. I'd left my mom, dad, and sister, along with two nephews and an awesome brother-in-law. Sophia had left a dance company and coach who had guided every step of her talented growth. And we'd all left behind lifelong friends who truly knew us.

I sat at that fireplace looking at my family and, in a moment of wisdom, said, "It's okay to feel sad." Immediately eyes began to well up. It was a surreal moment, but it allowed us each to accept that we can mourn and grieve changes even if they are for the better. It gave us emotional permission to cry over God's new direction for our lives. I'm grateful for that moment of wisdom and, most of all, that we experienced our grief together.

 DISCUSSION QUESTIONS

1 Think about some of the most impactful moments of grief in your life. Which stages of grief did you experience? How did that process hurt or help your ability to get through your pain?

2 Look over the seven strategies for grief work. Which would be most helpful to you in times of grief? Which could you use to help your child through theirs?

3 In the last chapter's discussion section, you described two experiences in your life that created lasting pain. Using those same experiences, explain how you knew you'd gotten through the worst of that pain. How can you be more conscious of recognizing your progress in the small moments?

4 Discuss how Romans 8:28 relates to grief work. How can relying on God help us find strength in our darkest moments?

We know that in all things God works for the good of those who love him. He appointed them to be saved in keeping with his purpose.

13

THE OPPONENT WITHIN

For the past few chapters, we've talked about the external factors that can cause us to deviate from God's path and choose a life of passivity and routine. If left unprocessed, negative or traumatic experiences can instill useless patterns of behavior that make us lose sight of our potential and our children's. And painful memories, whether the result of our own mistakes or of unavoidable tragedy, can even make life seem completely meaningless.

But although external factors can have a strong, lasting impact, they're ultimately not what causes the most damage in our lives. After all, we're the ones who avoid change and growth. We're the ones who push down those negative experiences instead of resolving them. And we're the ones who resist being all of who God created us to be. When it comes down to it, your biggest problem isn't your father's inadequacies, your painful experiences, or even life's unfairness. Your biggest problem is *you*—and the sin that lives within.

In Chapter 2, I gave a broad overview of the sin nature as it relates to fatherhood, along with the importance of engaging in your struggle with it in order to do fathering God's way. In this chapter, we'll take a deeper look at the specific attributes of sin and how to recognize its influence. There are two opposite perspectives to every circumstance you experience: you can seek God's will, or you can follow your own. The better you understand your sin nature, the harder you'll fight to adopt the first perspective and include God in your battles against temptation, and the more equipped you'll be to help your child in their own internal war.

WHAT IS SIN?

The easiest and most popular way of viewing sin is as a logical set of actions we should avoid at all costs: don't murder, don't lie, don't knowingly hurt others, and so on. But as sinful as those actions may be, they are not the primary problem. Sinful choices are simply the result of letting our sin nature take over our decision-making and control our actions. The real question is, where is our heart regarding a relationship with God?

In reality, sin is much more involved in our lives than we often think. It's like a powerful, destructive force that exists within each of us, working constantly to destroy every good thought or productive impulse we have. It seeks to infiltrate every area within us in order to drive us toward self-centered and pleasure-oriented behaviors and away from God's plan. In other words, it separates us from a holy God. And worst of all, it does most of this completely under the radar. Our sin nature encourages us to maintain a simplified, incomplete view of it, because that keeps us right where it wants us—unaware of its influence and completely unguarded.

Not only does our sin nature blind us to its own influence, it also blinds us to how sin may be affecting our children. At the very least, it stops us from doing anything about it. We often prefer to do what's comfortable and easy, which can lead us to avoid the tough work of parenting our children when they act up. Besides withholding the guidance they need to know how to manage their impulses and behaviors, this approach also causes us to set an ungodly example for them to follow. By letting sin control us, even when the outcome is simply passivity, we implicitly tell our children it's okay for them to do the same.

The first step in taking back that control is repentance. Go to God with humility and ask for His forgiveness. Ask Him to restore your strength. Ask Him for wisdom. Then you can use His guidance to understand the following four key characteristics of sin. The better you become at recognizing these characteristics, the quicker you can seek God's help the moment you sense its presence. And the greater your ability to manage your sin nature, the more active you will be in helping your child manage theirs.

1   Sin is proud.

The basic goal of our sin nature is to encourage us to focus solely on ourselves. It plays into our natural self-interest by convincing us that we're more important, worthy, or powerful and therefore don't need to follow the same rules as everyone else. Like we talked about in Chapter 3, God wants us to be like Him by internalizing His principles and working to live up to His standards. But our sin nature makes us want to *be* God instead. It instills a narcissistic belief that we're perfect and infallible and that our needs come before both others and God. As a result, we ignore our immaturity and shortcomings, depriving ourselves of any growth we could obtain.

2   Sin is pessimistic.

In our pride, our sin nature causes us to hold ourselves to a high standard of perfection. But as we discussed in Chapter 2, only God is truly perfect, which means we'll inevitably fail. But rather than see what we are in Jesus, our sin nature convinces us to focus on what we aren't, beating us down and making us feel like losers for not living up to an impossible standard. As a result, we careen into a deep sense of shame and give up trying altogether, believing the lie that we'll never be good enough. In our self-inflicted misery, we decide that we might as well stick to the negative behaviors we know will make us happy in the moment rather than taking a risk for something better.

3   Sin is persuasive.

Our sin nature continually seeks pleasure, and it will pull out all the stops to get us to do what it wants. No matter what argument you come up with, it will be ready with a counterargument. If you recognize that a behavior may be wrong, your sin nature will quickly tell you it won't hurt anyone (and besides, everyone else is doing it). If you point out the consequences of that behavior, your sin nature will immediately reply that it won't happen to you and that it's worth it (after all, doing it feels really, *really* good). If you say you don't want to start a bad habit, your sin nature will jump in, adding that you can just stop at any time (your own will-power is more than good enough). However, all of the claims above are nothing but lies. But unfortunately, those lies are often enticing enough to work.

4   Sin is pervasive.

Sin is most obvious in how it influences our actions, but the reality is that sin infiltrates *every* area of our lives. It hijacks our emotions, causing us to rely on anger and fear instead of mercy and trust. It inhibits our grief work, preventing us from mourning our losses properly and turning our pain into permanent feelings of sadness or inadequacy. It damages our bodies, convincing us to avoid exercise, put off seeing a doctor, and eat whatever we want. It warps our natural aggression, making us insensitive toward others, resentful, or even deliberately hurtful. And worst of all, it destroys our relationships both with God and with those we care about most, driving us to seek isolation and act in ways that make us difficult to love at all.

YOUR SIN

While it's important to recognize the characteristics of sin, doing so isn't enough to create a complete understanding. You must also discover how those characteristics manifest in your everyday life. Thankfully, as long as you're willing to look, its impact on your life can be pretty easy to see. Take an honest look at the following list of sin's common effects, and check off the ones you frequently struggle with or have struggled with in the past.[1] By owning up to these behaviors, you're taking the first step of acknowledging their negative influence on you, which will ultimately empower you to break free (1 John 1:9).

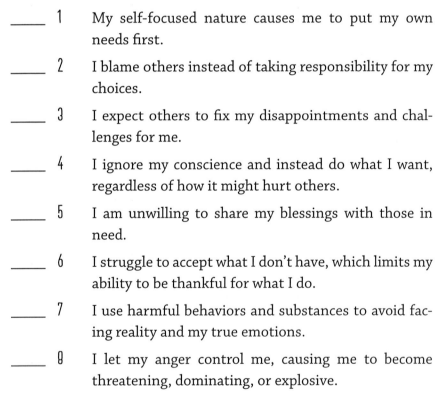

_____ 1   My self-focused nature causes me to put my own needs first.

_____ 2   I blame others instead of taking responsibility for my choices.

_____ 3   I expect others to fix my disappointments and challenges for me.

_____ 4   I ignore my conscience and instead do what I want, regardless of how it might hurt others.

_____ 5   I am unwilling to share my blessings with those in need.

_____ 6   I struggle to accept what I don't have, which limits my ability to be thankful for what I do.

_____ 7   I use harmful behaviors and substances to avoid facing reality and my true emotions.

_____ 8   I let my anger control me, causing me to become threatening, dominating, or explosive.

---

1   For a printable version of this checklist, visit liveupresources.com/fatherhood. You can also see this survey discussed further in *The Genesis of Manhood* video series at liveupresources.com.

_____ 9   I wallow in my disappointments instead of doing the hard work of facing reality, developing a new plan, and executing it.

_____ 10   I misuse my body and neglect my physical health.

_____ 11   I don't care for myself or my family by completing necessary tasks around the house.

_____ 12   I expect others to take care of me instead of taking charge and doing it myself.

_____ 13   I automatically distrust others instead of putting in the effort to get to know them.

_____ 14   I hang on to resentments regarding how others have hurt me instead of forgiving them and moving on.

_____ 15   I don't act on my love for others in ways that help them feel valued and cared for.

_____ 16   I am often prejudiced, which causes me to define those who are different from me as less valuable.

_____ 17   I say hurtful words with no regard for another person's feelings.

_____ 18   My anxiety and fear about what might happen in the future limit me from being present.

_____ 20   I deny or remain unaware of the circumstances and feelings around me in order to live in a comfortable fantasy world.

_____ 21   I internalize failure or criticism, which reinforces my sense of inadequacy and my belief that I shouldn't even try.

_____ 22   I feel worthless and ignore God's definition of me.

_____ 23   I pretend to be someone other than who I really am.

_____ 24   I don't control my self-destructive impulses or delay gratification.

If you're anything like me, you checked off quite a few of those behaviors. And right on cue, I'm sure your sin nature is telling you what a failure you are and how you'll never be able to begin to correct all those shortcomings. But God's truth always counteracts sin's lies. He says that your emotional, physical, mental, and relational aspects were created by Him to fit together and work in perfect harmony. So though you'll never fully escape your sin, every small step you take with Jesus in correcting the negative tendencies you checked off brings you closer to being the man and father God created you to be (Ephesians 4:22-24).

As we discussed in Chapter 2, by simply engaging in your struggle with your sin, you demonstrate a commitment to following God's way. You have access to His forgiveness, guidance, and love, all of which will give you the strength to persevere no matter how much your sin nature tries to sway you. And here's some more good news: you've already started the battle by honestly going through that checklist and recognizing how your sin nature has manifested in your life. Now it's time to take the next step—doing something about it.

Proverbs 28:13 puts it simply: "Anyone who hides their sins doesn't succeed. But anyone who admits their sins and gives them up finds mercy." In other words, it's not enough to just acknowledge your sins to yourself. You must also *confess* them, which means admitting your sinful desires and behaviors not only to God but also to others in your life (James 5:16).

As difficult as it may be, God wants us to share our struggles with each other for a multitude of reasons. For one, your confession can inspire others to share their own similar struggles. Relating to each other's challenges shows you that no matter how lonely your struggle may feel, you're never really alone. Through sharing, you also gain support and prayer, both of which become even more powerful as more people participate in them. And perhaps most importantly, others can hold you accountable for sticking to your goals and not succumbing to sin in moments of weakness.

Unfortunately, as vital as confession is in managing our sin, we can easily be blocked from engaging in it by our sin nature's pessimistic attitude. We all have a vision of the person God wants us to be, and having to admit our failures shows us just how far from that image we actually are. It can cause us to develop a lack of faith in God's view of us, making us wonder if we really are good enough. But instead of reaching out to Him to help us with our unbelief, we often beat ourselves up for our sinful desires and mistakes, which only makes it even more difficult for us to change them (Mark 9:24).

Another obstacle to confession is our hyperawareness of the potential for judgment from others. As a minister's kid, I saw first-hand that the line between the prayer chain and the gossip chain could at times be quite thin. Because of this, I never saw the church as very emotionally helpful with my sinful struggles. It seemed much easier to keep them to myself. As safe as this self-protection may appear, however, it ultimately does more harm in the long run. That's because while you may prevent yourself from having to face unfair and harsh judgment from some, you also cut yourself off from those who truly want to offer their love and support.

So how can we overcome these obstacles and be transparent about our sin, both to ourselves and to others? One effective solution I've found is to use another term for it. When I was writing *The Heroic Man's Journey,* a video program for men, God helped me find an alternative word for our sin nature that has helped many men struggling with this self-destructive aspect of themselves—the shadow. After all, sin's negative presence goes with us everywhere, even when we can't see it. And the closer we get to the light (God), the more clearly we can see our shadow's true form.[2]

I've seen the effectiveness of this term in many men's groups that used *The Heroic Man's Journey*. After the video lesson, the men break up into small groups, which we call campfires, so they can talk about the lesson. Occasionally, I'd walk around to the different campfires to briefly listen in and see if anyone had questions.

But more often, I was the one who was learning. What I heard in those groups was incredible. Because of the inseparable nature of a shadow, men had no trouble using this term to talk about their sins. They didn't doubt their shadow's existence or try to hide it. They felt safe enough to describe what was going on within them. As a result, they were opening up in ways they never had before, experiencing their emotions so deeply that some men were even crying. And in return, they were finally receiving the support they'd gone without for so long.

If using the word *shadow* doesn't work for you, I encourage you to develop a way to refer to your own sin nature that personalizes it so its effects become easier to observe. This will simply help you be more aware of it. Your sin nature isn't something to be proud of, but because of Jesus's sacrifice, it also doesn't need to define you. God knows it exists within you, and He loves you anyway. That's why He sent His Son to earth to die for your sins, and that's why He will forgive you for everything you've ever done wrong (John 3:16; Ephesians 1:7). Your sin nature may win a battle here or there, but as long as you always keep your focus on God, it will never win the war.

THEIR SIN

During the summer after my sophomore year of college, I met a woman several years older than me who I really hit it off

---

2   To learn more about the concept of the shadow or *The Heroic Man's Journey* series, visit liveupresources.com.

with. After driving her home one night, I found it incredibly diffi-cult to leave her behind and end our time together—so I didn't. I stayed and talked with her until just after midnight when we heard a knock at the door. To my surprise, it was my father—the last per-son an older teenager wants to see when they know they're doing something wrong. But he hadn't come to yell at me or punish me for being out so late with a woman. Instead, he simply said one sentence, a sentence I had heard several times before: "Very little good occurs after midnight."

I remember being embarrassed, though not because of him. I was embarrassed at myself, because I knew he was right. In the ex-citement of getting to know this woman, that truth had somehow become secondary in my mind. But thankfully, I had my father on my side. Even though I was technically an adult and arguably out of his care, he remained committed to helping me make the right decisions, no matter how it might look to me or others.

And that's exactly what your role is as a father. At the same time that you're engaging in the struggle with your sin nature, your child is also engaging with theirs—except, unlike you, they lack the wisdom and life experience to fully understand the struggle going on within them. Without your guidance, their only natural response is either to choose a self-destructive course of action or to conclude that there's something wrong with them. They think they must be the only person on earth whose willpower isn't enough, leaving them with a false sense of shame. Consequently, they de-velop a "why try?" attitude, which makes it even more likely that they'll continue to make self-destructive, sinful choices.

As a father, it's your duty not only to teach your child about their sin nature but also to actively help them manage it. To do this, you must engage with them regarding sin in several different ways. The first is through initiating conversations about it. Every concept we've discussed so far about your own struggle with sin is something your child needs to know as well, and you can't rely on the culture, school, or their peers to teach it to them correctly. You must be willing to step up and have that tough conversation so they can gain a clear understanding of what's going on within them.

However, especially for a young child, it won't be easy to understand such an abstract concept like sin. Children have a limited ability to think abstractly before their teenage years and often need concrete explanations or comparisons to understand a topic.[3] This means that a general explanation of sin likely won't be all that helpful and may even lead your child to personalize that explanation. They may start thinking, "My sin nature is bad, so that must mean *I'm* bad and worthless." While this may encourage them to apologize for their negative behaviors, it won't be out of true repentance. It'll be because they're overwhelmed by more than they can emotionally digest, whether what they feel is false guilt or simply fear.

The best way to prevent this misinterpretation of sin is to discuss God with your child during your conversations about it. As you describe the internal challenges they will face throughout their life, also explain that it doesn't change how God values them. Teach them that He will continually love them and empower them no matter what they do. By emphasizing this good news over the negativity of their sin nature, you will give your child both a realistic understanding of sin and a sense of hope and confidence, which will make it easier for them to recognize and manage this struggle in the future.

Besides reassuring your child of their value, talking about sin in the context of God's love also makes it simpler to explain. Our struggle with sin really boils down to one question: whose will takes precedence in your life—God's, or your own? Once you frame

---

3   For more on the cognitive limitations children face in their ability to understand the concept of sin and its relationship to their moral development, check out the theories of Jean Piaget and Lawrence Kohlberg.

sin in this way, you can then discuss with your child their need to accept God's help in this battle of the wills. It's only by continually identifying the areas that they give in to their sin nature's negative impulses the most and turning them over to God that they can truly resist them.

Another way to help your child understand sin is to discuss some practical examples of how it shows up in their life, like we did with the checklist. Basic rules and principles—such as a lie is wrong, taking something that isn't yours is stealing, and don't do to others what you don't want done to you—are all concepts your child should be able to comprehend, especially if you relate them to their everyday experiences. The Ten Commandments are also a good place to start (Exodus 20:2-17). God has provided these foundational identity structures for each of us to rely on, and internalizing them at a young age will give your child a head start on recognizing and managing their sin's influence.

Of course, your child won't always be so limited in their ability to understand abstract concepts, which is why it's important to continue to have conversations with them about making wrong decisions throughout their childhood. As their brain develops, so will their thought processes and emotional capabilities, which will allow them to understand the more complex aspects of sin.

In addition to having deeper discussions, you should also consider involving your child in various church activities where other children are processing the same concepts. Through interactions with their peers, your child will both understand the importance of community in their spiritual growth and learn to recognize how sin can challenge them relationally. Not only will this create questions within them that they can then bring to you, but it will also provide you with more opportunities to raise the topic with them when they don't.

As you know, your child won't be perfect in their struggle with their sin nature, so you also must be ready to confront them about their negative choices. When they're young, they won't experience as many natural consequences to their actions. If they purposely dump out the cat's food dish, the only one who's really affected is the hungry cat. Future rebellious actions, though, could lead to harsher consequences like losing friends, getting detention at school, or even facing prison time. By enforcing consequences when they're young, like giving them take a time-out or making them clean up the mess they made, you help them learn to resist their impulses and understand the areas where they still need to grow.

As you guide your child in managing their sin, you must also take care to be authentic and model through your own choices the standard you are holding them to. This begins with you humbling yourself and letting them see your repentant attitude toward your ungodly behaviors. The reality is that you won't always be perfect. At times, you will violate your standards in front of your child, no matter how hard you try not to. But instead of glossing over it, you should discuss it directly. By owning up to your mistakes, you will demonstrate a humility that will show your child how to seek God's strength and grace just like you do.

However, that's not to say you need to tell them everything. Being honest about your slip-ups is not the same as involving your child in your personal struggle with sin. They don't need to know the intimate details of your emotional turmoil, especially if they aren't yet mature enough to digest and relate to it. Oversharing can also make you dependent on your child to fulfill your relational needs, like your need for accountability, which is a role your wife or close friends should fulfill. This will only undermine the security your child has in you as their father. Rather than go into detail, simply share that you're experiencing the struggle with sin in general. That can be enough to help your child feel less alone and better understand the full negative power of their sin nature.

While all of the above tasks are vital in helping your child manage their sin, the most important one is providing the foundational, unconditional love we talked about in Chapter 5. Sin and God's love are incompatible with each other, and the more loving your relationship with your child is, the more empowered they'll be to manage their sin nature. When you accurately represent God in their life, your responses will be like His. And with that sense of security and support, your child can avoid internalizing their sin and letting it convince them they have no value. Instead, they'll trust in your love and know that they can rely on you to be there to guide them, support them, and help them start again.

The only way you can provide such unconditional love in the face of sin is to look to God's perfect example and mirror His love to your child. Whether it's through your caring actions or by teaching them important Bible stories that reflect God's love, you should continually find ways to share how He forgives them for any sinful mistake they make. Above all, help your child recognize that the one who is in them is ultimately more powerful than anything in the world—and that includes their sin nature (1 John 4:4).

Although our conversation about sin and its effects ends with this chapter, assessing your sin nature is not a once-and-done achievement. Because we are all constantly changing, and even more so due to our children's impact, we must continually evaluate ourselves so we can know which sinful desires are trying to take hold of our lives. Every so often, go back to the checklist in this chapter to see which areas you've improved on and which you still need to seek God's assistance with. The better you understand what's going on within you, the easier it will be to turn it over to God, ask for His forgiveness, receive His grace, and be empowered to try again.

As you engage in the struggle with your sin nature, always remember that because of Jesus's sacrifice, there's one characteristic of sin that no longer exists—permanence. This is the hope we all have (Hebrews 6:18-20). If you hold on to that, you will be able to help your child recognize that they are truly free. Then the brilliance God created for them can fully shine through.

ROBERT'S STORY

When Sophia was about four years old, I noticed a pattern in her behavior. Every time she did something wrong, she'd hide. Though she would occasionally tuck herself into a corner, completely out of sight, most often she would simply bury her face in a pillow or into her pretty little arms. She knew a lecture was probably coming, along with some type of disciplinary action that was *not* going to feel good.

I kept asking myself why she would hide instead of apologize or show remorse. Then I remembered Genesis 3, when Adam and Eve sinned and then attempted to hide from God, ashamed of their actions. Although they tried to duck behind trees and fig-leaf clothing, God exposed and properly disciplined them.

But then God did something amazing, something they couldn't do for themselves. He saw their inability to cover their shame about sinning and their nakedness, and He covered them Himself (Genesis 3:21). In other words, God taught them that though sin is indeed deeply offensive to Him and carries consequences, the solution is to run *to* Him, not away from Him. He is the only one who can properly heal the shame that haunts all of us.

As counterintuitive as it may seem, I realized that my job as a father was not just to punish the sin but also to offer emotional healing and restoration. I began to pray with Sophia whenever disciplinary action was required and teach her how to ask God for forgiveness. I exchanged loud, condemning words for loving truth and a continued relationship with her. I made sure she knew an embrace would always be available from me.

There's no doubt that sin is evil and rejected by God. There's also no doubt that God desires redemption over condemnation. Effectively, I began to teach my daughter the greatest lesson she would ever learn—how to repent. And that lesson goes a lot further than pretending she'll never break the rules.

💬 DISCUSSION QUESTIONS

1   Review your completed checklist of sins. In what areas does sin manifest in your life? What sinful desires or behaviors do you struggle with most?

2   How easy or difficult is it for you to confess your sins to yourself, to God, and to others? Describe how your sin nature is currently attacking you the most.

3   How have you described sin to your child in the past? What can you do to help them better understand their sin nature?

4   Discuss the directives given in Genesis 18:19 about how a father should guide his child. How do these directives help you understand your role in managing your child's sin nature?

I have chosen him. He must direct his children to live in the way that pleases me. And he must direct the members of his family after him to do the same. So he must guide all of them in doing what is right and fair. Then I, the LORD, will do for Abraham what I have promised him.

14

FIXED OR GROWTH?

Let me ask you something: are you having fun? Now, this might seem like an ironic question seeing as we've just finished talking about our father issues, grief, and sin—some of the least fun topics we could cover. But what I mean is, are you having fun as a father? Do you have moments of pure joy with your child? And not just when you play together or do something intentionally enjoyable. As fathers, we are blessed with the privilege of being part of a slowly unfolding miracle—our children's discovery of their personality, skills, and strengths. It's an awesome thing to witness, and if we're truly committed to fatherhood, we should be constantly amazed and delighted by every new experience or challenge our children encounter.

Unfortunately, not all fathers are, or at least not all the time. Life is filled with busyness, and we all have to-do lists that are simply too long to accomplish. And sometimes we can wind up seeing our children as just another task we need to check off. It's easy to get caught up in the natural stress of it all and lose sight of what's really happening, and not just with our children. As the well-known saying goes, "It's not about the destination; it's about the journey." Well, that's exactly what fatherhood is—a journey. And it's not one in which we're meant to arrive (1 Corinthians 13:12). As long as your child is learning and growing, so will you, often in the most unexpected ways.

However, growth isn't something that will miraculously happen just because you're a father in title, and it's not as simple as saying, "It's time to take more risks and be challenged!" While that's a good sentiment, you won't actually accomplish much unless you're intentional about it. And that means taking a deeper look at what may be limiting you in your own growth and preventing you from encouraging and appreciating your child in theirs. In the end, it's not just your knowledge of what's right and good that impacts your ability to grow—it's your confidence regarding whether or not you can.

TWO MINDSETS

Although there are many different beliefs we can internalize about life and ourselves, Stanford University psychologist Carol Dweck has identified two primary mindsets that relate specifically to identity formation—fixed and growth.[1] These mindsets are important to understand not only because of the impact they have on how your own life turns out, but also because of the influence they have on how you raise your child.

Your mindset will directly impact your ability to guide your child through their challenges and goals, encourage them in their struggles, and love them regardless of their choices and behaviors. For this reason, you must understand which one you currently have and how it dictates the way you treat both yourself and your child. Only then can you build on your strengths and manage your weaknesses, learning to see you both as God does.

As the name suggests, a fixed mindset is a static way of viewing yourself and others, like with the photograph we talked about in Chapter 8. When you have this mindset, you believe deep down that your life is confined by predetermined limits. You can only

---

1   Carol S. Dweck, *Mindset: The New Psychology of Success* (New York: Ballantine Books, 2016).

change and grow so much, which means you're ultimately unable to improve your natural abilities, intelligence, and talents past a certain fixed point. So once you feel you've hit your limit of growth, you stop pushing yourself. You don't seek out new risks because you don't want to have to face what you believe is inevitable failure, and you view others as threats, competitors, and sources of envy rather than resources for inspiration, support, and guidance. You willingly accept that change is not possible and simply give up trying at anything, thus completing the self-fulfilling prophecy that you can't achieve more than you already have.

Conversely, a growth mindset means you believe you can improve upon the capabilities God has given you through deliberate effort and experience. With this mindset, you trust God when He says that all things are possible for those who believe, which means you don't put limits on what you can become (Matthew 19:26). You're always looking for new ways to push your potential forward, regardless of how often you fail or succeed along the way. To you, the journey *is* more important than the destination, because as soon as you reach that destination, you'll simply set your sights on a new one.

As I'm sure you can tell, a growth mindset is the perspective we need to have if you ever want to reach your full, God-given potential. At first glance, obtaining such a growth-oriented belief system may seem like it's just about confidence. People with a fixed mindset don't believe in themselves, while people with a growth mindset do, right? According to Dweck's research, however, this isn't actually true. In positive, affirming circumstances, those with a fixed mindset are just as confident and optimistic as those with a growth mindset. The difference is found in moments of failure.

Here's a practical example to make this concept a little more relatable. Say there are two young men who dream of being photographers, one with a fixed mindset and one with a growth mindset. Both already know their way around a camera pretty well, and everyone they know says their photos are really good. So they decide to enroll in a college-level photography course to gain some more experience and eventually start a career in photography. Although the first few classes seem to go well, both men end up getting a C in the course overall. The instructor gives them similar feedback: creativity was lacking, and they limited themselves by safe subjects.

While both men's experiences were essentially the same, their responses are going to be completely different. One will take the feedback and do something about it, practicing taking pictures of new subjects at challenging angles and incorporating vibrant colors. He knows his passion is for photography, so he's going to work on his skills until he gets to where he wants to be. The other, however, will put his camera in a dark corner of his room and try to forget all about it. He'll feel that if that's what the world thinks of his work, being a photographer must not be his calling after all.

And that's the difference between the two mindsets. A fixed mindset encourages you to focus on proving yourself and displaying the abilities you already have, so when failure comes, it feels crushing and very personal. But a growth mindset isn't focused on performance at all. It's simply about the process of learning and developing—two direct byproducts of embracing any failure.

THE GROWTH MINDSET

There are several key components that make up a growth mindset, the most prominent being a continual commitment to looking for ways to develop. Not only do you enjoy learning, but you also constantly seek out new opportunities for it, even if it stretches you outside your comfort zone. As long as it can make you stronger, any discomfort or risk is worth it. Sometimes this approach will result in failure, but with a growth mindset, failure is just a temporary setback and a necessary step on the path to achievement. With a commitment to growth, you know you'll figure out a way to overcome the issue and try again.

The second component of a growth mindset is a willingness to put in the hard work necessary for growth. Rather than waiting for change to simply happen, you take responsibility for your own development and actively look for ways to improve. Though you appreciate your accomplishments and enjoy your success, you never stop asking yourself the tough question of "how can I become even better?" You seek out new strategies and willingly discard ones that don't elevate your gifts, even if they work well. We see this all the time with professional athletes. Tiger Woods, one of the greatest golfers of all time, has changed his golf swing many times in his career (often after winning a major tournament) in an attempt to get even just a little bit better. While his original swing worked well, he wasn't going to overlook an opportunity to grow and change.

A third component of a growth mindset is a realistic view of others. There will always be those more skilled or more successful than you, but rather than being angry or jealous, you use them as inspiration to work toward your own greatness. You willingly seek their external, objective perspective and use their feedback to help evaluate and build on the areas where you still need to grow. At the same time, you don't rely on their approval to validate your accomplishments or define your value. You appreciate their encouragement and support, but you know that only God and your own learning spirit can determine what you become.

GROWING YOUR CHILD

Besides affecting your own identity formation, your mindset will also impact your child and your ability to guide them well. When you have a fixed mindset, you view your child's flaws as a fundamental part of them and not as fluid traits they can grow beyond. You lose sight of the fact that they are constantly learning, developing, and evolving, instead defining them in a single fixed way that doesn't give them permission to be any different from how you already view them. Over time, this viewpoint will discourage your child's natural adventurous and curious spirit because they can sense your lack of faith in them. If you don't believe they can achieve much, why should they?

Besides limiting your child's potential, a fixed mindset also causes you to ignore the hard work of creating relational intimacy with them. You believe that any inability to relate to your child, understand them, or guide them well is a sign that you just aren't meant to be close or that you're too different to ever get along. As a result, you avoid conflict or any potential bonding experience, which only strains your relationship further and makes your child feel even more unworthy.

Conversely, a growth mindset allows you to view any imperfections in you or your child as something that can be changed (Psalm 92:12-14). You interpret your differences not as threats or obstacles to your relationship but as something you can both learn from. Rather than defining your child based on their mistakes or inexperience, you see their weaknesses as opportunities to help them learn how to bring out the best in themselves. Your commitment to love supersedes your desire for control or to always be right, allowing you to convey the truth that with God, they can achieve more than they could ever imagine (Philippians 4:13).

God wants both you and your child to keep working toward discovering your full potential, but you can only do so when you give up all traces of a fixed mindset. Any inability to see the unique capabilities of your child will limit their development. The only way to execute the vision of fatherhood is to instill within them a growth mindset. And the only way to instill a growth mindset in them is to develop it within yourself first.

UNCOVERING YOUR MINDSET

The first step in adopting and committing to a growth mindset is recognizing which mindset you currently have so you can better understand what your next step should be. However, that mindset isn't always easy to recognize or label, because it typically isn't something you've consciously developed. Like much of your identity, your mindset usually forms early in life based on guidance from your parents and teachers, your experiences in school, and your relationships with peers. Over time, the mindset those experiences generate gets so ingrained into your way of thinking that it becomes hard recognize its impact. In fact, you might even believe you have an attitude of growth, while deep down you've actually accepted a life of stagnation.

To see what kind of mindset you have, first look for its effects on your life. One way to do this is to pay attention to how your child reacts to your day-to-day treatment of them. Even if you don't directly convey a fixed mindset through establishing harsh rules or limitations on their behaviors, they will still sense when you aren't interested in their growth, don't believe in it, or simply don't have much room for them in your busy schedule. Their underlying resentment of this distance will cause them to react in one of two ways. They might reject your message of "you can't" by lashing out and dismissing you, seeking instead other relationships where they'll be heard and responded to. Or, even worse, they might actually accept your message and let it feed their own self-doubts to the point where they withdraw from all of their interests and goals, because like you, they simply believe they can't.

If any of this feels familiar to you, it likely means you have a fixed mindset, at least to a certain extent. And that's okay! As a result of our culture's emphasis on success and talent over hard work, most people grow up with a fixed mindset. It doesn't mean that you've failed in any way—it simply means it's time to turn the mirror inward. After all, a father's inability to expect and encourage growth in his child often stems from a similarly static view of himself. Due to unresolved negative experiences, relationships, or failures, he's lost his natural intrigue and excitement to learn, causing him to give up on even the idea that he could ever grow. Instead, he seeks the stability and safety of ordinary of life because he believes that without risk, he can never be hurt (Matthew 25:14-30).

When we're growing, we're naturally attracted to other growing things, and vice versa. So when we don't see ourselves as capable of growth, we can't help but see our discovery-oriented children as a threat. Their energy, imagination, playfulness, and curiosity fight against our belief that a person's growth is fixed and that we are all limited in what we become. Because of this conflict in perspective, it becomes impossible for us to find joy in watching them grow and develop.

The truth is that God has already given us countless blessings just waiting to be unlocked. And when we do, He will provide us with even more. But if we fail to apply the skills and abilities God gives us, we'll find those blessings fading quickly (Matthew 13:21). God won't pour out good things on someone who simply casts them aside. Our children are similar in this way. Why should they waste their time including us in their adventures if we've conveyed that we don't believe it matters?

In order to do fathering God's way, you must learn to adopt a growth mindset, which means embracing your own God-given gifts and rediscovering your passion for life. This is the only way to encourage your child's growth and development as well and help them achieve all God has in store for them. It won't always be easy, but thankfully God performs miracles every day in numerous small ways. I believe it's even a miracle when you're empowered to respond in a loving way when you would normally be irritated or angry. Though instances like this may not seem like much, it's these small miracles that create the environment in which bigger ones will occur. And from all those miracles combined, God will help you grow beyond your wildest expectations.

Don't believe me? Consider how God has already worked within you to open your heart to father your child like He does. Look at how your hard work has already caused you to progress much further on this journey than you initially thought possible. As we reach the halfway point of this book, push yourself one step further and let your new growth mindset really begin to take root. Continue to look at the discussion questions, pray for God's leading, and bravely enter into each upcoming fatherhood issue. You're on the right track. Keep up the good work!

 ROBERT'S STORY

One of my favorite characters I've ever played on film has been Javier from *Courageous*, primarily because becoming him was like stepping into my father's shoes. There was the accent, of course, and a few other circumstantial similarities. But most of the likeness came from one thing—both Javier and my dad were never afraid of working hard or failing.

As a Spanish-speaking immigrant in the '70s, there weren't many occupational opportunities for my dad. Some call it the Latino struggle. However, my dad never bought in to that concept. He taught me, just like his father taught him, that the only struggle that truly exists is the one against complacency, to keep believing in your ability to grow. And that struggle affects all humans regardless of heritage.

Just a few years after he'd arrived in America, my dad had taught himself English, learned two trades, opened his own business, found a wonderful wife, and began a family. Still today, at seventy years of age, my father has no plans of slowing down. He's my constant reminder that effort, above everything but God, matters most. Thanks to him, I know that I will be most effective for God and for my family when I push to keep a growth mindset.

💬 DISCUSSION QUESTIONS

1   Do you enjoy your role as a father? Think of three moments when you experienced pure joy regarding your child's growth. How can you be more active in their development?

2   Discuss the differences between a fixed and growth mindset. Which one describes how you view yourself? How often do you push yourself to grow and surpass expectations?

3   Which mindset describes how you view your child? How can you help them set growth-producing goals and achieve them? Do you believe in a God of miracles?

4   What does Psalm 103:13-14 convey about how a father should treat his child? What does it say about our duty to help our children grow?

A father is tender and kind to his children.
    In the same way, the LORD is tender and kind
    to those who have respect for him.
He knows what we are made of.
    He remembers that we are dust.

15

GUARANTEED SUCCESS

I don't think I need to tell you that growth isn't easy. It's filled with bumpy roads and unpredictable detours, not to mention the occasional flat tire. It often seems simpler just to return to the path you know. Sometimes you may even want to abandon your car on the side of the road and head off in a different direction altogether.

While a fixed mindset may give you a smooth and effortless journey, that isn't what God wants for you, and it's certainly not what He wants for your child. By their very nature, children are full of undiscovered possibilities and potential just waiting to be unlocked. But when you believe that their skills and capabilities are limited to a certain static point, it's like believing that a seed that hasn't yet sprouted can't become a tree—it's incorrect, damaging, and ultimately lacking in faith.

This is exactly why it's so essential to develop a growth mindset, and to know that doing so isn't a once-and-done accomplishment. As with many aspects of life, you will have to continually evaluate and challenge yourself to ensure you're responding in ways that live up to God's standards and keep you on His path toward growth. This can be a daunting task, but breaking it down into smaller steps makes it easier to stay true to your vision as a father. In this chapter, we'll unpack fifteen growth strategies that will help you continually grow as a father and guide your child well, no matter what obstacles arise.

STRATEGIES FOR GROWTH[1]

1   Acknowledge and embrace your weaknesses.

No one likes to admit to their faults, largely because it feels like we're acknowledging that there's something wrong with us—but that couldn't be further from the truth. Our weaknesses are not permanent character defects but rather a reminder of all the potential we have yet to develop. As long as you have the courage and humility to embrace this reality without letting your sin nature lead you into shame, you will gain the motivation to put in the effort to improve as both a man and a father.

Beyond growing yourself, this strategy will help you foster your child's growth and confidence as well. For one, even if you aren't declaring your growth to the world, your child will sense the effort you're putting into being your best for them, which tells them that they matter. Additionally, the more you embrace your own weaknesses, the easier it will be to accept your child's and help them learn how to grow beyond them.

2   Don't define your need to improve as failure.

We all want to be fully competent and prepared for every life challenge, especially when it comes to fatherhood. We think we'll know exactly what to do when our children get hurt on the playground or get in a fight with a friend. But life is more complicated than we think. And more often than we'd like, when an unexpected situation actually arises, we find ourselves at a loss for the best way to respond.

When you realize you don't know how to handle challenges like these, it can feel devastating. As a result, you may act defensively and deny your need to improve. You may even exaggerate

---

1   These strategies are modified from: "Fixed Mindset vs. Growth Mindset: What Really Matters for Success," Develop Good Habits, accessed August 18, 2021, https://www.developgoodhabits.com/fixed-mindset-vs-growth-mindset/.

a mistake by letting it define your whole identity. However, your need for improvement is not a statement of your worth but rather a call to action. Instead of pushing you down, it should stimulate your desire for growth so you can continue bettering yourself and working toward becoming the man God intended you to be.

Your child also needs to feel positive about the challenge of improving. While it's your job to point out their weaknesses so they can grow, you must always be careful to pace your criticism, control the intensity with which you give it, and avoid statements that might imply that who they are now is who they always will be. The goal is to create room for your child to improve without crushing their spirit in the process.

3   View challenges as opportunities.

Along with making us feel incompetent, unexpected life challenges can also seem impossible to overcome. In those moments, you must decide if you'll simply give up and accept your present limitations or if you'll trust God to help you grow. Jesus said it only takes a small bit of faith to move a mountain (Matthew 17:20). As long as you trust in Him, each challenge you step toward will reveal new lessons or help you recover a forgotten skill. Even when you feel like you've flunked one of these life tests, you will still gain the wisdom of knowing how to better prepare for it next time.

Besides embracing the challenges in your own life, you must also work with your child through your relational challenges. As your child gets older and learns more about themselves, your relationship will change as well, leading to natural moments of tension. They'll develop different viewpoints from you and will no longer like activities you once enjoyed together. Rather than seeing these changes as permanent divides, use them as opportunities to get to know your child better or to share your perspective with them. When you do, you'll find your relationship growing even stronger than it was before.

As your child becomes more and more independent from you, you must also actively encourage them to go after their own unique growth opportunities. Especially when they're young, the challenges they'll face can seem incredibly intimidating to them, even with new opportunities like entering a talent show or trying out for a sport. As their father, it's your job to ensure they don't let these opportunities pass by out of fear. Ask them about their concerns, and talk them through possible outcomes. They may still decide a specific challenge isn't right for them, but in discussing it with them, you'll help shape their perspective on life and strengthen their decision-making skills. And the next time a challenge arises, they'll feel more than ready to take it on.

4   Prioritize learning over seeking approval.

God created only one you, and He gave you a unique purpose that you alone can fulfill. This means you shouldn't try to change yourself to be what you think others want or worry about how they view you. Don't confine yourself to traditional ways of accomplishing something when it sacrifices your own individuality. Your child wants *you*, the father God gave them. As long as you focus on being that father, you will be more than enough.

Along these lines, you must also teach your child not to compare themselves to others and to always give serious thought to an idea before accepting it. While you will be a primary guiding resource for them, you won't be the only one. Teachers, coaches, peers, and even strangers will all play a role in your child's development, and their influence may not always be positive or effective. By being involved in your child's growth and asking them about their experiences, you will gain the ability to help them determine which lessons they should discard and which they should build on.

5   Learn from the mistakes of others.

While we shouldn't worry about how others view us or compare our growth to theirs, there are still plenty of ways they can help us grow. For one, we can find important lessons in their errors without having to go through the same challenges ourselves. As the saying goes, "Learn from the mistakes of others. You can't live long enough to make them all yourself." When you take the time to empathize with the failures, struggles, and pain of those around you, you can discover not only what emotions and decisions might have led to those circumstances but also a better way to respond if you ever find yourself in a similar situation.

This strategy can be even more helpful for your child's growth, as they have so few experiences of their own to learn from. Periodically talk with them about different choices and challenges in your family's history or in your own life in order to pass on those lessons to your child. Sharing these stories won't necessarily prevent them from making similar mistakes, but at the very least it can give them the advice they need to fix those mistakes when they do happen.

6   Embrace constructive feedback.

Another way others can help our growth is through sharing their perspective, whether it's through encouragement or confrontation. When done out of love and support, being confronted about where you need to improve can give you the nudge you need to fully invest in your growth. Jesus did this for Peter after he had denied even knowing Jesus not once, but three times (Matthew 26:69-75). Jesus then asked Peter three times if he loved Him, giving Peter the chance to resolve his previous mistake (John 21:15-17).

In the same way, we must embrace feedback so we can discover the truth in someone else's perspective and correct our negative behaviors. This is true even when the feedback comes from your child. As they develop their internal processes, they'll realize you're not perfect and will be more than willing to tell you so. Instead of dismissing their input because you believe you know best, you should learn to recognize when they might be right. Besides allowing you to grow, accepting your child's feedback builds their self-confidence and shows them the importance of being accountable to godly standards.

In addition to receiving feedback, you must also consistently give it to your child, who will need plenty of it as they learn to navigate life. Just be careful to do so in a way that doesn't sugarcoat the truth or cause them to internalize their mistakes. And be willing to accept that they may not always agree with your perspective. Keeping an open and honest approach to communication in your relationship is more important than determining who's right. So instead of getting into a power struggle, ask them why they disagree. Even if you don't manage to reach a middle ground, having a calm and thoughtful conversation regarding your feedback will still achieve the goal of getting your child to think through their behaviors. More importantly, it will show that you respect their right to think differently and make decisions for themselves.

7   Celebrate effort and action over skill and achievement.

An important part of having a growth mindset is learning not to define your success by the outcome of your efforts but rather by how hard you try. When you have a fixed mindset, you tend to overvalue your present skills and abilities, causing you to only go after tasks you know you can achieve and that reinforce the skills you already believe you have. A growth mindset, on the other hand, values genuine effort and well-placed action, which inspires you to always push yourself to keep trying. By celebrating your hard work, you will develop an attitude of optimism toward what you can accomplish. Even in your failures, you will focus less on what you did wrong and more on what you learned and how you can do better next time.

This strategy is especially important when it comes to your role as a father. While it may make your child feel good at first to hear you praise their knowledge of history or their singing ability, having that be the only way you affirm them will actually hurt their self-definition. Complimenting fixed traits after an accomplishment tells your child that they've reached the limit of what they can do. So when they get a hat trick in their soccer game, celebrate all the hard work they put into practice to prepare for that moment. Or if they don't get accepted to their dream college, help them see it as an opportunity to figure out what they're really passionate about. The God of possibilities created them to achieve much more than you'll ever know. Helping your child see the value of their efforts, even when they result in failure, will reflect that truth to them in everything they do.

8   Recognize the changeability of your brain.

Despite the fact that your brain stops growing in size around early adolescence, it doesn't actually finish developing until your mid-twenties. And even after that, due to what scientists call neural plasticity, you're still able to retrain and reorganize it no matter how old you are. In fact, through deliberate effort, you can actually change some of your genetic makeup, which scientists previously believed permanently embedded certain traits and behavioral patterns within us.

The study of epigenetics shows that although what you do *is* influenced by your genetic predispositions, the actions you choose can also change the influence your genetics have over you. A common example is that when an alcoholic consumes greater amounts of alcohol, his brain structure can actually change to make him crave alcohol more and more. It's then possible for him to pass that created genetic structure on to his children as well. All of this goes to show that just as new theories are discovered and old thought processes are discarded, you are never done growing and discovering new ways you can apply your brain.

Regardless of how you may feel about your own capacity to change your brain structure, there's no arguing that a child's brain is fully in a stage of development. As a father, the worst thing you can do for your child is let them be passive in this growth. You must always be searching for activities or resources that will help develop the thought processes, emotional management, and behavioral patterns they'll need to navigate life. Whether it's learning a new game, having an interesting conversation, or going somewhere you've never been before, there are countless ways you can help them develop their ability to process life.

9   Never stop learning.

Whether we realize it or not, as we get older we all slip into an I-already-know-it-all mindset. The problem is, only God knows it all (Psalm 147:5). And since you're not God, you have to continually search for ways to increase your knowledge. Besides expanding your understanding of the world, continuous learning will also exercise your brain in ways that broaden your horizons and increase your ability to survive in or adapt to any situation.

We all have specific subjects and activities that inspire us, and there's nothing wrong with focusing on these interests in order to develop your unique gifts. However, putting all of your eggs in one basket will ultimately limit what you can achieve, because everything is interconnected. Topics that may seem irrelevant to your everyday life can still teach you principles or skills that you can apply to your current challenges. At the very least, they can give you a greater appreciation for the complexities of this world, not to mention the people living in it with you.

Thankfully, fatherhood can make continual learning easier, as long as you're open to its opportunities. As we discussed in Chapter 8, by going on your child's journey of growth with them, you get to experience the same discoveries they do. And by seeing life through their optimistic eyes, your own fears and limitations will no longer blind you.

You must also take care to both encourage your child to follow their curious mind and actively guide that curious mind yourself. Answer their many questions about even the most mundane topics, like what you do at work or what makes a car run. Listen intently as they share their latest excitement, and encourage them by responding with observations or questions. Take them to science museums and art exhibits to introduce them to new ideas. Show them books about history, chemistry, politics, and geography. Encourage them to try new hobbies like bike riding or learning an instrument. Most importantly, teach them about the wonder of God's Word, and help them understand how they can apply it to their growth.

In addition to all of these external topics, you should also encourage your child to learn about themselves by continually considering their thought processes and emotional responses. Help them evaluate how well they're doing in these areas by occasionally asking them what they're thinking about and assessing how well they're able to express it, or by discussing a situation that happened at school and the emotions that everyone might have been feeling. By having these conversations, you will take a more active role in shaping your child's personal development, making it easier for them to recognize their growth and continue to pursue it.

10   Learn how to learn.

As encouraging and enlightening as school can be for a lot of students, for many others it is demotivating and overwhelming. The stress of tests, academic expectations, and social challenges can spoil all learning for us, causing us to see it as boring or distressing. As a result, we repress our curious minds, and over time, we forget how to even learn at all.

There are several practices you can follow to become more

intentional about learning. One is to evaluate any idea or opinion you come across rather than immediately accepting or dismissing it. Besides giving you a chance to determine for yourself if an idea is true, this approach will deepen your understanding of it. You can also attempt to generalize information so as to see how it could apply to seemingly unrelated topics or situations. In this way, you can gain a new perspective in multiple areas and increase your ability to apply it in everyday life.

You must also pass along these same strategies to your child before they begin to repress their own curious mind. Imparting a desire to learn is one of the greatest gifts you can give your child. Emphasize that not learning is not an option, and set aside time to allow them to develop their interests and abilities unrelated to school. Additionally, because learning shouldn't stop once they graduate, you should encourage them to regularly set goals related to their interests, such as practicing the guitar or learning the names of plants. This approach will foster their general interest in learning and will help ensure they stick with it over the course of their life.

11 Understand your own unique learning style.

Part of learning how to learn is becoming aware of your own learning style. Trying to conform to a standard way of learning will only hold you back. Think about whether you learn best through watching, doing, or hearing. Does it help you to keep journals, write lists, or develop memory tools? Do you like to listen to music, put on a sports game, or work in complete silence? It doesn't matter how unorthodox your learning style is, as long as it works for you.

Your child must also learn the way that works best for them. As you become more involved in their growth, you might discover that they have a different style from you. Rather than trying to teach them to learn the way you prefer, you should work with their style as best you can. This includes being aware of any learning disabilities they may have and assisting them in developing coping mechanisms to help them discover their world. If your child is still relatively young, you can try out a variety of teaching techniques so you both can discover what works best for them. And if they're older, ask them for their perspective on their learning style so you can better adapt to their needs.

12   Choose learning well over learning fast.

It's part of our human nature to want to rush through experiences just to get to the other side. But the faster you try to get through a lesson, the less likely you'll be to actually understand it and thus apply it. Learning isn't about what you know. It's about how well you learned it and how you apply that knowledge to your life.

Jesus repeatedly pointed out this flaw in the church leaders of His time, telling rabbis and priests that they didn't know the Scriptures even though they had spent their lives studying them (Matthew 22:29; 23:2-3). His point was that if we know God's Word but don't live according to it, do we really know it at all? Even though it will feel tedious at times, we have to learn to slow down our learning, think through the "whys," and apply one detail at a time. Only then can we maximize our knowledge by making it real and putting it into action.

When it comes to the less concrete lessons we must learn, learning well also means accepting that the process will take time and plenty of mistakes. But these mistakes aren't something to be ashamed of. They're actually part of the learning process, and by making them, you will gain a better understanding of the lessons you need to build into your life.

You can apply this growth strategy to your fatherhood in a few different ways, depending on your child's developmental stage. Sometimes you may need to slow yourself down as you teach them. Because your child is still in the process of figuring out how to function in life, they might not always progress at the pace you think they should. But rushing them through any learning experience won't help. For them to truly learn how to do math, hit a ball, read, or even use the potty, you must practice patience. Graciously walk them through each difficult developmental step without huffing or sighing, and celebrate with them when they finally reach their goal.

Other times you may need to slow your child down instead. Because their emotions aren't yet regulated, children often get so excited or so annoyed in a learning experience that they barrel through it so they can jump right to the cool stuff, or right to the end. When this happens, try to talk your child through the learning process. Ask them why they're feeling rushed so they can practice identifying and labeling their internal processes. Then explain the importance of taking their time. The more they slow down, the more prepared they'll be when they finally get to the part they're excited about, and the less likely they'll have to repeat the stuff they hate.

13 Apply and reflect on your learning every day.

What good is learning a lesson if you don't remember it? James 1:23-24 compares it to looking at your reflection and then immediately forgetting what you look like. Sadly, remembering important details is a big problem for us men. That's why we need to be deliberate about it by creating tricks and devices for retaining life lessons.

There are many different tricks you can choose from. You could write down a concept that's important to you and put it on your desk at work. You could relate a goal to a concrete example that makes it more memorable, like imagining yourself strapping on your superhero cape to carry out your fatherhood duties. You could read a short passage of the Bible every morning during breakfast to make sure you remember God's Word. Or you could set small goals that reinforce your learning throughout the week, such as vowing to leave work early every Friday to spend more time with your family. No matter what you do, you should always continually pray throughout your learning. Besides helping you maintain your focus, including God in your growth efforts is the best way to ensure you actually achieve them.

Because a child's brain is still developing and working a mile a minute, they're even more likely to forget important lessons. As their father, it's your responsibility to continually reinforce the principles that remind them of who they are and what is expected of them. Of course, your child will also need to develop their own way of remembering lessons, but that will happen naturally over time, as long as you're there to guide their learning process.

14   Cultivate a sense of purpose.

A key part of having a growth mindset is continually working toward improving yourself, but doing so will be hard if you don't feel driven by a greater purpose. God wants each of us to be like Jesus in everything we do and to serve others as His representatives, and that calling should drive all of your goals (1 Peter 2:21). You can only truly appreciate your achievements when they fully reflect who God created you to be.

Of course, God has a different plan for each of us, one that we may never fully understand (Jeremiah 29:11). But no matter how unclear it may seem, we must continually seek to pursue it. Whether your goal is to become a mechanic, create a nonprofit, or yes, become a father, having a sense of the grander purpose behind that goal will help you make choices that are congruent with your values and God's standards. Not only will this make life more enjoyable, but it will also motivate you to make it what you truly want it to be, filling you with a greater purpose in the process.

When you become a father, part of this purpose must include looking after your child's well-being and helping them discover their own God-given calling. For much of their early life, your child will struggle to look outside themselves at all, let alone begin to understand the abstract idea of finding their purpose. That's why it's your job to pay attention to their deepest feelings and help them evaluate their motivations. When you do, they will eventually recognize what matters most. And once they've reached maturity, they'll be ready to pursue God's great plan for them.

15 Focus on the process, not the end result.

Just as your journey toward godly fatherhood will continue until the end of your life, learning shouldn't have an end point. It's not meant to ever be fully achieved until the moment you leave this earth. At times that may feel frustrating, but accepting this reality will actually give you the freedom to embrace life more fully. You will recognize that the time it takes to practice a new skill or reach a goal is the time God has set aside for you do so, and you'll understand how the various stages of life provide challenges and learning opportunities. By trusting His pacing of your life instead of trying to rush through it, you will learn more than you ever could have imagined.

God is also in charge of the pacing of your child's life, and we must trust that process rather than trying to dictate it ourselves. This goes back to what we discussed in the last chapter. You must play an active role in guiding your child's growth and development, whether that means instructing them directly, answering their questions, or simply encouraging them through a challenge. But ultimately, you're limited in how much you can truly influence their life. At some point, you have to learn to simply sit back, trust in God, and enjoy the miracle unfolding before you.

While the strategies outlined in this chapter are essential to your growth as a father and to your child's development, they only scratch the surface of what we need to do to continue our growth, especially for us as men. In the next couple chapters, we'll delve deeper into the specific topic of manhood growth and the role it plays in our fatherhood. The more you work to become God's man, the more you'll grow into the father He created you to be.

ROBERT'S STORY

There's a famous saying you've probably heard before: "If you give a man a fish, you feed him for a day. If you teach a man to fish, you feed him for a lifetime." These words represent a good portion of my parenting philosophy. Just like I believe repentance is a better lesson than "do not sin," the process and effort required for success is far more valuable than the success itself.

When Sophia won her very first national dance competition, everyone praised her for her performance, and rightfully so. She was absolutely incredible. However, the effort it took to get to that position was something I wanted her to relish even more. So I took her little face in my hand, looked her straight in the eyes, and said, "You put in the time and rigorous effort to get to this position. While others did just enough to get through class, you practiced at home until you had it down. You struggled in your first regional competition but bounced back more determined than ever. Today, you *earned* this title."

Sophia often reminds me of how much that affirmation meant to her. Years later, she told me that it was better than all of the praise she'd ever received from others, because it wasn't about the title. Rather, it was about who she is and what she can accomplish. With my words, I showed her what to value most. And since then, she has pushed herself to achieve even more than I could have dreamed.

💬 DISCUSSION QUESTIONS

1   Review growth strategies 1 through 7. Which strategies can you improve on so you can be a better example of a growth mindset for your child? How can you use the support and feedback of others to help you grow in this regard?

2   Review growth strategies 8 through 15. How easy or difficult is it for you to learn? What are some ways you can better embrace continual learning? How can your role as a father help both you and your child become better learners?

3   Do you have a sense of purpose in your life? If so, how does that impact the goals you set for yourself? If not, how can you rely on God to help you find it?

4   Discuss the directives given in 1 Timothy 3:2-5. How well do you live up to this standard of a leader? How can you use the fifteen growth strategies to become more like the father described in this verse?

A leader must be free from blame. He must be faithful to his wife. In anything he does, he must not go too far. He must control himself. He must be worthy of respect. He must welcome people into his home. He must be able to teach. He must not get drunk. He must not push people around. He must be gentle. He must not be a person who likes to argue. He must not love money. He must manage his own family well. He must make sure that his children obey him. And he must do this in a way that gains him respect. Suppose someone doesn't know how to manage his own family. Then how can he take care of God's church?

16

BEING GOD'S MAN

I have to warn you, I'm about to say something shocking to all the fathers reading this—you are a male. Totally mind-blowing, right? Well, okay, maybe not. As I like to say, all you need to do to determine if you're a male is to look down. However, just because you're a male doesn't mean you're a man. While you're born with the elements that make you a male, manhood isn't something that comes automatically—it's something you have to earn.

For the past few chapters, we've talked about growth in a general sense, discussing concepts that apply to everyone regardless of age, gender, or role along with strategies we can use to guide our self-development. But if you truly want to be a good father, there are also specific ways you need to grow beyond those general principles. And one of the biggest of those ways is in your manhood.

In this chapter, we'll look at what it means to be a man and the steps and resources we need in order to earn that title. Fatherhood and manhood go hand in hand, and unless you put in the work to strengthen each element of manhood, you won't be able to achieve your full potential and become the best father you can be. It's only by recognizing the true value of manhood that you can fully engage your growth mindset and uncover all God has in store for you and your child.

MANHOOD AND THE FATHER

If you were to ask a group of men to describe themselves, they'd all probably use completely different words, depending on their individual values and viewpoints. One might define himself by his occupation, another by his sense of humor, and another by his dashing good looks. But no matter how different they are, I can guarantee you one thing—each would consider himself a man.

All males have an instinctual desire to become men. That drive is an intrinsic part of our identity and plays a huge role in our decision-making, our principles, and even our relationships. The problem is, a lot of men don't have a good understanding of what godly manhood actually is. I'd bet that if you asked that same group of men to describe what being a man means, their definitions would vary just as greatly as their definitions of themselves. One might say it means being strong and brave. Another might define it through success and accomplishments. Still others might believe it simply is what it is, meaning there's no point in trying to describe it further.

However, true manhood is so much more than any of this. It requires going through the fortification process of embracing challenges and facing hardships head-on. It demands putting in the work to develop yourself internally and learning to recognize and express your emotions. In this way, it's not just a state of being. It's a continuous journey of self-discovery where you seek knowledge, learn to be open with others, take in their feedback, and then make the effort to change.

None of this is impossible to achieve, but unfortunately the world is constantly working to stop us from even trying. Our culture's definition of manhood directly opposes God's definition, depicting men in movies, television, and advertisements as simple, sexual, and aggressive. The modern age of technology further enforces this false image by plastering it on every screen, making it virtually inescapable and instilling within us the belief that a man's value is determined by his muscle size and sexual prowess. Not only is this standard completely untrue, but it's also impossible to attain, which leaves many males feeling inadequate and searching for wholeness in all the wrong places.

The culture's definition of manhood is dangerous for any male, but it's especially damaging for boys with absent or disengaged fathers. Without someone to counter the culture's messages and help them define manhood accurately, they're forced to try to figure it out themselves, which often leads them to become even more entrenched in the culture's definition. In turn, they never learn to guide their natural sexual and aggressive impulses in positive ways.

Even worse, they often don't want to. Because the culture has taught them that their impulsivity is simply part of being a man, many males wind up hurting themselves and others trying to prove their manhood. If you look closely at many of our cultural problems, whether it's pornography, dictatorship, poverty, or violence, you'll almost always find an immature male at the source.

This is exactly why pursuing manhood is so essential, not just for yourself but also for your fatherhood. Since manhood is a desire you already have within you, connecting it to your fatherhood will make taking on challenges and fulfilling your responsibilities simply what you expect of yourself. What once felt exhausting or unappealing in your role as a father will become just a natural expression of who you are as a man.

The more you work on developing godly manhood, the more His standards will be reflected in how you treat your child. To be a man is to be noble and honorable, which will make you committed to doing what's best for them. It means being strong and perseverant, which will lead you to embrace challenges and step outside of your comfort zone. It means being self-sacrificing, which will drive you to always put your child above yourself, even when doing so doesn't feel natural or easy.

To be an effective father is to be a man, but this is only possible if you put in the work to move past any false definitions of manhood. When you learn to appreciate, develop, and protect your true manhood status, you will grow strong enough inside to be the father your child needs. It certainly won't be easy, but it's like I always say—real men do what's hard.

MANHOOD AND THE FAMILY

When we fail to live up to God's definition of manhood, we hurt ourselves in many ways. Our passivity causes us to succumb to a life of boredom and comfort, preventing us from achieving our goals and reaching our full potential. Our isolation limits our ability to create the loving, intimate relationships we need to fully enjoy life. And our underlying sense that we should somehow be and do more, buried beneath our fear of actually going after it, leaves us feeling restless, unfulfilled, and empty.

However, we aren't the only ones who suffer as a result of our immaturity. You may think I'm talking about your child, but they're not actually the person who's the most impacted by your manhood (or lack thereof)—it's your wife.

Now, I know you picked up this book to become a better father, not necessarily a better husband, so this may come across as unsolicited marital advice. But your manhood is part of *all* the areas of your life, not just the one you're focusing on now, and how you treat your wife does actually have a direct impact on how you guide your child.

As you may or may not know, in choosing to marry you, your wife had expectations for how you would treat her as her husband (1 Peter 3:7). And let's be real—those expectations are not that difficult to meet. All she wants is a life partner who treats her as the valuable woman she is. She wants you to go on dates with her, to listen to her, and to make plans for your future together. She wants you to be a parent to your child so she doesn't have to do it all on her own. And she wants to be a part of the powerful legacy you create together for your child.

Unfortunately, this isn't the kind of man many women receive in marriage. Instead of a partner who loves and respects them, they find themselves committed to males who only care about themselves. These males don't help out in the home or family, placing all of the burden on their wives. They make plans for themselves, spend their money on themselves, and only pay attention to their family when it benefits them in some way. And in failing to meet their wives' expectations, they do a lot of damage along the way. Many women are afraid of men, often because they've been hurt by them, and they consequently find it difficult to trust any men at all, including the ones who are supposed to love them.

When faced with this kind of treatment, do you think women are going to passively sit by, just waiting for us to come to our senses and treat them like they deserve? Of course not! Because immature males don't step up, women have had to take on burdens they shouldn't be asked to bear. They've had to adopt roles meant to be shared by their husbands. They've had to start cultural movements like feminism simply to get the respect they have always deserved but rarely received.

God calls all men to serve and protect the women in their lives, but unfortunately, many choose to engage in violence or to violate women instead. As a result, our culture has decided to take matters into their own hands to keep women safe by "domesticating" us and repressing the natural aggression we so often mishandle. And because the evidence of how men harm women is so obvious, many of us feel guilty and willingly cooperate with that domestication process rather than simply learning to manage and express our aggression in healthy ways. However, by succumbing in this way, we're not really eliminating the problem. We're actually just redirecting the abuse away from women and onto ourselves.

The reason this issue is so long-lasting in our culture is because we keep passing it on through the generations. God wants both men and women to be respected, valued, and strong, and accepting His definition of our worth has to start now, not only for the benefit of you and your wife but also for your child (Galatians 3:28). By disrespecting your wife and not being involved in your family, you teach your daughters that they are less valuable than men and therefore deserve abuse or neglect, which makes it more likely they will wind up in relationships with abusive or neglectful men. Similarly, you teach your sons that it's okay to violate the value God has given all women, a mindset that will limit all of their relationships in the future, but especially their marriages.

Besides passing on an attitude of abuse to your child, you can also harm them through your refusal to emotionally connect with your wife. Each parent should be the most important resource for the other's emotional intimacy needs, but an immature male doesn't have the relational ability to be open with his wife in this way. As their relationship grows more distant, he instinctively seeks out other ways to fulfill his needs. And if he's not careful, he can end up becoming emotionally dependent on his child in ways they are not developmentally equipped to handle.

In recovery counseling, we refer to this dynamic as *emotional incest*. A father is supposed to support and guide his child, not the other way around. If he relies on his child emotionally, he keeps them from developing their own ability to create emotional intimacy with others, which will stunt their overall identity development. This makes it more likely that they'll never reach their full potential—just like him.

The only way to stop this cycle of abuse and cultural lies is to develop your manhood as God defines it. This means taking your time to hone all of your relational, emotional, and mental capabilities so you can form a truly intimate bond with your wife, giving you both the support and love you need to navigate the challenges of life and parenthood. It means building and maintaining appropriate boundaries within your family so you can be the best husband and father possible. It means choosing the actions and behaviors that will teach your daughter not to tolerate mistreatment from any male and how to form strong relationships with men in the future, whether with friends or her future husband. It means being an example of manhood for your son, showing him that a true man never demeans anyone, let alone women, and teaching him to define and treat them as valuable as God does.

If you work on your manhood in this way, it will naturally result in a healthy marriage with your wife, which will then provide a positive foundation for your child's eventual lifelong relationship. Part of God's path for most of us is to one day leave our parents and become one with our wives, but as I'm sure you know, that's not exactly a simple process (Genesis 2:24). In order to create a mature adult relationship with another individual, your child needs to understand the advantages of an intimate bond and what it takes to have one. And a big part of their ability to do that comes from the strength, love, and commitment they learn through observing your marriage.

You're probably well aware by now, but your child's well-being directly depends on you. And you can't rise to that responsibility unless you are willing to take on the challenge of developing your manhood as God sees it. As I stated at the beginning of this chapter, manhood isn't something you're born with. The question is, are you ready to earn it?

BECOMING A MAN

The need for developing manhood should now be pretty clear, but knowing exactly how to do so isn't quite so cut-and-dried—especially when you've spent years, maybe even decades, internalizing an unhealthy definition of it. That's why I've divided it up into three areas of personal discovery: the process of developing manhood, the elements of manhood, and the internal structures we need to build our identity on.

This section will focus on the first, breaking down the specific steps you must take in order to develop your manhood. It's only by putting in the work to change your perspective and your way of thinking that you can know how to internalize and apply the elements and principles you need to become a man of God.

1 Understand and apply your need to move.[1]

Sadly, many males these days are content with their recliner and their remote, deliberately spending as little effort as possible on any other pursuits. But this passive lifestyle wasn't what God had in mind when He created you. If I asked you to describe your childhood, you'd probably reply with story after story of running around the playground, running on the football field, running around the house, and even running through the halls at school. That's because God designed men to *move*.

While this characteristic may seem like nothing but a quirk, it actually plays a huge role in our development, especially as children. You may notice that boys often react in physical ways to their environment and circumstances, like bouncing their legs when they're nervous or flailing their arms when they're excited. This type of response may actually indicate that they rely on their muscles and nervous systems to think and express themselves much more than girls naturally do.

This innate need for movement is also evident in the ways boys learn and grow. When we first learn to read, our leg muscles twitch at the word *run*, and our brain registers the word *slug* as if we're actually feeling something slimy and squishy or seeing something slow and slithering. To our teachers we may seem restless,

---

1   Much of the research and information referenced in this step is taken from: Louann Brizendine, *The Male Brain* (New York: Harmony Books, 2010).

but these physical associations are all helping us internalize and remember what we learn.

Movement can also improve our spatial ability, which is how well we can visualize objects and move them around in our minds. This skill comes in handy with reading a map, as we're able to mentally turn and manipulate the flat features of the map to figure out where we are or where we want to go. We can also employ the same technique in attacking more abstract puzzles, such as solving math problems. In a study of students in a grade-school math class, researchers found that the boys finished problems faster than the girls. When those boys were asked to explain how they found their answers, many of them used gestures instead of words, indicating that even when working in their minds, they were completing this task in a physical manner. Even more interestingly, when the girls were taught to explain their math problems in the same way, they caught right up to the boys.

While this male penchant for movement is clearly key to our development, not everyone sees it that way. Our modern education system requires students to sit still and be quiet, and many teachers (especially female teachers) see our desire to move as disruptive rather than vital to our learning process. In order to develop our manhood, however, we must redefine our desire to move so that it can fulfill its true purpose—to drive us forward and make things happen.

There are many simple ways you can start to do so in everyday life. Let yourself gesture as you work through a problem at your job. Take a walk or exercise once a day to unwind and refocus your mind. Most importantly, make time to play with your child. As we discussed in Chapter 1, a man's natural physical style of play benefits a child's development in a number of ways. The more you recognize and apply your need to move, the more active you will become in your fatherhood, and the better you'll be able to push your child in ways that only a father can.

2   Learn to accept "what is" rather than getting lost in "what should be."

As we've discussed before, every one of us has experienced some form of disappointment. Sometimes things don't always turn out as we wish, and if that happens frequently enough or painfully enough, we can come to the conclusion that we should just give up hope altogether.

However, that doesn't get rid of the feeling that there's something unfulfilling about our lives, that there must be something more. But rather than looking at reality and how we could change, we focus on how we believe life should be and how we're not getting what we think we deserve. This allows us to deflect the responsibility for the outcome of our lives away from ourselves and ultimately succumb to passivity. Instead of actively setting goals and developing our potential, we indulge in behaviors that provide instant gratification, such as pornography or excessive video games. Such behaviors let us live in a fantasy world in which no trials or disappointments exist, numbing all of our capabilities and limiting our self-awareness even further.

Rather than letting reality defeat us, we must simply accept it, which begins with acknowledging that God is ultimately in charge (Isaiah 45:6-7). There will always be circumstances that are out of our control, but know that whatever happens is all a part of God's plan. And no matter what has happened up to this point, no matter how much you think you've failed or how little hope you have, God still loves and values you. He knows what you can achieve—and He still wants you to achieve it.

When you can acknowledge what is, accept that you don't like it, and see the truth that God has greater plans for you, you will feel a natural drive to change your circumstances, either by improving yourself or by taking charge of the situation. And because the fact that you're a father is also part of what is, this acceptance will allow you to improve your fathering. You can't change the mistakes you made in the past or the distance those mistakes have caused in your relationship with your child—but you can *always* move toward a better future.

3   Hone and develop your natural initiative.

Just as God created men to move, He also created them to initiate. Men are not meant to sit there and just accept (or ignore) everything life has to offer (Proverbs 10:4). God wants us to make a difference, which includes taking risks and seeking out new learning. As boys, this initiative is what leads us to take apart the toaster just to see how it works, climb a tall tree just to see if we can, or explore an unknown cave just to see what's inside. And as men, it's what drives us to find ways to apply our unique God-given gifts to honor Him and contribute to the world.

However, while we're born with a natural desire to initiate, we don't instinctively know how to manage it. When your parents found you on the floor surrounded by toaster parts, I'm sure their first question was "Why would you do that?" And your answer was probably a shrug and a sheepish "I don't know."

Thanks to the hormone testosterone, we all struggle with some level of impulsivity, which, when combined with our initiative, can cause us to jump into action without giving it any thought. (For many of us, as we look back on the chances we took and the choices we made, it's clear that it's only by the grace of God that we're alive.) And unfortunately, many of us didn't have the best mentors growing up to help us reign in our impulsivity and guide our initiative well. Some of us were told to repress our initiative in order to conform to the rules. Others were simply brushed off with a "boys will be boys" mentality without any instruction on guiding their impulsivity.

But neither of these approaches help turn a male into a man. Instead, they instill a sense of weakness, encouraging him to use his initiative to attempt to express a false sense of power. In turn, he never learns how to say no or think through consequences, which only makes him more likely to involve himself with harmful friends, negative sexual behaviors, or other self-destructive actions.

If you find yourself struggling with impulsivity, it's time to learn to evaluate your motivations and determine which to follow through on and which to resist. And if your initiative seems to have disappeared entirely, it's time to discover it once again and restore it to its former glory. Think about your goals for yourself and for your family, and determine what steps you need to take to achieve them. Then go out there and do it.

4   Learn to label and guide what's going on within you.

Introspection isn't a skill that comes naturally to most men, but it's one we all need. Though it may not always seem fun, learning to label your internal thoughts and feelings is the key to becoming more responsible in your decision-making. We all have a unique way of thinking that influences how we process situations, how we interpret them, and how we decide to respond. The better we understand and guide this internal system, the easier it will be to make the right choices in any situation.

The same is also true of our emotional reactions. Our feelings are much more fluid than our thoughts and can bleed into each other more easily, which means something that happened earlier this morning, last week, or even years ago can impact your reaction to a present situation. For instance, an unresolved fight with your wife may have you feeling a little insecure, which can make you unnecessarily defensive when your boss brings up some minor feedback at work. It also doesn't help that emotions are contagious, leading us to become emotionally stimulated by what others are feeling. The more attuned you are to your own feelings and the better you can label them, the less reactive your responses will be to a person or situation, and the easier it will be to reply rationally and appropriately.

Since movement is so natural to us as men, going through this process of labeling may initially feel painful and pointless as it requires us to slow down and look inside. Our impulsivity causes us to want to immediately fix a problem or go after a goal, and taking a moment of consideration can feel like we're preventing ourselves from maximizing our abilities. However, over time you'll find that the more work you put in now to understand what's going on within you, the faster you'll be able to move in the future. That's because you'll automatically know what you need to do and why you need to do it—and you'll have fewer mistakes to clean up later.

Additionally, the better you learn to label your own thoughts and emotions, the easier it will be to identify what's going on within your child and to help them understand it. More importantly, getting in tune with your emotions will allow you to relate to your child's experiences, whether it's celebrating with them over passing a test or sitting with them through losing a pet. In the end, that's what your child will remember most—the moments where you truly expressed your love for them.

5   Create rules that will hold you accountable to God's standards.

If I were to ask you if you liked rules, you'd probably react automatically with a resounding "No!" That's because even after we become adults, we primarily associate rules with the annoying restrictions our parents or teachers placed on us as children. But I'm sure that if you were really honest, you'd admit that they were probably right to guide you in that way. The rules they imposed, and the principles those rules instilled in you, likely taught you a lot about how to take care of yourself, treat others well, and navigate life, even if you didn't realize it at the time.

While rules can often feel limiting, the reality is that we all need a way to organize life and establish patterns of behavior so we don't become a big chaotic mess. Rules give us a strong foundation of truth that consists of what we believe is right, what we expect of ourselves, and what we expect from life. Whether our rules are broader and more abstract (such as "don't knowingly hurt others" or "don't ignore someone who needs help") or more direct and concrete (such as "always be on time" or "don't make big, impulsive purchases"), having them prevents us from always needing to make a decision when these situations arise. Instead, we can simply act, which gives us the freedom to engage more fully in life and focus our energy on more important endeavors.

Ideally, your parents would have taught you many of these rules of life as you grew up. Unfortunately, however, many parents don't, either because they never established guidelines for themselves or because they simply aren't willing to put in the work to create structure in their children's lives. It takes effort to establish rules, enforce consequences, and face the relational tension that can come with doing what's right for your child. It's often easier for parents to take a passive role in their child's development, in turn giving them implicit permission to make up their own rules, most of which, not surprisingly, *don't* live up to God's standards.

Regardless of the rules you were raised with, you must consciously identify, evaluate, and correct or solidify the rules you live by now. Not only will committing to living as God desires help you become a better man, but it will also allow you to instill within your child the rules they need to reach their full potential. Our children always assume we know best, and they will take in and repeat without question our viewpoints and behaviors. You must do whatever you can to ensure that this influence is positive, even if it means finally following some rules.

6   Build a support team.

No one is meant to do life alone, and the same is true for all men, no matter how much you may want to be a lone ranger (Hebrews 10:24-25). When you have a team of men who are willing to listen to your challenges, support and advise you through your struggles, call you out for your mistakes, and celebrate your accomplishments, you will naturally begin to develop into the person you've always wanted to be. Your value may come from God, but it is your band of brothers who will help you realize it. With them, you don't have to be beaten down by the seemingly relentless negativity of life. Instead, together you can rely on God to stand strong and power through anything it throws your way.

Sadly, outside of school and the military, there are few places we can naturally find a team like this. Although church is meant to be a community (and most churches are), few create or invest in a men's groups that focuses specifically on men's issues, leaving the average man feeling somewhat isolated despite the other resources churches offer. Many of the few men's groups that *do* exist only meet once a month for a prayer breakfast, allowing little room to build the comradery we need. I know that if my Penn State Nittany Lions saw each other that infrequently, they would never win a football game.

Manhood is something to be earned, but it's also something to be granted by other men. Friendships between men remind each other of what is expected of them, allowing their sense of manhood to never stop growing. You need other men in your life to push you in this way, not only to become a man but also to commit to *always* being one. When you have such support in your life, you will feel empowered to be the best man, husband, and father you can be, because you know that no matter what happens, you will always have a safety net to catch you.

. . .

As you go through your manhood journey, always remember that God is there with you, showing you the way. He is continually moving toward you. He accepts where you are even as He empowers you to go after who you can become. In His Word, He's given you specific instructions on how to be a man by His standards, and through prayer He gives you with the strength to keep going. He initiates regular conversations so He can guide you in your fatherhood, and He provides rules and structures that will help you serve your family well. Above all, God wants to be on your team. Seek Him out. Include Him in your struggles. If you do, He will show you exactly what it means to be His man.

 ## ROY'S STORY

When I became a father, one thing I didn't anticipate was how often my children would push my boundaries. Growing up, Nick loved lollipops, and so we'd always stick a bunch of them into every birthday cake. On one memorable birthday, he grabbed a lollipop and began licking it with great intent. And then he did something I didn't anticipate—he put the lollipop up to *my* mouth.

Now, given that I'm a little obsessive-compulsive, this is not something I would normally respond well to. And everyone at the table knew it. They all watched with bated breath to see what I would do—lick it or push it away?

Much to my surprise, I licked it! It seemed God gave me strength I didn't realize I had. Laughing, Nick licked the lollipop back, and we continued to share it until it was gone. And you know what? I was glad I did. I could tell that this new way of relating to each other filled his heart with joy.

As men we're supposed to be strong, but being strong doesn't mean being unyielding. Sometimes the toughest thing we can do is humble ourselves and step outside our comfort zone, especially when it's for our children's sake. When they have a request, our default response should be yes, not no, unless there's a good reason otherwise.

Throughout his life, Nick continued to do things that tested my limits as a way of expressing his desire to be close to me. During these moments, I'm happy to say God gave me the strength to oblige.

💬 DISCUSSION QUESTIONS

1   How do you define manhood? Do you consider yourself to be a man? How could strengthening your manhood improve your ability to father your child?

2   Think about your relationship with your wife or your child's mother. How well do you live up to her expectations for you as a husband and a father? How does your manhood impact her? How does it impact your child?

3   Review the six steps toward developing manhood. Which come naturally to you? Which do you need to improve on?

4   Discuss how Micah 6:8 relates to the concept of manhood. How do you live up to the standard God lays out in this verse?

The LORD has shown you what is good.
    He has told you what he requires of you.
You must act with justice.
    You must love to show mercy.
And you must be humble as you live in the sight of your God.

17

BUILDING MANHOOD

Imagine you're building a house. Everything goes smoothly at first. You plan it all out perfectly, organize your approach to the last detail, and put it all together without a hitch. But then, after living in it for a little while, things start to go south. Suddenly the floorboards are rotting and the roof is caving in, and you realize that you were so focused on getting the job done quickly and efficiently that you made one fatal error—you forgot to use the best materials.

It's the same with building manhood. If you neglect any element of your manhood, it will undermine your entire identity, making it easy for one impulse or one temptation to pull you away from your God-given design. The good news is, the materials you need to build godly manhood are already available to you. It's just a matter of recognizing, understanding, and using them properly.

As with a sturdy house, the first step toward building your manhood is constructing a strong foundation, as it's your foundation that will determine how well you'll be able to withstand the challenges of life (1 Peter 2:5). In this chapter, we'll go over the elements and principles of manhood that go into that strong foundation. These are the materials that will fortify your manhood and enable you to truly guide and protect your child well, empowering you both to stand strong no matter what winds blow.

ELEMENTS OF MANHOOD

In the last chapter, we imagined asking a group of men to describe themselves, guessing that they'd all give different answers based on how much they valued their occupation, personality, or appearance. The funny thing is, while I used that example to display how those characteristics aren't really what defines us as men, they actually *are* included in our manhood. No matter how insignificant any aspect of you may seem, it's still part of who you are. Therefore, it plays some kind of role in how you shape and express your identity.

To achieve your own God-given potential and help your child discover theirs, you must learn to recognize and express all of your skills, gifts, and abilities. After all, the elements that make up your identity are the same ones that make up theirs. By building that firm foundation for yourself, you don't just become all of who God called you to be—you also show your child how to do the same.

There are too many elements to cover in one chapter, so I've chosen just a few core ones to help you get started on your journey of self-exploration.[1] Use the following list to begin to think more deeply about the main aspects of your manhood and how they affect your fatherhood. It's only when you understand the pieces that make up your identity that you can really be able to sort through them. Then you can form them into the structure that will make you a better man—and an amazing father.

1   Your armor

Living in a sinful world requires you to actively protect yourself against threats to your standards, well-being, and identity in Christ. However, there are both immature and mature ways to do this. An immature male encloses himself in firm, unyielding armor

---

1   For more on the elements of manhood and building a strong identity, check out our books and video programs at liveupresources.com.

that barricades him from everything in the world, both the good and the bad. Instead of standing strong and relying on his strength in Christ, he flees from his problems, engaging in denial and blame and ignoring his weaknesses (James 1:6-8). Worst of all, his armor is so thick that it completely blocks him off from others, which may help him avoid any potential for pain and rejection but ultimately deprives him of necessary love and support.

A man, on the other hand, is only as defensive as he needs to be in any given situation. His armor is as flexible as it is strong, which allows him to use different defense mechanisms for different relationships and circumstances. As a result, he can enjoy life even as he's prepared to defend himself against it, and he can be vulnerable with others even if it leads to disappointment.

The more intentional you are about developing this type of armor, the easier it will be to form close relationships with others. And as you do, you'll find yourself extending your armor to cover them as well. Nowhere is this more apparent than in fatherhood. As you develop your own armor, you'll begin to personalize your child's welfare and maintain a vigilance for anything that might hurt them. But more than that, your example will teach your child how to develop a sense for when they need to defend themselves, giving them the tools to start developing their own armor to protect themselves when the time comes.

2   Your filters

Because of the unique experiences, influences, and memories that shape our viewpoints, we each have a unique way of perceiving life. You see the world through a filter system that helps you process life and respond to it, and those filters directly influence your everyday decision-making. As with your armor, this can be both helpful and hurtful. Many of your filters are either created from painful memories or formed without your knowledge. And when you don't resolve them or consciously recognize them, these filters can hijack your internal processes, distorting your perception of reality and weakening your ability to respond appropriately.

As we've discussed throughout this section, part of being a man is learning to readjust your filters by taking responsibility for what once was so that, with God's help, you can take an active role in shaping what will be. And when you reconcile with your past by consciously reinforcing its positive aspects and redefining its negative ones, you will gain an even greater understanding of the weight of your influence on your child. You'll recognize that each interaction with them creates an opportunity to instill positive memories that will lead them to develop healthy filters, allowing them to carry on the legacy you're working so hard to leave them.

3 Your mind

A mind is a terrible thing to waste, though it's certainly easy to take it for granted. But I'm not talking about intelligence as defined by our culture. No matter what areas we naturally excel in or how old we are, we all must consciously develop our minds in order to continually expand their capabilities. You do this primarily by gathering and organizing information, sorting through what's truthful and what's not, and figuring out how you can apply those truths to your life. This is how you create opinions about yourself and the world, which will allow you to navigate and respond to life more effectively.

Besides taking in new information, you must also develop your mind through introspection. Thinking through the potential positive and negative consequences of your actions can help you evaluate your decision-making so you can strengthen it for the future. Furthermore, it can increase your ability to see past your impulses. As you develop your mind, you will gain the ability to consciously slow down, reign in your misplaced passion, and then follow more positive pursuits.

Having a strong mind will also make it easier for you to

engage in your child's mental development rather than being intimidated by it or dismissing it out of disinterest or misunderstanding. Through different approaches like joking, questioning, and teaching, you can help them discover the flaws in their thinking and hone their decision-making skills, allowing them to avoid some of the same mistakes you had to learn the hard way.

4   Your heart

As important as developing the mind is, it's useless without also strengthening the heart. While your mind helps you gain understanding and create noble goals, it's the passion in your heart that will motivate you to actually apply that understanding and work toward those goals. When you tune in to your God-given passion, it will energize you not only to make your ideas reality but also to push yourself to pursue goals beyond survival. You will uncover what truly motivates you, what your real priorities are, and the values they represent. Only then will you be able to take action to follow through on them.

Consciously developing your heart allows you to tap in to your emotional strengths and true passion, which will naturally lead you to become a better servant-leader for your loved ones. You'll gain a caring resiliency, enabling you to persevere through your child's various moods, struggles, successes, and needs. Even greater, you'll uncover the passion behind your vision for your child, allowing you to respond to them as they need, not simply as they desire. Instead of automatically agreeing to make them happy, you'll learn to carefully assess what's best for them and respond accordingly.

5   Your body

While our bodies are the temples of the Holy Spirit, we don't always treat them as such (1 Corinthians 6:19-20). It takes a lot of effort to consistently exercise and eat healthy foods. And though we all want to be strong physically, it's simply easier to claim we're strong than to put in the work to actually be strong.

But in order to be a man, you need to actively build up your body, and not just so you have the strength, energy, and physical ability to accomplish your goals. Your mind, heart, and body all interact with each other constantly, which means your body has a tremendous influence on your mental, emotional, and relational capabilities. For instance, when you don't get enough sleep, you become sluggish and tired, limiting your ability to think clearly or feel excited about anything. By strengthening your body, you strengthen your ability to engage with all the other elements of manhood and maximize them to the fullest.

Working on your body also improves your fatherhood in many ways. Besides increasing the chances that you'll be around for a long time to take care of your family, it also allows you to take advantage of your desire to move. The more in shape you are, the easier it will be to engage in your naturally active style of play, which teaches your child self-control, strengthens their physical development, and builds up their confidence in their body's abilities. With such strength and confidence, they'll be able to persevere through any pain or discomfort until they achieve success.

6   Your soul and spirit

God created each of us with a desire for a relationship with Him. As a result, your soul is constantly searching for something that will give your life meaning and empower you beyond your own willpower. Because God's law is written on our hearts, we inherently feel His presence even when we aren't aware of it or don't have a relationship with Him (Romans 2:14-16). Even so, He leaves it up to us to put aside our self-interest long enough to recognize our soul's search, follow its leading, and accept His love.

While a man's soul points him toward God, his spirit is what allows him to connect with the Spirit of our Creator (John 3:6-7).

Until you make that connection by accepting Jesus into your life, your spirit remains dormant within you. But when you allow Him to bring it to life, your spirit will seek every opportunity to stay in contact with God's presence, inspiring you to immerse yourself in His Word and His ways and work to understand and apply them to your life.

Following your soul's leading and letting God fuel your spirit also enables Him to work through you to guide your child as well. Because of your sin nature, what's best for your child won't always be your first response. However, God will empower you to slow down your impulses, keep their best interests at heart, and work to always do right by them. He will help you treat your child as He does, which means that no matter how they behave or how they respond to you, you will never lose sight of their God-given value.

7   Your self

Simply put, a man's self *is* his identity, which organizes and controls all of the other elements of manhood. The elements described above provide input to your self, and your self uses that feedback to make the choices that define who you are. When you've explored each area of your manhood well, your self will be able to accurately weigh the importance of the feedback each element gives it while always keeping an eye out for your sin nature's corrupting influence.

The stronger your sense of self, the better your decision-making will be, including the decisions that affect your child. All of your manhood elements working together will help you evaluate and understand how to best guide your child. And when you have a well-developed self that is grounded in who God is, you'll be able to create and refine the developmental goals that will help them reach their full potential.

PRINCIPLES OF MANHOOD

Along with recognizing and developing each element of manhood, a strong foundation also requires internalizing godly principles. These are the "rules" we talked about in the last chapter that will structure your identity and allow you to use the elements above appropriately. Through my discussions with God while developing men's programs for LiveUp Resources, He revealed what I refer to as the 15 Principles of Manhood.[2] While you must work with God to decide for yourself which principles you should build your manhood on, these can help serve as a starting point to begin the process of doing so. As you read them, consider how they relate to your manhood and how you can apply them to your fatherhood. Then reach out to God and start building your solid foundation.

1   FORGED – Males are born, while men are forged.
(1 Peter 1:7)

Becoming a man isn't easy. It only comes from a deliberate process of being heated and fortified through the hardships of life. From that suffering, he develops all of his abilities and his toughness, making him fully capable of facing the realities of life—and that includes fatherhood. A man embraces any challenge in his relationship with his child and is willing to step up to take care of their needs. When he's been forged, his child can sense that he is trustworthy and dependent, giving them the stability they need to experience safety, guidance, and love.

---

2   Visit k21.men/principles to view the complete definition for each of the 15 Principles of Manhood and the images associated with them. To purchase these posters or check out our other resources that discuss the 15 Principles of Manhood, visit liveupresources.com/men.

2   CHOICES – A man is responsible for all of his choices.
(Haggai 1:5)

Even when life's events feel completely outside of his control, a man understands his responsibility to maintain command of his attitude and responses. He approaches fatherhood with optimism and remains aware of the impact even his smallest choices can have on his child. If his responses aren't positively influencing his child, he takes the time to change strategies and seek advice for how to father them more effectively.

3   CHANGE – A man's world is constantly in motion.
(1 Corinthians 9:19-20)

Because the world and our culture are always changing, a man makes sure to develop his full capabilities so he can adjust to any circumstance he finds himself in. He demonstrates an adventuresome spirit that encourages both him and his child to continually discover and explore the numerous possibilities that exist. He works with his child to adapt to the changes in their relationship as they grow older, taking care never to get caught in the past and to always focus on the person his child is blossoming into.

4   WORTH – Men are amazing; every man is of infinite worth. (Matthew 10:31)

Despite life's attempts to beat him down, a man accepts his own value and recognizes the unique gifts God has given him to contribute to the common good. He understands that God created him to be a father, which means he embraces this role with enthusiasm. He also takes care to pass on that sense of purpose to his child, finding ways to continually compliment, encourage, and reinforce their value. He praises their good choices and confronts their bad ones in order to ensure they keep moving toward an amazing future.

5   COURAGE – Men do whatever it takes. (Matthew 16:24)

Because he serves the God of miracles, a man believes all things are possible (Luke 1:37). However, this doesn't mean he passively waits for good things to happen to him. Rather, he consistently follows through on what needs to be done to give him and his child the best lives possible, no matter how much work it takes. He willingly exercises self-discipline to fulfill their needs by sharpening his decision-making skills, exercising his body, honing his emotional courage, deepening his relationships, and applying his faith.

6   LEARNING – A man is dedicated to continuous learning. (Proverbs 1:5)

A man never assumes he knows it all. Instead, he constantly studies God's Word and seeks feedback from others so he can always improve on how he's living and how he's fathering his child. He instills this same growth mindset in his child and takes care to encourage their God-given, curious mind. As he leaves his comfort zone and puts in the effort to learn new skills, he inspires them to do the same.

7   REFLECTION – Only the true you will get you through. (Deuteronomy 4:9)

While a man recognizes that fully sharing all of who he is at any given moment may not always be socially appropriate, he also understands that his private self and public self must be congruent with each other. In more common terms, who he is behind closed doors is the same as who he is when he's around others. He knows that being anything but fully authentic in any area of his life would make him inconsistent and unreliable, creating a sense of distrust in his child. Instead, he makes a point to honestly express himself in order to be a supportive resource for his child and to set an example for what they themselves need to become.

8   CONTROL – A man shapes the world more than the world shapes the man. (Romans 12:2)

As unfair as the world can be at times, a man doesn't simply accept a victim mindset. He sets goals, outlines the steps to complete them, seeks a support system, and then gets it done with God. He works with his child to make the home environment better for the entire family, and in the process, he demonstrates the positive work ethic they will need to achieve their desire for self-fulfillment and success.

9   CALLING – The best way for a man to predict his future is to create it. (Ezra 10:4)

While a man accepts that God is ultimately in control, he also recognizes that much of what he experiences is influenced by his own choices. Through goal setting and constant self-assessment, he teaches his child how to dream and then apply themselves in practical ways to make those dreams come true. Just as importantly, he guides them to act proactively to avoid harming themselves or others through unnecessary mistakes.

10   STRENGTH – A man accepts that to live is to be challenged through crisis and hardship. (James 1:2-4)

Failure is inevitable, but a man doesn't let it defeat him. He prepares for unexpected challenges by creating a backup plan and perseveres through the pain to complete the task at hand. As a father, he teaches his child to handle crises with the same courage. He shows them that failure, when kept in perspective, can lead them to find opportunities they otherwise never would have discovered.

11   ACCOUNTABILITY – A man never stands alone unless he is taking a stand. (Proverbs 17:17)

No matter how strong a man is, he knows that any strength he has is ultimately meaningless if he tries to do life alone. Instead, he builds a support system he can rely on through hardships and challenges, in turn demonstrating to his child the importance of relationships. He assists them in developing their own relational skills, teaches them how to assess their relationships to figure out who's safe and who's not, and guides them in setting the proper boundaries.

12   HUMILITY – A man knows when to say, "I was wrong," and humbly faces his errors. (Luke 14:11)

A man knows he isn't perfect. But rather than run from his mistakes, he does what he can to make amends and improve his actions. He isn't afraid of apologizing to his child when he knows he's hurt them, and he teaches them the importance of doing the same with others. And when his child makes a mistake, he encourages them to ask for forgiveness and take the necessary steps to make up for their negative actions.

13   PERSEVERANCE – A man does not always get it right the first time, but he keeps on trying until he does. (James 1:12)

No matter how much he prepares, a man knows life won't always go according to plan. He is willing to continually adjust his approach to life and to fatherhood. When his child stumbles, he encourages them to get back up, shake it off, learn from it, and try again. He doesn't accept excuses, and he provides consequences that will help his child choose better alternatives in the future.

14 CHARACTER – A man lives by his principles. (Genesis 39:3)

A man sets specific standards for himself and commits to living up to them, and he expects the same of his child. He teaches them the Word of God and helps them internalize its principles so they can use them to improve their decision-making. And when they violate these standards, he confronts them to ensure they understand that compromising who they are is simply not an option.

15 SUBMISSION – A man submits to an authority beyond himself. (1 Peter 5:6)

A man recognizes that his willpower is never enough, and he willingly submits to the one true God instead of to the false gods of the world. He also shares about God with his child, introducing Him as both an authority figure and a source of love and empowerment. Because he bases everything in his life on who God is, he teaches his child to do the same, giving them their best chance to become all they can be.

God has called all males to become men. After all, a family needs a godly man who can lead them sacrificially. But because of the many forces in the world attacking manhood, you must intentionally seek out God's plan for you and fight to become the man He created you to be. Develop all the elements that make up your manly identity. Internalize and follow godly principles. Study the model God has provided us through His Son, Jesus, and live accordingly to this holy example. When you do, His blessings will pour out on you, your manhood, and your child.

ROY'S STORY

I'll never forget what my dad said to me the day I passed my driver's license test. It was my second attempt at it, and we were both feeling proud of what I had accomplished. As I drove us home, my father first congratulated me. Then he said something that surprised me. He told me that there's a difference between being able to pass a test and being a good driver. And while I had achieved the former, I was only just beginning the journey of discovering what kind of driver I was going to be.

What he was saying is there is a big difference between knowing how to drive and actually creating a lifestyle that regularly applies the rules and principles of the driver's manual. When it came down to it, my habitual choices as a driver would eventually define me more than my intentions.

My father's words have stuck with me all these years, not just as a driver but also as a man. Just like good driving habits, character and integrity don't just happen. It takes creating positive structures and living them out to truly become a man of God. Thankfully, I had a father who could help me do so, but not all men do. I've heard from numerous men in prison who've gone through our ministry programs and studied our Principles of Manhood say, "This is what my dad *should* have taught me." Growing up, they never had any instruction or guidance on forming a strong identity or developing good decision-making skills. As a result, they made self-destructive choices that came with extreme consequences, upending their lives and hurting those they loved most.

However, while these men are an example of what happens when you don't build strong principles in your life, they also prove that it's never too late to do so. Each one had willingly served God by participating in our five-year men's program, and each one had put in the hard work of developing themselves, forging strong relationships, and learning to apply God's Word to their lives. As my dad told me after getting my driver's license, you get to decide what kind of man you're going to be. And that's a decision you make every single day.

DISCUSSION QUESTIONS

1   What do you think about the idea that every aspect of you is part of your manhood identity, no matter how insignificant it may seem? How does this change the way you see yourself?

2   Review the seven core elements of manhood. Which do you feel you've already developed well? Which do you need to work on? How can doing so strengthen your fatherhood?

3   Choose three of the manhood principles and discuss how they relate to your fatherhood. How can building them into your identity increase your ability to help your child develop theirs?

4   Discuss how Deuteronomy 28:1-2 relates manhood. How can obeying God help you become the man you want to be?

Make sure you obey the LORD your God completely. Be careful to obey all his commands. I'm giving them to you today. If you do these things, the LORD will honor you more than all the other nations on earth. If you obey the LORD your God, here are the blessings that will come to you and remain with you.

18

SO NOW WHAT?

I know the men who read this book are all doing so for many different reasons. Some soon-to-be fathers are doing their homework well and making sure they start out strong on their fatherhood journey. Others are far into their fatherhood and have hit a natural parenting challenge or obstacle that has made them realize their desperate need for God's guidance. And still others have made irrevocable mistakes, pushed their children away, and simply don't know where else to turn.

The first two sections of this book have focused on repairing yourself as a father so you're better able to guide your child well, an approach that may seem to assume you still have a salvageable relationship with your child. But what if you've royally screwed things up? What if your decisions have caused your child so much pain that there seems to be no hope of restoration? What if it's just too late to fix things?

Well, I can promise you, it's not. God is in the restoration business. No matter what you've done, He already has a better future planned for both you and your child, and He is standing by ready to help you achieve it. You just need to be willing to own up to how you've failed your child, face the issues you've been trying to so hard to ignore, and finally turn it all over to God. It's His love and empowerment that will help you make the necessary changes to allow your dreams for your fatherhood to finally become possible.

THE BREAKING POINT

He entered my office alone. It had taken him years to reach that point. I could tell he would've rather been anywhere else, but he was tired of feeling defeated, incompetent, and rejected. He knew that seeking out counseling was the only shred of hope he had left.

His desperation and brokenness were evident in the unaccustomed tears streaking down his face as he described his situation. He admitted to all the ways he had failed his family through his poor choices and how his life and relationships may never be the same as a result. He described how angry his wife and children were at the ways he had treated them and how their trust in him was completely nonexistent. He told me his children had simply moved on, wanting nothing to do with him.

"I want to change," he then announced, as if it would be easy.

And I wanted to believe him. I could tell he truly recognized the selfishness and failure of his lifestyle. He even acknowledged how his unhealthy actions mirrored that of his own father's. I sensed, however, that his newfound desire to change was more about improving his own life than the lives of his loved ones. He didn't seem to fully understand the difficulty and depth of the change process.

He confirmed my hunch a moment later. Finished with his story, he looked up expectantly and asked, "So now what?"

I have had this same discussion with fathers over and over again in my counseling career, and I've found that the devastating reality is that many men simply refuse to accept the responsibilities of being a father. Some ignore the emotional, physical, or mental needs of their children, while others actively abuse them as a result of misdirected anger, depraved sexual impulses, or neglect. These fathers claim to love their children, but in reality they truly care only about themselves.

And before long, the consequences of their actions catch up to them. They have hurt and disappointed their children so many times that these children have realized and acted on their need to take care of themselves, typically by cutting their father out of their lives and maybe even replacing him with a more caring father figure. Having finally broken free from his negative influence, they have little interest in letting him back into their lives. In fact, many of them would be happy never to see him again.

Many men who feel this hurt and disconnection from their children want to make things right. But at the same time, they don't really want to do all that it takes to change. That's because they aren't sad for how they've hurt their child—they're sad for how the consequences of their actions have hurt *themselves*. And a father who grieves only for himself will fall back into old habits the second his pain and discomfort go away.

For a man to truly change, he must willingly admit to and take responsibility for how his selfish choices have harmed others. His pain needs to stem in part from the damage he's caused them. It's only when he desires to improve both his *and* their lives that his motivation will be strong enough to lead to lasting change.

So I called out my client for his selfish tendencies. I told that him his children were right to have distanced themselves from him. I told him that he was no good for them if he stayed the way he was, and that if he tried to reconnect with them now, he would only hurt them again. I told him that if he truly wanted things to be different, he had to commit to changing his negative behaviors and selfish ways and start putting their needs before his.

"It's your choice," I told him. Then I leaned back in my chair, looked him straight in the eyes, and turned his question back on him: "So now what?"

IT STARTS WITHIN

Over the years, I have counseled countless men who, after deciding to change, temporarily get their act together and then revert right back to their negative behaviors. I've even seen men who've gone through this cycle several times. It's a little confounding. These men want to change. They want to be better fathers. And yet they fail again and again. So what's the problem? Are they simply incapable of embracing godly fatherhood?

Well, that's clearly not the issue, since we established back in Chapter 1 that God designed all men for fatherhood. The real problem is that men often have a lack of self-discipline. We aren't good at managing our impulses, and we aren't interested in anything that requires too much work. And we may actually get away with that lifestyle for a while. People are typically willing to give others the benefit of the doubt at first. However, once someone hurts or disappoints them too many times, they become skeptical of whether that person's word means anything at all.

When a man establishes such a reputation of instability, his wife and child will understandably have a hard time trusting his desire to change. Consequently, they'll continually challenge him, either indirectly through silent judgment or directly through criticism. And without the external affirmation he believes he deserves, it becomes harder for him to even want to follow through on his commitment to change.

That's why this commitment can't be done simply to please someone else. Becoming a better father begins with changing because *you* want to. While your desire to restore your relationship with your child or to fix the pain you've caused them are good enough motivating factors to jump-start the growth process, they aren't enough to sustain your motivation throughout it. That's because a man who chooses to change for others always expects something from them in return, and your child won't always be willing to give it. No matter how much you change, they may choose to reject you anyway, making you feel like all your hard work wasn't worth it after all.

When you base the success of your growth journey on whether you restore your relationship with your child, you only make it more likely that you'll fall right back into your old, comfortable lifestyle when things don't go as you'd hoped. A father can only achieve lasting change when he takes full responsibility for himself, his behaviors, and his growth, because it's only then that he'll truly want to be different. You must let your displeasure with your past actions and attitudes be what fuels your growth process, taking the pressure off your family either to force you into change or to make it worth it. When you focus on instituting the change *you* want to make and forming an identity *you* can be proud of, you will set yourself up to create a better future for yourself and your family, regardless of whether they accept the new you.

Changing for yourself means becoming a man of character, like we talked about in the previous two chapters, which requires developing a strong sense of integrity and then continually making the tough choices that express that integrity. It requires letting go of your need for control and learning to value relationships over power. And it requires giving up your self-focus and sacrificing your needs for the needs of others—especially those of your child.

WEATHERING THE STORM

While the manhood characteristics above go against many of your preformed tendencies, adopting them is the only way to eventually restore your relationship with your child. And in order to do so, you will have to undergo a painful transformation process. Until now, you've ignored the complex potential God created you with, choosing instead to act in immature ways that allow you to avoid emotional risk and remain comfortable. If you truly want to change, you must be willing to leave your comfort zone and enter into a period of suffering as you confront your mistakes and accept the pain you've caused. It's only by fighting to take control of your life and purging yourself of your negative behaviors, beliefs, and perspectives that you can develop better, godlier ones in their place.

If this uncomfortable process sounds like the last thing you want to do, you're not alone. As with any worthwhile challenge, it will be a long, difficult journey. Even before you start on it, you need to fully consider whether you're willing to pay the price of undergoing such a deep level of personal change. Each time you commit to changing and then back out, you will kill a little of your child's faith in you until, eventually, they won't bother getting their hopes up at all.

For this reason, it's actually better for you not to try to restore your relationship with your child right away. Instead, you should wait until after a period of measurable change in your lifestyle. One reason for this approach is that recovery is not a straight line, and you will likely make several missteps as you learn better ways to live. Though these mistakes are part of the development process, they still have the capacity to hurt your child, who may see them as signs that you're not actually committed to changing.

Additionally, a younger child's tendency toward temper tantrums, constant questioning, and lack of social skills can make it difficult for even the best parents to respond maturely. For a recovering father who's used to behaving immaturely, it might feel impossible, which will make it even more difficult or potentially damaging to keep trying to mend the relationship. By achieving a basic foundation of development first, you will gain the resiliency you need to keep moving forward no matter what relational challenges come your way.

Ultimately, the biggest key to initiating real and lasting change is to develop an intimate relationship with God the Father.

As we've gone over in great depth, God's powerful definition of love provides the perfect example of a caring father, and a relationship with Him will instill a sense of humility and repentance within you. It's through understanding His definition of love that you will finally realize that while you might have *wanted* to love your child, you have fallen desperately short compared to His standard.

In this way, your relationship with God will motivate you to be honest with your family, sacrifice for your children, and care for them as Jesus would. He will help you search your heart and recognize the negative behavioral patterns you once ignored (Psalm 139:23-24). As this awareness grows, your narcissism, shame, and self-centeredness will give way to a desire for God's way. You will seek His forgiveness for your failures and rely on His Word to know what to do instead. Over time, His empowerment will help you detach from your past sinful choices and replace them with the positive behaviors you need to finally be the father He created you to be.

In addition to love, guidance, and support, God will also help you have faith as you navigate the struggles associated with trying to change. Life has no guarantees, and no matter how hard we try to be different, there's no promise of a positive outcome. However, God is a good God (Psalm 31:19; 34:8). As long as you remain steadfast in your faith and maintain your goal of self-development, He will help you become the man you need to be to then begin the process of restoring your relationship with your child.

STEP BY STEP

Once you recognize the ways your choices have hurt your child, fully commit to changing from the inside out, and achieve a basic level of development, you're ready for the next step, which is a process I call *refathering*. While a father can't go back in time and change how he treated his child or alter what they think about him, he can move forward by working to establish a new definition of what his presence means in their life, thus *refathering* them in a completely new way.

As much as you may want to rush through this process to get right to a reconciliation, it will take time. Even though your child desires their father's love, years of intermittent and unpredictable support have taught them not to expect it. Many children in these situations build solid emotional walls and may even begin mirroring their father's worst traits, such as anger, withdrawal, or defensiveness, closing them off to the refathering process. They may also lash out verbally or physically in a preemptive attempt to reject their father before he can reject them again. When barriers like these occur, you must decide: will life continue to be all about your own feelings and issues, or can you be like Jesus and consistently maintain this new unconditional love for your child?

While refathering will be different for each man depending on the specific ways he hurt or let down his child in the past, there are three basic requirements every father must understand and adhere to in order to rebuild his relationship with his child. First and foremost, he must give his child a chance to freely express their sadness, pain, and anger. This means that at the beginning of the refathering process, you must take time to sit down with them to ask how you've hurt them, and then listen to their answer—no matter how painful it may be to hear.

If your child is in fact willing to engage in this conversation (which is often *not* the case), remember that the conversation is about them and their feelings, not about you. As your child shares their pain, you must put aside your need to dominate or control the interaction and listen without making excuses, trying to explain your perspective, or rushing to ask for forgiveness. Your child's perceptions are real to them, and arguing about the extent of what they felt will just cause them to feel assaulted or rejected once again.

Instead, you should only respond when your child indicates they are ready to hear it. Letting them lead the conversation in this way will convey your willingness to give them control of the future of your relationship, including when and what they want to forgive. Working at their preferred pace allows them to assess the authenticity of your motivations and attempts to change. Then they can decide if they are comfortable enough to move forward in the refathering process.

If they *are* open to progressing, the next step is to schedule regular times for honest evaluation of the relationship in order to give your child a chance to directly address and process any negative tendencies that they sense are starting to reemerge within you. Two specific questions you should ask are "How are you feeling about our relationship?" and "Is there anything I need to ask forgiveness for?" These questions will help your child begin to feel safe enough to express their honest responses to your actions and treatment of them. On a larger scale, your continuous commitment to having these conversations will show your child that you're taking responsibility for the restoration process, which is an important step toward building mutual confidence and a foundation for trust.

However, it's not enough simply to have conversations about your negative behaviors. The second refathering requirement demands that you are completely vigilant in avoiding negative behaviors in the first place. Your child has grown to expect inconsistency and unpredictability from you due to your past actions. Even one small adverse action can have a tremendously harmful impact on your relationship, telling your child that you won't or can't change. This is especially true when they already have a lack of trust in you, which will cause them to magnify common relational mistakes that would normally be tolerated. As you rebuild your relationship, be aware of the potential impact of all of your actions and constantly fight your natural impulsivity. That way you won't accidentally misstep and cause a setback in your progress.

While you may feel the urge to do whatever it takes to regain your child's trust and love, you must stick to the third refathering requirement: do not become overly solicitous. A child's distrust will only increase if their previously abusive or disengaged father suddenly attempts to reconnect with shallow displays of affection or a showering of gifts. They'll likely see it as a tactic to manipulate or buy back their love or, even worse, as a trivialization of their pain.

Instead of trying to win back their love, you should engage in behaviors that will allow you to *earn* it back. True relational healing and recovery must be rebuilt brick by brick through your commitment to consistently live out the godly characteristics described in the previous two chapters. When a man gives love freely, without expecting immediate affirmation or reciprocation, he proves his authenticity and dedication, and his child will finally start to feel valued by him.

One effective way to do this is to engage in activities with your child outside of the restoration process. Relational restoration is heavy and often emotionally draining, and it can be useful at times to take a break from it to have some fun. Activities such as going to museums, taking a road trip, or even reading a book together give you and your child a chance to relax, laugh, and simply be yourselves. During these moments, your child's emotional walls will temporarily come down, allowing trust to grow where it might not have otherwise.

However, despite the casual nature of these moments of fun, keep in mind that your actions can still have consequences. Your child is continuously evaluating you, and that won't stop simply because you're playing video games together instead of having a serious conversation. Furthermore, just because your child could enjoy your time together for a brief moment doesn't mean they'll suddenly feel like everything is fixed. If they shut you out again after the moment of connection ends, don't get discouraged. Rather, remind yourself that God has His own pacing, appreciate the moment for what it was, and continue attempting to move forward in the relationship.

WHEN THE GOING GETS TOUGH

Unfortunately, the reality is that the refathering process won't always flow smoothly. Your child may be reluctant to be refathered and therefore may turn every conversation into a confrontation. Younger children especially often lack the ability to understand and control their emotions. But even if your child is seemingly old enough to think logically and rationally, you must always remember that you are the adult. That means you should be the first one to step back from an argument, especially if you start to feel defensive or angry. If both you and your child take time apart to think, it will open the door for an even more honest and controlled conversation later.

Additionally, you may find that even after everything you've worked toward, both with your development and your relationship, your child is simply unwilling to forgive you. In this difficult situation, it's vital for you to respect their decision, learn to forgive yourself, and celebrate any small successes you have made in the relationship (Ephesians 4:32).

Of course, your child isn't the only one that can get in the way of reconciliation. No matter how much effort you put into changing, it's always possible for you to return to your negative past behaviors. If this regression happens, your child will see it as evidence that the cycle of inconsistency is beginning again and will likely shut you out to protect themselves from further disappointment. Even if you recognize your mistakes and work to recommit to changing yourself, the damage is already done. While the refathering process can continue or begin again, it will be much more difficult this time.

In extreme situations, fathers who are not confident in their ability to stay away from past habits of addiction, crime, self-destruction, abuse, or other harmful behaviors may need to take the courageous and selfless step to voluntarily remove themselves from their loved ones' lives (Matthew 18:6-9). At the beginning of the refathering process, the father must clearly discuss this possibility with his child by saying, "If I continue down this path, I am dangerous to you and to me. I may have to do what's best for you by staying out of your life." Sometimes simply recognizing this as a possibility can motivate a father to truly change.

While refathering is a demanding and extensive process that can feel impossible at times, it is worth the effort. When a man commits to seeking God's guidance, practicing patience, and praying for the strength to do the right thing, his family relationships can be restored. But to do so, you must completely reconstruct your life and behaviors so you can pour out God's love and character (Matthew 9:17). You must create new habits and strengths and accept God's empowerment to navigate the long, tough road ahead. With His help, you can turn around right now and begin to be the father your child needs and deserves. Only then will you be able to answer that lingering question: "So now what?"

 ROY'S STORY

It's been no secret that my father and I had a tumultuous relationship. Throughout my childhood I felt neglected and abandoned by him. We had moments of connection, and I won't deny that he was a very wise man, but I never felt like I truly had a loving and supportive father. Then, at the end of his pastoral career, he made a series of negative decisions that repeatedly put him on the front page of our local newspaper—including having an affair.

I'm sure you can imagine the pain it caused me knowing that he would inflict such embarrassment on his family due to his own self-centeredness.

Now, let's fast forward to seven years after this happened. I was an adult fully on my own and had been working to build a retreat center on my 150-acre property that would be open to pastors, missionaries, and other leaders to come and be refreshed. However, my neighbors were vehemently opposed to my plans. They were concerned about increased traffic and, as they put it, what kind of people would be filtering through the retreat center. As a result, they dragged me through numerous court hearings and made up all kinds of stories about my wild parties and how I was building a secret prison. The local feud got so bad that the newspapers even wrote about it several times. It was, quite frankly, one of the worst experiences of my life.

Then one day in the heat of it all, I got a call from my father. He asked how things were going, and I shared some of my challenges and frustrations with him. At the end, he said, "This is going to be a problem for me. You see, Roy, we have the same name, and I'm going to get really tired of you making me look bad in the newspapers."

We both laughed, partly because it was a good joke, but also from relief. You see, we had never really talked about how he hurt me and my family so many years ago. His bringing it up was an acknowledgment of his negative choices and of how we needed to resolve it in order to truly repair our relationship. While he couldn't go back and undo how he'd acted throughout my childhood, he could start now, by being present for me in my adulthood. Even though it was late, it was much, much better than never.

💬 DISCUSSION QUESTIONS

1   Name some of the ways fathers harm their children and their relationships with them. Have you made any choices that have hurt your child? How has your natural impulsivity impacted their well-being?

2   How can you be a better example of God's love for your child? What do you need to change about yourself in order to become a better leader in this regard?

3   What is one failure or temptation you have participated in that makes it hard for you to believe that God can forgive you? How can you integrate God's fatherhood into your life to help you overcome this shame?

4   Discuss how Colossians 3:13 relates to the refathering process. How can seeking God's forgiveness help you work toward restoring your relationship with your child?

Put up with one another. Forgive one another if you are holding something against someone. Forgive, just as the Lord forgave you.

part III

FATHERHOOD REFINED

"He is like a father who trains the son he is pleased with."
—*Proverbs 3:12*

19

A FATHER'S INFLUENCE

There's a word I've used in just about every chapter in this book so far, which goes to show how essential it is to fatherhood. The word is *influence*. In all areas of life, we're surrounded by a myriad of different influences, many of which we've already talked about here. Our sin nature, childhood experiences, environment, friends, and mentors all impact what we do, think, and ultimately become. And with how sinful and damaging the world is, there's no guarantee this influence will always be positive.

For us fathers, this can be a terrifying thought. When our impressionable and trusting children are submerged in a culture where lies, addiction, and narcissism are considered normal, how will they ever discover and live out God's purpose for them? When so many factors are influencing them in ways that seem to be outside of their control, how will they ever be able to determine the direction of their own lives?

The answer to that depends on you. While it's true that all children are influenced by many outside factors, both good and bad, it's their parents that create the foundational pillars they build their identity on. The character and decision-making you exhibit will lead your child to internalize either godly values or negative cultural standards, and the type of support you give will impact whether they push themselves or give into passivity. In other words, the more positive your influence is and the more active you are in wielding it, the better equipped your child will be to create a positive future for themselves no matter what else tries to pull them in a different direction.

In the rest of this book, we're going to focus on your influence as a father and how to use it to help your child grow. In each of the topics discussed, we'll unpack how to actively teach your child in these areas as well as how to guide them through your example and actions. But before we can get into the specifics, we need to go deeper into what it really means to have influence as a father. It's only by understanding the many nuanced ways you impact your child and the weight your influence carries that you can maximize it to help them become all God intended them to be.

LEVEL UP

By now, you should be well aware that the influence you have over your child is both direct and indirect. As we go about life and make decisions, our children follow in our footsteps whether or not we directly instruct them to, assuming that how we behave must be the right way. What this means is that your influence can't be something that simply happens. It must be a daily, deliberate choice not only to express who God created you to be but also to act as a constant guiding light to help your child do the same (Matthew 5:14-16).

It's pretty easy to choose to *become* a father. But to truly *be* a father, you must accept the responsibility that goes along with it and commit to being a continual part of your child's ever-changing life. This commitment of fatherhood can be broken up into the following five levels, each of which build off of each other. All fathers start at either level one or level two. After that, it's up to you to decide how high you will go.

1   The physical father

Physical fathers are those who bear the title of *father* in biology only. While these fathers provide the sperm that help create their children—either as a result of a one-night stand, an extramarital affair, or a brief relationship—doing so is not their intention, and so they flee in order to avoid the responsibility of fatherhood. A desire to be a father doesn't always prevent this abandonment, though. Some physical fathers actually do want to be fathers, but when the reality of that role sets in, they realize they aren't ready and decide to bail.

In this way, physical fathers deny both their own and their child's need for an emotional connection (1 Timothy 5:8). That's why children of these men, especially those who don't even know who their father is, often refer to them only as "the sperm donor." After all, that's all they ever received from the man who was supposed to care for and guide them. Consequently, they grow up feeling abandoned, confused, and inadequate. Sadly, they can't help but believe that if they were good enough, their father never would've left in the first place.

2   The positional father

Unlike the physical father, the positional father makes the active choice to accept his role as a father, whether it's to a biological child, foster child, adopted child, or stepchild. This means that he feels responsible for his child's welfare, at least on some level, and he acknowledges his duty to provide for their basic needs, often with the expectation that they will obey and respect him in return.

However, while the positional father does take care of his child and may even work hard to provide for his family financially, he doesn't involve himself in their development any further than that. He may periodically engage with his child on the weekend, but ultimately he's not involved in their daily life and doesn't recognize the value of progressing to a higher level of fatherly attachment. As long as he's fulfilling his child's basic survival needs, he considers his duty as a father complete. His child, on the other hand, craves a more intimate relationship. And when it fails to happen, they'll feel the sharp pain of rejection, no matter how well their father provides.

3 The principled father

Taking it one step further than the positional father, the principled father *does* accept the role he plays in his child's development. He recognizes his need to help them internalize godly principles, develop their gifts, and hone their decision-making, and so he involves himself in their day-to-day growth. He works hard to teach, affirm, and guide them in all areas of life, which in turn helps direct their development in a positive direction (Deuteronomy 11:19). This includes regularly planning activities with his child that will strengthen their skills and broaden their knowledge to set them up to create the best future they can.

Unfortunately, while the principled father is present for his child physically, he is still only engages with them cognitively. Whether he tends to keep conversations superficial, eliminate any intimate expression of affection, or even avoid verbally stating his love for his child, he subconsciously puts up barriers to limit emotional intimacy in their relationship. And like with the positional father, his child will be left wanting more. Even as they appreciate the quality time they spend together, they'll still experience a sense of emptiness, yearning for a deeper connection their father simply isn't willing to give.

4 The passionate father

Like the principled father, the passionate father actively participates in teaching his child life skills and fostering their development. However, he doesn't just want to provide rules and structures for them to live by. He also wants to connect on an emotional level. He knows that for his child to truly thrive, he needs to provide them with the love, affirmation, and support that will give them the confidence to persevere. And that means helping them work through life's failures and rejections, taking time to celebrate their achievements, and listening attentively as they open their heart to him. With this type of connection, his child will be empowered to charge headfirst at any challenge that pops up, because they know that no matter what, their father has their back.

5   The spiritual father

While the passionate father does all that is necessary for his child's mental and emotional growth, the reality is that something is still missing. For a father to truly maximize his influence, he needs to take that final step and become a spiritual father. In addition to guiding his child in the exact same ways as the passionate father, a spiritual father also recognizes that fatherhood is part of God's divine purpose for him. Furthermore, he understands that God has a purpose for his child as well, and he accepts his responsibility to help them develop every capability God created them with (Proverbs 22:15). He involves God in all aspects of his fatherhood, relying on His guidance to make the choices that will fulfill his child's needs and help them achieve their God-given purpose.

The spiritual father further recognizes that he represents God to his child, which is why he continually strives to become more like Him. He confronts his selfish tendencies and learns to sacrifice his desires for the success of his child. He enters into difficult conversations that will stretch him to become a better father. He accepts that he is not perfect and willingly apologizes to his child for his mistakes so they can move beyond them, allowing them to continue to help each other develop their God-given potential.

Above all, the spiritual father helps his child learn who God can be in their life, using their own intimate relationship to point them to an even greater relationship with God. He discusses the importance of faith, meaning, and godly values with them, though he ultimately accepts their right to develop their own beliefs. Regardless of his child's choices, the father has confidence in knowing that with God's guidance, he has provided a strong spiritual foundation upon which they can build the rest of their life (Proverbs 19:18).

As with most of life, it's not where you start with your child but where you end up (Philippians 3:13). No matter what level of fatherhood you're currently at, you are fully capable of becoming the spiritual father your child needs, because that's the father God created you to become. So set your standard high, and then pursue it with all you have. When you do, you'll find yourself becoming more and more of a godly influence on your child, and you'll start to see how that influence can change the direction of their entire life.

A UNIQUE TYPE OF FATHER

A father's influence depends not only on his commitment to his role as a father but also on what the nature of that role really is. While I've talked about the previous growth topics primarily from the perspective of a biological father who's married to his child's mother, the truth is that not all fathers have taken this route to fatherhood. And while all types of fathers have the same responsibility to influence their child in godly ways, the approach to that influence will look quite different depending on their specific situation.

While it's difficult to fully dissect every possible nuance in different fathers' relationships with their children, I want to take a moment to define the main categories of fatherhood, the unique challenges they bring, and how these challenges can impact the father's influence. The following descriptions are not meant to be comprehensive but to help you begin to think more deeply about your own approach to fatherhood. The greater understanding you have of the circumstances that impact your influence, the better you can apply the topics discussed in the rest of this book to your fatherhood.[1]

1   Traditional fathers

What I'm calling a traditional father is a biological father who is married to and living with his child's mother. This type of relationship brings with it the benefit of getting to see his child every day, which makes it easier to be involved in and influence their life. Additionally, because their relationship begins the moment the child is born, there likely won't be predeveloped barriers, such as the child's past trauma, that could limit the intimacy of their relationship. And when he has a strong, loving connection to his wife, he gains the benefit of a partner to support and assist him as they work to raise their child together.

However, because these blessings are simply a part of the father's natural relationship with his child, it can be tempting to take them for granted. Since a traditional father has full-time access to his child, it can be much easier for him to assume their relationship will just happen with no energy exerted on his end. Instead of intentionally putting effort into spending time with his child, he relies on the brief interactions they have while passing each other at home. And since the mother is an equally active partner in parenting, many traditional fathers are happy to let her take over the relational work of parenting and be their child's sole source of emotional support and intimate communication.

But the reality is that a traditional father has an equal amount of work to do as any other type of father, just as his choices have an equally weighty impact on who his child becomes. And because

---

1   For more great resources on different types of family relationships and their impact on parenting, check out the organizations FamilyLife (familylife.com) and Focus on the Family (focusonthefamily.com).

they're physically living together and even share some of the same biological tendencies, his indirect influence becomes that much more powerful. He must take advantage of this unique opportunity to guide his child by closely monitoring his behaviors and carefully honing his influence over them. Only then can he ensure that every aspect of it points them toward who God created them to be.

2   Divorced fathers

Divorces aren't fun for anyone, not the father, not the mother, and certainly not the child. No matter how "clean" a divorce may be, it still creates a huge disruption in a child's life and causes many parts of it to change, leading them to experience any number of different feelings, opinions, and reactions to the divorce. They may blame their mother and latch on to their father, or they may blame their father and refuse to have anything to do with him at all. They may be angry about the entire situation and become distant and combative to both parents, or they may become overly affectionate and compliant in an attempt to make everyone happy again.

All of these reactions can make it difficult for a father to use his influence effectively, because they are all ways the child is attempting to avoid the emotional turbulence within them. No matter how much he may want to fix things for his child, the father must learn to adjust to their healing process even if it means accepting their anger toward him. Trying to force a positive attitude or relationship onto the child will only make them resent him more and inhibit their healing process. Instead, the father must be willing to offer his support and love and let the child choose how they want to respond.

At the same time, he must not allow his child's response to dictate what type of father he is. Especially if he doesn't get to see his child every day, a divorced father can try too much to become a friend, often by showering them with gifts, in an attempt to get them to like him or to cheer them up. But even though their physical time together may be reduced, the father is still responsible to do what's right for his child, which means teaching them important life skills, challenging them on their negative behaviors, and disciplining them when needed, no matter how much they may dislike it.

Another challenge to a divorced father's influence is simply the process of custody and coparenting. Due to the mother's own anger and resentment, she may try to undermine his influence out of spite, either by badmouthing him to their child or by limiting how often he sees them. And even when the mother is fully cooperative, custody is still likely to be split, hindering the father's ability to influence his child's day-to-day life. Rather than feeling frustrated and defeated, the father must learn to take advantage of the time he *does* have with his child. He can't control the mother or what happens when he's not there, but he can control how he responds to and interacts with his child. And at the end of day, that's what matters most.

3   Widowed fathers

A widowed father faces a similar challenge to the divorced father in that he and his child are facing a life-changing disruption, but the difference is that his wife, their mother, is completely gone from their lives. They are both forced to reconcile with that loss, and while their grief may bring them closer together, it can also limit the father's influence over his child. His own grief can overwhelm him, making it hard to take care of himself, let alone his child. And due to his child's undeveloped state, they may end up lashing out or closing themselves off in an attempt to find relief from their pain.

As with the divorced father, the widowed father must adjust to his child's healing process and go at their pace while still accepting the responsibility of being their father in the tough moments. With the mother gone, he is the only pillar his child has to rely on, which means his influence has become even more powerful. His child needs him now more than ever to step up to do what's right for them through loving them, disciplining them, and guiding them. But as I've stated before, you can't give what you don't have. If a father wants to help his child through their grief, he must face his own first. Only then can he help both of them move forward.

4   Stepfathers

I've never understood why some men decide to marry a woman who has a child and yet have no plans to create a relationship with that child as well. Maybe they don't feel like it's their place to be a father figure to the child, or maybe they don't know how. Sometimes, though, these men simply have no interest in being fathers, which I believe means they have no business marrying this woman in the first place. A woman's children are a vital part of who she is, and if a man wants to love her well, he must love her children well too.

The truth is, a stepfather *is* a father. Because he is a part of his stepchild's life, he will influence them whether he intends to or not, and that influence becomes even greater if he's living with them. To ensure that his impact is positive, a stepfather must not only be willing to actively parent his wife's child, but he must also work to love them as if they were his own. I've never had a client who had a problem with their stepfather loving them as much as their biological parents did. But I *have* had several clients whose stepfathers' indifference or outright dislike caused emotional wounds that took many, many years to heal.

At the same time, the stepfather must let the child take their time deciding how they want to define their relationship with him. Especially if their biological father has passed away, they may not be looking for a replacement father. They may even be resentful of the stepfather's presence. This doesn't mean that the stepfather shouldn't try to strengthen their relationship, but he should recognize that he must adjust his influence based on what the child needs. As long as he focuses on loving them, without expecting the love to be returned or to be called "father," he can maintain a positive influence and keep an open door for the possibility of one day building a great relationship.

5 Other nonbiological fathers

Men can become fathers through a variety of means other than biological, whether they adopt their child, become foster parents, or take over guardianship. For those whose children are babies at the start of their journey together, their relationship will be similar to that of a biological father for much of their children's lives. But for those whose children are older and can remember their lives before, forming a relationship will require careful navigation. Like with the stepfather, the child may not accept the nonbiological father as a replacement for their birth father. He will have to earn their trust through patience, kindness, and unconditional love.

Furthermore, the child may have trauma that can make opening up to the father difficult. Children aren't separated from their birth parents or previous home without a reason, which means they may have faced any number of issues, including the death of a parent, gross neglect, physical or emotional abuse, or exposure to drugs. In these cases, the father's influence will matter even more, as he must not only guide them in their growth but also help them heal and unlearn the negative lessons they've already internalized. By accepting the child's pain and learning to go at their pace, over time they will begin to accept his influence.

6 Honorary fathers

While most fathers are active in their child's day-to-day life to some extent, not all father figures are in a direct parental role. Many children who don't have fathers or whose fathers are emotionally absent yearn for a male influence and grow attached to a prominent man in their life, such as an uncle, a family friend, a coach, a teacher, or another type of mentor. Because of this attachment, these men have a fatherlike influence on the child whether they intend to or not.

At the same time, they're limited in their influence due to the fact that they aren't actually the child's father. In many areas where the child may want more involvement or intervention, these men feel like it's simply not their place to step in—something the mother or father may remind them of when they attempt to. However, these limitations won't necessarily stop the child from seeing this man as a father figure, nor will they prevent him from influencing them in the areas he can. Whether it's inviting them to his classroom during a study hall or giving them one-on-one coaching on the baseball field, there's always a way to provide the guidance, support, and love they crave. And if the child's parents support the relationship, he can work with them to spend more time with the child in appropriate ways, which will further deepen their relationship and allow his influence to have even more of a positive impact.[2]

MAXIMIZING YOUR INFLUENCE

Regardless of what category of fatherhood you fall into, all fathers must consciously decide to make their influence count. While that influence will look different from father to father, every child needs the deliberate, intentional impact of a father in their life. It doesn't matter how little you can physically be with them—as long as you are part of that child's life, you are influencing them. And it's up to you to decide what that influence will look like.

No matter how your fatherhood journey begins, there are a few aspects that are universal to establishing a positive influence.

---

2   For more on creating a strong mentoring relationship, check out my book *Pass It On* at liveupresources.com.

The most important factor is comprised of everything we spent Part II of this book talking about. The only way to ensure that you have a positive influence on your child is to develop your character, decision-making abilities, relational skills, and identity structure. Besides strengthening the example you set for your child, working on your own growth will also increase your ability to love them as God does, which can make all the difference in guiding them to reach their full potential.

In addition to developing yourself in these areas, you must also hone your communication style. While it's true that your indirect impact on your child guides them in countless ways, it's your ability to talk to them directly about the many challenges and decisions in life that will help them process their experiences and internalize godly standards. Life is undoubtedly busy, but if we don't set aside a specific time to focus solely on our children, their development will suffer. Even something as simple as reading to your child every night can create a positive relational experience that stimulates them mentally and encourages them to grow. To this day, I still remember those few but priceless evenings when my father would read me either *Tom Sawyer*, whose many slang words delighted me at a young age, or *The Pilgrims Progress*, which encouraged my spiritual interests.

As one part of a parenting duo, your influence must also work in conjunction with that of your child's mother. And that starts with your relationship with her. Parental conflict can tear a child apart emotionally. Because the child loves their mother and father equally, it hurts them to see them fight unnecessarily. Additionally, the parents' inability to manage their own emotions during conflict causes emotional instability within their child, leading them to lash out in unhealthy and unproductive ways. No matter what tension might arise, you and their mother must find a way to resolve it maturely, both to set a good example for your child and to avoid stunting their growth.

Besides strengthening your personal relationship, you and your child's mother must also work together to become a solid parenting team. Children rely on both of their parents to help them achieve the necessary level of development, so you must work together to decide how to best exert your parental influence. When a child receives mixed messages from their parents, it can limit their ability to learn vital life lessons simply because they're not sure who to listen to. But when their parents work as a unit to present a positive example, the child can better internalize the intended lessons and act on them in growth-producing ways.

Working with the mother is especially important for divorced fathers and stepfathers. For divorced fathers, it can be easy to give in to resentment, but personal feelings about the mother have no place in their fathering. The child still loves her even if you don't, and you must take care not to voice any jealousy or anger that would undermine the vital mother-child relationship or, even worse, cause your child to think you might feel the same resentment toward them too. A child's growth should always be your priority, which means you must do what you can to build a strong coparenting team with their mother despite your differences.[3]

Unfortunately, however, sometimes the mother's cooperation won't seem all that likely. When that's the case, trust God to help you and your child through it. You can't control what happens when your child is with their mother, just as you can't control what happens when they're at school or at a friend's house. Rather than growing overly frustrated by your coparenting situation, focus on being a positive influence your child can learn from when they are with you. With your guidance, they can develop the ability to behave in godly ways no matter what environment they're in or who they're around.

If you're a stepfather, working with the child's mother will

---

3   For more on effective coparenting, check out *Co-Parenting Works!: Helping Your Child Thrive after Divorce* by Tammy Daughtry.

mean having to navigate both of their feelings and receptiveness to you to figure out how to step into a father role. Mothers can be protective of their children, and especially if they experienced a rough end to their previous relationship, they may be reluctant to allow the stepfather any authority in raising their child. For the sake of the child, you must accept her rules and work within those boundaries to love and engage with the child. Over time, she will learn to trust your desire to father her child and will begin to work with you to become the best parenting team you can be.

No matter the specific challenges you face or how much life gets in the way, you must never stop trying to be that ultimate spiritual father. Matthew 28:19 tells us to "go and make disciples," and that's exactly what being a father really means. God has called every father to mentor, discipline, develop, counsel, and coach his child into adulthood. He is waiting to help you move from being a physical father to a spiritual one, a father who fully acts like God in his child's life. All you have to do is say yes to His call.

 ROBERT'S STORY

I recently had one of those melt-your-heart moments watching Angelina play with a friend. They were on the playground, and I was keeping an eye on them from a bench a short distance away. After racing each other to the swings, it appeared Angie's friend became upset because Angie had won. She crossed her arms and stomped off play on her own.

This is where the "melting" began. Angelina jumped off her swing, walked up to her friend, and begin to say something. Doing my best not to distract either of them, I inched my way closer to listen. I heard my little Angie say, "Why are you mad? Is it because I won our race? You don't have to be upset. Sometimes I lose when I try doing something too. I'm sorry I made you feel bad. I didn't mean to. Let's ask Jesus to forgive us, and maybe you can forgive me too."

I almost couldn't believe it. All those conversations that felt like words going in one ear and out the other had actually stuck to her. All those times I tried to show her that we need to experience God's forgiveness to truly forgive others were finally bearing fruit. Angelina was valuing her relationship with her friend the way I valued ours—and it worked. She and her friend actually prayed together, which was the most adorable thing I had ever seen. Moments later, they began to play together again.

I learned a valuable lesson that day—never think your child isn't listening to or learning from you. You are the greatest influence they will ever have, even when you don't see the impact right away. In all things, lead them to Christ, and they may one day lead others to Him too.

💬 DISCUSSION QUESTIONS

1   Discuss the importance of a father's influence both within the family and within the culture. In what areas should a father help his child reach their God-given potential? In what ways are you spiritually influencing your child?

2   Which level of fatherhood are you presently at? How does that affect your relationship with your child? How can God help you move toward the commitment of spiritual fatherhood?

3   Describe your relationship with your child's mother. How is this similar or different from how your parents got along? How can you work together to maximize the influence you both have on them?

4   Discuss the instructions given in Deuteronomy 6:6-9. What do they say about how a father should apply his influence?

The commandments I give you today must be in your hearts. Make sure your children learn them. Talk about them when you are at home. Talk about them when you walk along the road. Speak about them when you go to bed. And speak about them when you get up. Write them down and tie them on your hands as a reminder. Also tie them on your foreheads. Write them on the doorframes of your houses. Also write them on your gates.

20

A FATHER GUIDES

I want to tell you something I'm not particularly proud of—I am hopeless when it comes to anything mechanical. I know, it's not very "manly" of me to admit. But I'm telling you, I can make a problem in a car worse just by looking at it. If Kim were to ask me to help her change her oil, I'd send her straight to the mechanic. While I'd love to be able to help my daughter solve all her problems, there are just some areas of life I know I'd better leave to the professionals.

Now, if Kim were to ask me to take her fishing, I'd be on my way over before she could even finish the request. I've been fishing since I was a kid, and there's nothing like the serenity of sitting on the water as you wait for a bite or like the satisfaction of reeling in the first catch of the day. I will always treasure the times I've gotten to spend with Kim, just her and me, fishing on the pond by our house.

I'm sure you have certain activities you like to do with your child just like I have, as well as those you'd rather avoid. For hobbies or skills that aren't vital to everyday life, there's nothing wrong taking a back seat in these areas when it comes to your involvement with your child. The problem is, a lot of fathers don't stop there—they also take a back seat in the big areas, the ones their children need them to show up for. Many either aren't good at or aren't interested in being involved in their children's education, their unique interests, or even their emotions. "Their mom can handle it," they say. "I'll stick to what I know."

But that's just not good enough. If you want to achieve the highest level of fatherhood and be a truly spiritual father, you have to be involved in *every* area of your child's life. In this chapter, we'll break down the main realms you must engage in to ensure your child develops the full capabilities they need to succeed in life. While I'll only touch the surface of some of these topics, even a basic knowledge will help you better understand your role in guiding your child through them—and how exactly you can do so.

THE EMOTIONAL REALM

While a father is responsible for helping his child develop their cognitive abilities, he must also be active in guiding them to manage their emotions and appropriately express their feelings. This is a relatively easy task when their emotions are positive, but when it comes to the negative ones, we're often tempted to run the other way. After all, we men don't even like to face our own negative emotions. How are we supposed to navigate someone else's?

The fact is, God calls you as a father to help your child cope with *all* of their emotional responses, which includes feelings like anxiety, sadness, grief, shame, and anger (Romans 12:15). In Chapter 22, we'll discuss more about how to help your child develop their general emotional capabilities, but here I'll focus specifically on how you can guide them through some of their more intense negative emotions.

As happy as your child may seem, you never know when they'll experience a life challenge, failure, or trauma that causes these emotions to rear their ugly heads. And when they do, you have to be ready, because your child will need your help to defeat them.

The following three negative emotional states are common

ones that can overwhelm a child and disrupt their development. Always be on the lookout for their warning signs so you can help your child work through them—before they let their emotions push them too far off track.

1   Depression

Occasional feelings of sadness are normal, but sometimes that negativity can send us into a downward spiral. If your child starts to demonstrate an attitude of helplessness and hopelessness, or if their normal sleeping and eating patterns have changed, it might be a sign they're going through a period of depression. Unlike sadness, depression can't simply be overcome by a positive attitude or a good cheering up. That's because your child isn't just sad. They also have little hope for a better future and no faith in their ability to change it.

2   Shame

Though children certainly make plenty of choices they should rightly feel guilty for, it can be easy for them to exaggerate normal life failures. In their minds, the fact that they deserve consequences for their negative choices or mistakes means there's something wrong with them. The shame that comes as a result of such a negative self-definition can cause your child to feel overwhelmed, insecure, and inadequate. Rather than trying to improve their behavior or control their emotions, they beat themselves up over every tiny error, eventually convincing themselves there's no point trying at all.

3   Anxiety

Despite the reality that God created your child with great potential and the gifts needed to achieve it, they may at times obsess over their perceived inadequacies. Sometimes the source of their anxiety is external, like a bully who makes fun of them or a friend who rejects them. Other times it comes from within, such as when they interpret a life challenge as utterly insurmountable. But no matter where it comes from, the result is the same—your child feels alone, believing they're incapable of making the right choices or coping with life at all.

It's never fun for a father to see his child struggle, especially when he doesn't know what to do about it. But just because your child may feel hopeless in their depression, shame, or anxiety doesn't mean you have to as well. Regardless of the intensity of their emotions, there are a few key approaches you can take to guide them through it. The first is to work slowly and not expect a quick fix. Because the emotional realm is internal, your child is the only one who can really process what they're feeling. Sometimes this can cause your attempts to help to feel pushy to them, like you're not really listening, and it may lead them to shut down even further.

Instead of immediately offering a solution, you should focus on helping your child define their experience and develop their own strategy to manage it. Slowing yourself down in this way requires deliberate effort on your part and an awareness of how your child is responding to your guidance. It won't always be easy, but when you demonstrate patience, you tell your child that you're here for them no matter what. And as long as they have that love and support, they'll know they can get through anything, even their own negative emotions.

Another key approach has been a common theme throughout this book: simply be present. As your child engages in their struggle with their emotions, you must act as a pillar of support and stability for them, not trying to take charge of the problem yourself but just continuing to love them through it. By being supportive rather than attempting to take control of the situation, you convey an important message: "God is here, and you can do this." And that quiet message can encourage your child more strongly than words ever could.

A third vital approach is to attempt to feel what your child is feeling. The funny thing about emotions is that although they're contagious, and though everyone can experience the same feeling, how and when we each experience it is often completely different. An event that seems fairly insignificant to you might feel life altering to your child. To help them process such an experience, you must learn to empathize with them and accept that their emotions are real to them, even if you see the situation differently.

Engaging in empathy will also help you identify patterns in your child's emotional state and the way it impacts their responses, which will allow you to tailor your own response to them. Do they lash out in anger over minor grievances? Helping them navigate what they're angry about will give them permission to face the disappointment they experienced and acknowledge their own unmet needs. Do they obsess about doing a task completely perfectly to the point that they freak out if they don't? Teaching them a better way to define success and achievement will increase their self-worth and decrease their unachievable expectations. By learning to sense your child's frustration before it erupts in a strong negative emotion, you'll be better able to enter their emotional world with them and help them navigate through any turmoil.

The more effort you put into approaching your child's emotional realm from these angles, the better equipped you'll be to make talking about emotions a regular practice with your child. Like Jesus with the woman at the well, you may need to approach the topic more indirectly at first to ease your child into being comfortable enough to address the main issue (John 4:4-42). You might not get there in a single conversation, but eventually, through careful listening and well-placed questions, you'll help your child define their emotional experiences and develop their own strategies to finally start working through them.

THE SOCIAL REALM

Because they directly influence our overall satisfaction and fulfillment, relationships are the most important aspect of life, which means that part of your role as a father is helping your child develop the ability to establish healthy, supportive relationships. Besides teaching them relational skills, which we'll discuss further in Chapter 23, this includes guiding your child in choosing the right friends. As Proverbs 10:7-13 implies, there are both good people to spend time with and people who should be avoided. You have more life experience than your child does, and you must use that experience to help you spot any red flags in your child's friendships that you've seen in your own past negative relationships. By steering them away from harmful influences, you can prevent them from having to experience that same pain.

At the same time, however, you must be careful not to interfere too much in your child's relationships. Not only will forbidding certain friendships make them seem even more interesting to your curious child, but it will also limit their ability to think for themselves. Sometimes the only way for them to really learn about the dangers of certain types of friends is to experience the consequences for themselves. As hard as it may be to watch your child experience this pain, you must give them the responsibility of managing their own relationships. The earlier they learn these tough lessons, and while you're still present to help them through it, the more equipped they'll be to create stronger relationships with the right people in the future.

However, letting your child take the lead in choosing their friendships doesn't mean being completely hands off. If your child is struggling with a relationship, support them as they manage their sad, anxious, or angry feelings and advise them on what steps to take next. If they've been hurt by a friend, encourage them to forgive so they aren't held hostage by the pain. And if that friend wants to reconcile, help them discern if the relationship is safe enough to be restored.

No matter the issue, you can always use your own relationship with your child to provide the support they need to handle any relational challenge well. Ultimately, that's the best way you can help them in the social realm—by building a strong, loving relationship with them. Without such a positive relationship in the home, a child is more likely to be relationally hungry and seek to get their needs met by their peers, some of whom will take advantage of their trust and hurt them even further. This is often most apparent in young girls. If a daughter doesn't get the love she craves from her father, she's more likely to attach to the first man who shows her any type of affection, despite any obvious shortcomings or inconsistencies.

A child's relationship with their father is the one of the most important relationships in their life. Besides indirectly showing them how to build their own relationships with others, it also gives them the love and support they need to create a secure foundation they can build their identity on. The stronger that foundation is, the more you'll see your child's friendships thrive, and the greater success they'll find in life.

THE PHYSICAL REALM

While a father is responsible for taking care of his child's physical health for most of their childhood, he must do so in a way that encourages them to take responsibility for their own body in the future (1 Corinthians 3:16-17). Through active play, you teach your child to continually develop basic physical skills such as coordination and control. Through establishing rules and reminders, you instill within them personal hygiene habits, such as brushing their teeth every morning and night. Through scheduling regular medical and dental checkups and regulating their food and sleep, you help them internalize the importance of always taking care of their body.

The physical realm isn't only about your child's health, though. It also involves their physical interests. Whether it's ballet or baseball, hiking or lacrosse, it's your job to support them no matter how different their physical skills are from yours. Being there for them as much as you can during their competitions, practices, or hobbies is another way you can put your love into action. When your child can share their excitement and passion with you, they'll be more likely to turn that passion into success.

However, while you should be involved in your child's physical activities, be careful not to try to live vicariously through them. This is especially relevant when it comes to men and sports. When I was in college, I volunteered to run a flag football league for elementary-school kids, thinking it would be a lot of fun. On the contrary, it was a nightmare. The kids were great. It was their dads who really got to me. Instead of cheering for the kids on the field, they constantly fought with each other over plays and berated the referees and coaches over the smallest issues. That's not what supporting your child's physical growth looks like. Regardless of their interests, always make sure to keep the activity about their learning, growth, and enjoyment—not about you.

THE ENVIRONMENTAL REALM

Though we may not always realize it, a child's environment plays a huge role in shaping the person they become, and so a father must do his best to create the most positive environment he can for them. Unfortunately, many areas of the environment are outside of your control, like the negative cultural messages that will inevitably seep into your child's life. However, there's still a lot you *can* do, especially in your own home. You can prioritize your child's safety by locking away guns or other hazardous materials.

You can establish order by making rules and structures your child can rely on, and you can keep the house clean and organized to limit distractions. Above all, you can promote a positive attitude that will continually encourage your child to chase their passions, hone their skills, and make new discoveries every day (Proverbs 16:24).

As for the environmental areas you have no control over, you can use them as life lessons for your child. Rather than trying to hide them away from the evil and hardships within the world, take time to sit down with them and explain your environmental challenges to them (but only at an age where they can begin to understand). Children are perceptive, and if you don't address these issues head-on, they may end up internalizing the culture's attitudes of selfishness, hopelessness, and harm. Use your influence as their father to help them see these issues and successfully navigate through them. With you by their side, they will be empowered to face and overcome every aspect of the complicated environmental realm.

THE EDUCATIONAL REALM

For at least the first eighteen years of their life, a child's world is dominated by school. And that means that regardless of your own negative memories of school or your limitations in certain subjects, you must be as involved in your child's education as possible. Don't just help them with their homework. Teach them how to understand the practical value of even their least favorite subjects, and assist them in getting through those subjects as successfully as they can. Even further, serve as a sounding board for their decision-making in areas of their school life that aren't directly related to learning, including which teams or clubs to join, which classes to take, and which peers to build relationships with.

However, a father's involvement in his child's education doesn't stop with school. Intelligence isn't just about how much you know or how good you are at memorizing information. It also involves how you think about and process life. To help your child develop in this way, continually ask them good questions that stimulate their thought processes. Ask them about their feelings and experiences, about their hopes and fears, and most importantly, about God. Teaching them about His Word and how they can apply it to their daily decision-making will help prepare your child to always do what's right, even when you aren't around.

THE OCCUPATIONAL REALM

Naturally, after a child finishes school they will enter the world of work. However, a father's involvement in this realm begins long before his child starts to even think about getting their first job. Although your child will only be able to learn certain skills through training and occupational experience, there are still several helpful soft skills you can teach them at a young age, starting with the other realms we've already discussed. Guiding them in the social realm will enable them to work well with others and be a productive, contributing teammate. Helping them in the emotional realm will teach them to manage their feelings so they can gracefully handle feedback and improve their approach to any task. And encouraging them in the physical realm will help them build the endurance and work ethic they need to persevere through any challenging project.

You can further instill the importance of a strong work ethic in your child both through your example and through direct instruction. Seeing how you commit to your own job and listening to stories about your work will show them what it takes to be a good employee. The rules you set in your home will prepare them to follow similar structures at a future job. And simply assigning them chores around the house will give them a head start on developing the skills they need to be a productive employee, especially when you give them feedback that helps hold them to a standard of excellence.

Since your child will probably be working for the majority of their adult life, it's also important that you teach them how to enjoy it (Colossians 3:23). The biggest way to do this is to encourage them to find a career that fits within their natural skills and interests. As the saying goes, "Do what you love, and you'll never work a day in your life."

However, no matter how much a person loves their job, there will always be days or tasks that are simply difficult to get through. For this reason, you should teach your child to see the value of each task they do and feel pride in completing it. As you assign them chores, work with them on school assignments, or include them in your own projects, explain to them the reason behind each task and how completing it benefits either them or others. Understanding work in this way will help your child learn to define it as something they *should* do rather than something they *have* to do. With that mindset, they'll be empowered to take on any task, no matter how unenjoyable it actually is.

THE FINANCIAL REALM

Just like with work, a father should teach his child the value of money before ever even talking about finances. There are many ways to do so, but the most important one is to help them learn how to control their impulsive desires and differentiate between their needs and wants. While this typically means simply not buying your child everything they ask for, it can also mean negotiating with them or giving them a choice in the matter. By providing an allowance they can use however they want or having them choose between a candy bar now or dessert after dinner, you will force them to think carefully about their decisions and what's most important to them. And if they choose incorrectly, they'll learn how to make a better decision next time, a lesson they can apply to their finances once they have money of their own.

You can also demonstrate good money management through your treatment of your own finances and resources. Turning off lights, saving up for important purchases, or wisely deciding how often you eat out all show your child the importance of being careful with your purchases (Proverbs 21:20). Even subconsciously, they will take in what they see you doing and will one day find themselves, perhaps to their annoyance, scolding their own children for "wasting electricity" or telling them that "we have food at home," in turn passing on your legacy to the next generation.

THE SPIRITUAL REALM

The spiritual realm is the most important realm in your child's life, but it actually isn't a separate realm at all. The spiritual realm involves finding meaning and connection with God, who wants to be a part of every area of our lives, which means that spirituality is actually part of each of the other realms discussed. Even when we aren't aware of it, they all provide an opportunity for God to work in our lives and bring us even closer to Him.

To help your child maximize God's empowerment in every realm, you must teach them about the benefits of a relationship with Him. In their toughest challenges, point them to God by discussing how our own willpower isn't enough and how we all must reach beyond ourselves for a solution. And when they feel disappointed in themselves or in life, remind them that God created them with amazing gifts and will use everyday life experiences to help them develop and achieve wondrous success.

Of course, a father can only help his child in their spiritual realm when he does the work in his own by regularly talking with God and applying His Word to every area of his life. The wisdom you obtain through making mistakes, giving them to God, and using His guidance to get back on your feet is what allows you to help your child do the same. If you let God infiltrate all of your decision-making, your relationship with Him will blossom, in turn becoming a standard your child can use to develop themselves as well.

LEARNING TO DISCERN

How you guide your child through each of these life realms will be different based on your individual situation, but generally speaking, you'll do it by being present, communicating your love through listening and good questions, and sharing your wisdom. This method of guidance should typically hover right in the sweet spot between hands-off parenting and hands-on, empowering your child to take responsibility for their choices while still allowing them to rely on you when they need to.

Sometimes, however, you will have to swing more toward one end of the spectrum either by stepping back further or by becoming more involved. Guiding your child is relatively easy when they ask for your advice or seek out your support, because their openness allows you to point them in the right direction even as you let them make choices for themselves. But sometimes your child won't be open to your input, or they'll be in a situation you know they must experience in order to learn a lesson fully. So what do you do then?

As hard as it is to hear, the answer is often nothing. Sometimes in order to love and support your child through their challenges, you must resist giving them advice or pointing out their potential mistakes. After all, you won't always be present to assist them through their challenges, which means they must learn to make their own decisions, even if it includes experiencing failure once in a while. It's hard for a father not to intervene in a situation he knows could hurt his child emotionally. But in the long run, it's the right thing to do, because it's only by going through the heat of life that they can be forged into something stronger.

However, this approach should only be taken when the decision being made is one that is not physically dangerous, potentially harmful to others, or likely to lead to long-term consequences. A child doesn't always inherently know what's best, nor are they often able to recognize their need for assistance. When you notice your child exhibiting self-destructive emotional, mental, relational, or physical responses, you must step in even if means creating tension. Sometimes we have to pay the price of conflict with our children in order to make sure they don't make decisions that lead to irreversible damage.

All humans have a tendency to be prideful, and it can be especially strong in children, who have a constant desire to prove themselves and their abilities. Even when they're in immense pain, they might still resist your help. They're like a UFC fighter who gets hit square in the face by his opponent. Rather than going down, he just smiles and pretends everything is perfectly fine. Just as God pursues us even when we don't seek Him out, there will be times when you need to force yourself into a situation despite your child's desire to hide or withdraw. Assess the situation carefully and decide if you need to intervene through a conversation, discipline, or another method. And then do it as you do everything else—with love.

Learning to identify the best way to guide your child in any situation and within any realm is tricky and will take time to master. But it is absolutely vital to godly fatherhood, not just for how it can help your child in the present but also for how it increases your ability to guide them into the future. A teenager or adult is most likely to respond positively to their father's outreach when he has been consistently present in his guidance and reliable in his love. You must learn to recognize and take advantage of these holy moments in your child's early experiences. When you do, you can become the father they need, both in this moment and for the rest of their lives.

 ROY'S STORY

For several years when I was young, my dad would take me to a Youth for Christ meeting most Saturday nights. We'd watch the teenagers quiz each other on the Bible, and then we'd participate with them in the music and the message. It wasn't anything special, but that didn't matter to my father. He just wanted time to create conversations with me about life and God and give me a chance to see the type of young adult I should grow into.

We'd typically end these evenings at a local ice-cream shop, where I'd almost always get a banana split. Sometimes we'd chat some more, but more often my father would start conversations with the staff about their lives. And just as often, those conversations would naturally turn into a discussion about faith, allowing him to talk about God in a nonthreatening way and connect with these people even more deeply.

I didn't think much of those nights at the time. But as I grew up, I found that talking about God came easily to me, even with those who had different beliefs. It didn't take me long to realize that much of it had to do with my weekly time with my father and God. Through this Saturday night ritual, he helped me better understand God's Word and how He relates to us daily. And through the ice cream conversations, he showed me that I could be comfortable sharing Jesus with anyone. As a result, I learned to integrate my faith pretty well into every area of my life. At this point, I don't think I could separate it even if I tried.

 DISCUSSION QUESTIONS

1   Which of the life realms do you struggle with the most? How can you strengthen yourself in those areas so you can in turn help your child through them?

2   How much do you engage with the spiritual realm? What can you do to strengthen your relationship with God? How can you rely on Him to help you guide your child effectively?

3   Discuss a situation where you either took a step back in guiding your child or became more deeply involved. How did doing so help or hurt your child? What could you have done differently?

4   Discuss how 1 Chronicles 29:17 relates to a father's need to be involved in his child's life. What role does honesty play in guiding your child?

My God, I know that you tested our hearts. And you are pleased when we are honest. I've given all these things just because I wanted to. When I did it, I was completely honest with you. Your people here have also been willing to give to you. And I've been happy to see this.

21

A FATHER'S MIND

If you're like most people, you probably don't give too much thought to how your brain works. And I don't blame you. The brain is a complicated organ. In fact, it's so complicated that even after centuries of research by thousands of different scientists and scholars, there are many questions we still don't fully know the answers to, such as how neurons communicate with each other or why certain neurological disorders occur.

Such a complicated piece of us can feel impossible to even begin to understand, which is why I like to simplify it down to one basic concept. Think of it this way—we all have two brains that each serve a basic purpose, the brain that thinks and the brain that feels. Now, our brain isn't literally separated, of course, but it does have two distinct internal processes going on within it at all times, which most people refer to as our thoughts and emotions. Together they work to help us evaluate our circumstances, take in details, and calculate the best way to respond.

As fathers, understanding how our brains that think and feel work is vital to helping our children develop, because it's their ability to control their emotions and think through their decisions that will dictate what they can accomplish. In this chapter, we'll start with the more straightforward of the two: the brain that thinks. By breaking down the role your child's thought processes play in their mental development, you'll increase your ability not only to encourage that growth but also to teach them how to put it into action.

HOW TO THINK

There are many people in this world who love to discover new information, and they seem to have an uncanny ability to remember almost all of what they learn. If you asked them to tell you the plot of Shakespeare's *Macbeth* or to list all the US presidents and their accomplishments, they could give you a detailed explanation with no hesitation. However, if you asked them what their opinion was on the subject, they'd probably draw a blank. Or maybe they'd offer you an opinion, but if you asked them why they believe that, they'd likely just shrug.

Too often people learn greedily in an effort to gain knowledge without actually evaluating and understanding it for themselves, which leads them to simply mimic other people's opinions without really knowing why. It's not surprising, considering we live in a culture that values appearing to be right over actually being right. But God expects more of us than that. As 1 Peter 3:15 reminds us, "Always be ready to give an answer to anyone who asks you about the hope you have. Be ready to give the reason for it." It's not enough simply to believe in God, to agree with a fact, or to hold a certain opinion—we must have such a deep understanding of *why* we feel the way we do that we could defend ourselves without hesitation against anyone who challenged us.

For this reason, our role as fathers isn't just to show our children how to take in information—we're also responsible for teaching them what to do with it. Their brains are designed to both process facts and details and integrate them into their daily life in practical ways. That's why they don't stop at "what" questions but go further to those persistent "why" questions. Rather than dismiss them, we must engage with our children's natural curiosity and use it to help shape their thought processes in useful, godly ways. And that means teaching them how to discern between which information to keep and which to discard, coaching them in integrating it with the knowledge they already have, and most importantly, guiding them in using it to shape and strengthen their opinions and perspectives.

A great way to guide your child's brain that thinks is to help them learn to see the story behind the story. Compared to you, your child knows very little about the world. Information that you might take for granted, such as how trees grow or why we have to brush our teeth, is still completely foreign to them. It can be easy to give them simple explanations that satisfy them enough and allow you to move on, especially when you're in a rush or in the middle of another task. But while those explanations may answer their questions, they won't expand their thinking or further their mental development.

Instead, you should see every activity and conversation with your child as an opportunity to deepen their understanding. At any doctor's visit, explain why you're taking them and how going frequently can help them stay healthy. After interactions with others, either friends or strangers, point out to your child what you learned from the other person. When you're playing around with a hobby at home, show them what you're doing, how it works, or what you enjoy about it. In this way, you will not only increase their knowledge but also activate their thinking processes, giving them a foundation to build their perspectives on and strengthen their brain that thinks.

As you communicate with your child, you should also encourage them to think through the different angles of a subject. I did this with Kim when she was a teenager through a designated "argument time." After her church youth group meeting every Wednesday night, I'd take her to an ice-cream shop where we would discuss various life scenarios and problems. I'd let her pick the side she believed in, and then I'd take the opposite position to challenge her stance and get her to think more deeply about it. We had a lot of fun coming up with creative arguments about each subject we chose. I like to think that challenging her in this way had at least some impact on her ability to think analytically and eventually become the excellent psychologist she is today.

Another good way to develop your child's brain that thinks is to turn to their childhood tendency back on them—pepper them with "why" questions every chance you get. Asking questions that cause your child to seek out difficult answers not only stimulates their thinking but also helps them develop an independent mind. You won't always be available to give them the answers, which means they'll need to be equipped to one day figure them out for themselves.

So when you're reading a book to your child, ask them why they think a character made the choice they did. When they complain about their homework, challenge them to consider why learning this subject might be important. And when they ask you one of those "why" questions, encourage them to give their answer first. Then you can help them recognize where their thinking is accurate and gently correct them in areas where they need to do more learning.

As you begin to work with your child on their brain that thinks, you may find them voicing ideas you don't necessarily agree with. Sometimes these ways of thinking are simply incorrect and need to be adjusted. Sometimes they aren't necessarily wrong but are just different from yours. And other times they may be your child's way of testing out new information. I know a woman who used to try out newly learned swear words on her parents, not out of disrespect, but just because she wanted to see their genuine reaction. To her, that was a much better gauge of how bad those words *really* were than simply asking her parents if it was okay to say them.

Whatever your child's intention, it's important not to become threatened or emotionally distressed about the ideas they're expressing. Childhood is a time of experimentation and discovery, and often your child is just trying out a certain perspective to see how it feels. What safer place to do so than in a dialogue with a father who's trustworthy, patient, and loving? Even when it's something you don't want to hear, always encourage your child to voice what they're thinking. After all, they're already thinking it anyway. By giving them the freedom to express it, you give yourself the chance to challenge what they believe and guide them in a better direction before that belief becomes too ingrained.

THINKING ABOUT THINKING

Along with helping your child develop their mind to take in and process information, you must also teach them to evaluate the way they think. For the most part, our perspectives, opinions, and general thought processes aren't meant to be set in stone, simply because it's impossible for anyone to know everything. Even once your child is fully developed, there will always be ways they can improve or correct their ways of thinking. Are they overlooking any perspectives that would be worth considering? Where are they being inconsistent with their thinking? Do they have any ideas that once seemed good but now need to be reconsidered?

One way to help your child engage in self-evaluation is simply to ask them questions about their behaviors. For instance, why didn't they clean their room when you asked them to? Why did they ignore a friend on the playground today? How might their teammates feel if they decided to skip the game? Whatever the situation, the key is not to always tell your child what to think or do. Children value their independence, and they may react more strongly in the opposite direction if you guide them with too heavy a hand. Focus on sharing your perspective and guiding your child to think more in-depth about their own thoughts. Then trust that God will help them discover what's right.

In addition to asking them questions, you should also regularly remind your child that their brain that thinks doesn't always interpret information accurately. There are many different cognitive biases and distortions that can lead us to believe something that really isn't true.[1] Your child won't always be able to avoid these biases, but by learning to constantly evaluate their thinking, they will develop a healthy sense of skepticism and self-questioning, preventing them from ever growing so rigid in their thinking that they refuse to consider new ideas or perspectives.

The best way to teach your child to be skeptical about their thinking is to point them to God. Because God is perfect and omnipotent, only He has a full understanding of the world (Psalm 147:5). For your child to fully develop their brain that thinks, they must learn to submit their thinking processes to Him (James 1:5). As you guide them in self-evaluation, use the Bible to highlight how powerful kings and leaders continually sought out God's wisdom, even during times of prosperity (1 Kings 3:1-15). Through their examples, your child will learn to rely on God, not just to shape their thinking but also to help them know what to believe and what to do when the answer isn't clear.

BE S.M.A.R.T.

Besides organizing information and shaping our way of thinking, our brain that thinks is also responsible for strengthening our decision-making. That's partly why young children typically struggle with making the right choices. Because their brain that thinks is still underdeveloped, they lack the ability to really think through what they want or understand how to get it—especially when their

---

1   To learn more about common cognitive biases and distortions that can happen in the mentoring or fathering relationship, check out my book *Pass It On* at liveupresources.com.

natural desire for instant gratification is so strong.

For this reason, part of helping your child strengthen their brain that thinks is guiding them to develop a plan, create the steps to implement it, and follow through. There are many different ways to teach them this, but a simple and concise one is to train them to be S.M.A.R.T. Each letter of this acronym represents a characteristic your child should work to apply to every decision they make and every goal they set. As long as they adhere to these guidelines, they'll be able to achieve whatever they set their mind to—and know how to make adjustments when they trip up.

SPECIFIC

If we want to achieve our goals, we must focus on the task at hand and eliminate the numerous distractions of life. This means being as specific as possible by outlining exactly what we want to achieve, why we want to achieve it, and the individual steps or smaller goals it will take to do so. The more specific we are in our goal setting, the better we'll commit to our plans and follow through on them.

One of the biggest aspects of specificity is learning to establish priorities. We can all get carried away setting goal after goal and trying to work on them all at once, but the reality is that we're really only capable of completing a few at a time. And by keeping the insignificant goals on our to-do list when we don't have the time for them, we allow them to distract us from achieving the most important ones.

This can especially be a problem for children, whose schedules are often jam-packed with activities, lessons, and events. When your child is younger, it's good to allow them to try a wide variety of hobbies and interests to see what appeals to them and fits their skills the most. But as they grow older, they'll have less time for all of those options and will eventually have to pare down what they want to pursue. Encourage them through this process by discussing their values or dreams for the future with them. The more clear they are about what they want, the easier it will be to cut out certain goals, allowing them to devote more time and attention to the ones that truly align with who God created them to be.

Along with their big goals, you should also encourage your child to prioritize their smaller tasks. One way to do this is through being specific when you assign them their chores. Instead of giving them a long list of tasks to get done over the weekend, pick three to five that are the most important. By telling them to focus on getting their homework done, doing the dishes, and vacuuming the living room, you will prevent them from being so overwhelmed that they rush through their tasks—or fail to do any at all. Over time, your child will internalize the value of prioritization and begin to take on the responsibility of deciding what's most important for them to work toward.

Along with prioritization, chores are also helpful for teaching your child how to be specific about completing a goal. Instead of just saying, "Clean your room," break down exactly what you expect from the assignment, whether it's putting toys away, moving clothes from the floor to the hamper, or making the bed. Outlining your expectations in this way will both teach your child the standard they should work toward and demonstrate to them how they can likewise be specific when approaching their bigger goals.

MEASURABLE

A key part of creating any goal is establishing a way to assess our progress. After all, we want to be able to know for certain when we've completed it. But even more than having a clear vision of what achievement will look like, you should also have markers along the way to help you gauge your own performance and identify when disruptions or challenges have come into your path. This evaluation will help you measure whether you're still on course to achieve your goal, enabling you to make any necessary adjustments to ensure you stay on the best path.

Your child will need a lot of help in this area at first, which may create tension as you assess their progress and encourage them to work harder. But even though they might not like it, it's important to let them know that the time they're taking or the effort they're expending isn't living up to your expectations, because it will help them make adjustments before it's too late.

Along with calling them out on their substandard behaviors, you can also teach your child to self-evaluate simply by being their sounding board. Your child will have many ideas about what they want to do, but they won't always know what to do about them. By allowing them to share with you, you gain the ability to work with them to predict or troubleshoot any challenges that may occur as they go after their goals.

However, keep in mind that no matter how many adjustments your child makes, life won't always cooperate with their plans. Part of creating measurable goals is learning to accept that failure and disappointment may happen. When it does, discuss it directly with your child so they don't internalize it as a shameful definition of who they are. Then assess the failure together so you can pinpoint exactly what went wrong and uncover the lessons to be learned. When they can work through disappointments in this way, your child will be encouraged to move on and start again without repeating the same mistakes.

ACCURATE

When we develop our goals, we must always make sure they align with both our character and God's plan for us. As we discussed with being specific, it's not enough just to make a list of priorities—you need to pick the *right* priorities according to God's standards and values. It doesn't do you any good to narrow your focus if what you've decided to spend your time and resources on pursues worldly achievements instead of godly ones. If all you care about is popularity and wealth, you will inevitably find yourself looking back one day and feeling like you've wasted your life.

I'm certain you've already taken some needless detours in this area and have had to face the consequences, which means you're well-equipped to know how to guide your child away from pursuing negative desires. But just as importantly, you should also teach them not to be distracted by positive ones. One of the hardest things to do is to say no or not now to a goal that feels important, but sometimes it's what's necessary not only to succeed but also to do it in a way that lives up to God's standards.

Children feel a lot of pressure growing up to make friends, get good grades, and even please their parents, and it can be tempting for them to take shortcuts for the good of such noble goals. But if they achieve a goal by taking the easy route or by breaking God's standards, they haven't really achieved anything. You must instill within your child the value of doing what's right above all else— even if it means they don't get to reach their goal at all.

God has a unique vision for each of us, but the one goal He desires all of His children to achieve is for us to serve each other (Matthew 25:35-40). And that means you must confront your child's self-centeredness, encourage them to recognize and consider the feelings of others, and teach them to experience the pleasure of giving. When they do, He will help them set goals that align with His great plan—to work through them as they serve others.

REALISTIC

Your child was born a dreamer, and those dreams are what will motivate them to stretch themselves beyond their comfort zone and figure out what they're really capable of. At the same time, however, many of their dreams are either simply unachievable or not a good fit for their skills. As their father, your role is not necessarily to point this out to them but to be present as they discover what inspires them and figure out which goals fit their true potential. They may never defeat all the evil in the world like Captain America or Wonder Woman, but there are still many other ways they can help a hurting world or even a single person.

While you shouldn't directly tell your child their goals aren't realistic, you can still help them figure out for themselves if a goal fits them by having them look at both the end goal and the steps it will take the achieve it. Sometimes your child may be so excited about one aspect of a goal that they don't realize just how much another aspect doesn't align with who they are. For instance, they may want to be a surgeon because they like the science of the human body, but if they also can't stand the sight of blood or don't work well under pressure, they won't get very far. Because of your outside perspective, you have a better ability to see these inconsistencies, which means you can encourage them to consider a career that's more conducive to their attributes.

Other times it's not the goal itself but rather the steps of the goal that don't align with who your child is. Let's say I suddenly decided I wanted to be a UFC fighter. I mean, I've watched a lot of fights in my lifetime. I should be pretty good at coming up with various strategies to fend off an opponent who has certain advantages over me. Unfortunately, there are two factors that would make such a goal extremely difficult for me to achieve. First, I absolutely hate to exercise, and second, I'm old. I'd likely collapse from fatigue after the first few minutes of training, let alone be able to withstand hit after hit in the ring.

While any goal we set should push us to grow in ways that won't always be comfortable, that growth should always be rewarding. If you notice that your child is burned out, continually struggling with their workload, or spiraling emotionally, it's time for you to step in. Together you can work out what's wrong, make adjustments to their approach, and even decide if it's time to move on to something new altogether.

TIMELY

No matter how hardworking they are, everyone at some point falls victim to a classic human condition: procrastination. Even the best jobs include certain tasks or projects that we just can't stand, and while we know we have to do them eventually, we put them off for as long as we can. If you have older children, I'm sure you've noticed this with their homework or chores. Children will do *anything* to avoid these boring, annoying tasks, to the point where they may wind up not doing them at all.

Unfortunately, they'll have to face unpleasant tasks their entire lives, even once the homework and chores are gone, which is why you should teach your child to complete their responsibilities as early as possible. The best way to help them do so is to make them feel responsible for the task by giving them space to succeed or fail. This means outlining what needs to be done, highlighting the standards that must be met, providing a timeline for completion, and then leaving it up to them. Depending on your child's age, you may want to remind them of the deadline occasionally, but for the most part it should be up to them decide how to use their time. With such clear expectations, they have no excuse for not meeting the goal (barring any extenuating circumstances).

Part of establishing a timeline for your child is explaining the potential consequences of not meeting it, whether those consequences are natural (such as a failed grade if they don't study for a test) or imposed (such as no TV for a week if they put off their chores). In the future, there will always be consequences for missing a deadline or not following through, and so your child must learn to accept the pressure of getting things done before their casual attitude or procrastination can get them in trouble. By both stating the consequences up front and then following through when a deadline is missed, you will help your child internalize the truth that their actions impact the outcomes they experience in life, even if they don't like you for it in the moment.

THE FATHER'S MIND

Just like your child, your brain that thinks is always working, creating internal dialogues that help you process and interact with life and, for the most part, become a better father. As you focus on guiding your child, you also are taking in the information around you and sorting through it to make sure the relationship you create with your child is the best it can be. And when you set S.M.A.R.T. goals for both yourself and your child, you not only model to your child how to create their own goals. You also strengthen both of your capabilities and develop your God-given potential.

However, despite all the benefits your brain that thinks provides, it can also limit your ability to father well if you're not careful. The biases and distortions that can happen to your child can also happen to you, and they can fool you into thinking you always know what's best and don't need any help. Rather than being open to feedback or advice that could help you improve your fathering, it can be all too easy to dismiss it out of arrogance, defensiveness, or overconfidence.

Perhaps the biggest way your brain that thinks can hurt you is by distracting you from being fully present. Truly listening to your child can be hard, because a person's brain that thinks works much faster than anyone could ever talk. As you wait for your child to get to their point or find their next word, your mind often races ahead, already thinking through several things they might say. While this may help you feel productive, it can actually limit you from hearing what they're actually trying to tell you or, even worse, make you miss their point on an emotional level.

To prevent your brain that thinks from getting in the way of fathering your child well, you must invite God into your internal dialogue so He can disrupt your self-centered ways of thinking.

God's view of life is unobstructed, which means He can see both the bigger picture of life and the minute details that make it up much better than any human can. When you turn your brain that thinks over to God and pray without ceasing, your internal conversation will change, your actions will improve, and your satisfaction in your walk with Him will increase (1 Thessalonians 5:16-18).

Even better, when you rely on God in this way, everything will begin to slow down. You'll get less caught up in maximizing your time and will instead develop a stronger sense of patience, allowing you to listen to your child without trying to expedite the interaction. More importantly, you'll increase your ability to hear *everything* they're saying. Like God, our children are constantly talking, either through their words, actions, feelings, or body language. Just as you learn to hear God through countless methods, you can also learn to tune in to the different ways your child communicates, allowing you to engage with them more fully and become even more involved in their growth.

As you work with your child on developing their thought processes, keep in mind that this isn't the only part of their brain that needs guidance. In the next chapter, we'll talk about the second aspect of our brain, the brain that feels. It's just as important to help your child understand not only their emotions but also how their two brains work together in intricate, empowering ways. When you strive to fully develop both of these brains within you and your child, you'll find out what it truly means to have the best of both worlds.

 ROY'S STORY

During my senior year of college, I was dating a girl who I'd been with for about a year and a half. As graduation neared, I took a brief visit home to talk to my father about possibly marrying her. It seemed like I was at the point in my life where I should, especially since just about everyone else my age was getting engaged and married. But when I asked my father about it, he didn't necessarily agree. Instead, he replied, "Roy, what does it mean that you're asking me that?"

That difficult question helped me understand that if I needed my father's opinion to help me make such a vital decision about a relationship I would build my life on, then I probably was not emotionally ready for such a decision. I realized that if I was going to be an adequate husband, I needed to learn to think independently from my family. And so rather than proposing, I decided to develop myself further and really figure out if I was ready to make such a permanent commitment to this woman.

Well, let me tell you, it was a good thing I didn't propose, because that very summer I met the woman who *would* become my wife. This time, I didn't need my father's help deciding if I should marry her. I knew exactly what I wanted to do. And you know what? Given that we've had more than forty wonderful years of marriage, I believe my brain that thinks helped me make the right call.

💬 DISCUSSION QUESTIONS

1   Discuss the different attributes of the brain that thinks. What can you do to encourage your child's mental development?

2   What goals do you have for yourself, both for your own growth and for fatherhood? What goals does your child have for themselves? How can you better support and guide them to think through these goals?

3   In what areas are you most likely to fool yourself or succumb to distorted or biased thinking? Discuss how seeking God's wisdom and engaging in His Word can strengthen your brain that thinks and your ability to father well.

4   Discuss what 1 Timothy 4:12 says about the value and potential children have. How does this concept relate to your child's mental development?

Don't let anyone look down on you because you are young. Set an example for the believers in what you say and in how you live. Also set an example in how you love and in what you believe. Show the believers how to be pure.

22

A FATHER'S HEART

When you think back to your childhood and adolescence, what memories stand out most? Maybe it's talking to your first crush and stuttering over your words because you were so nervous, despite how many times you'd practiced in the mirror. Maybe it's playing in a big basketball game where you were so excited just to be on the court that you took a shot in the wrong hoop. Or maybe it's being so stressed and overwhelmed by your final exams that you ended up unintentionally taking it out on your best friend, causing a fight that lasted for days.

Those weren't exactly fun situations, where they? And yet you can still remember them clear as day, all these years later. That's because they were all charged with emotions or, as I like to say, driven by your brain that feels. They're examples that as hard as you may try to ignore your feelings and shove them down, your brain that feels will always be there to complicate your plans.

However, our emotions don't exist just to get in the way. In fact, without them we wouldn't have any passion for life or motivation to pursue any goals at all. When you're excited about your job, you're driven to work harder. When you're worried about a friend or a situation, you're inspired to lend a helping hand. And when you're angry about an injustice, you're empowered to protect yourself and others.

The difference between whether your emotions are helpful or

hurtful is in the development of your brain that feels. When your child is young, their emotional regulation is virtually nonexistent. They let their emotions take over their decision-making, and they verbalize and act on what they feel without worrying about consequences. It's your job to help them tune in to their gut reactions, label them with words, and then express them in more productive ways.

The thing is, you can't do this without first learning to manage your own brain that feels. The more you to label and understand your own emotions, the better you'll understand others, know what to say or not to say, and speak the truth in love (Ephesians 4:15). In this way, you can become a pillar of strength for your child, providing the encouragement, comfort, support, and confrontation they need to develop their own brain that feels and become successful in all areas of life.

EMOTIONAL REGULATION

Although your brain that feels plays a huge part in how you navigate life, emotions can often feel elusive, complicated, and intimidating. Unlike thoughts, they're fluid and undefined, overlapping with each other in inconvenient ways and defying any logical box you try to put them in. As with many men, I'm sure you've struggled with knowing how to manage or express your emotions at times. And with that struggle comes a question: if our emotions are so tricky, how can we hope to help our children with their own?

Well, as I've said before, it starts with you. Because emotions are contagious, any emotional response can trigger a similar response in you. And if you don't have a well-developed brain that feels, your emotions can easily overwhelm you, preventing you not just from guiding your child through their emotions but also from connecting with them at a deep emotional level.

In order to develop your brain that feels, you must learn to continually practice the following five processes of emotional development. The more you engage with these processes, the better you'll be able to manage your emotions, and the more equipped you'll be to help your child do the same.

1   Regulate the intensity of your emotions.

Part of what can make emotions difficult to understand or control is the power with which they hit us. In order to manage and positively express them, you must first develop your ability to recognize what you feel, assess why you feel that way, and find methods for keeping your emotions from overwhelming you and causing you to react impulsively.

2   Label your emotions.

By learning to regulate your feelings and calm yourself down, you allow your brain that thinks to step in and help label what exactly you're feeling. There are six basic categories our emotional responses generally fall into: tenderness, excitement, fear, sadness, happiness, and aggression.[1] Learning to differentiate between these categories is vital for making the right decisions, because if you label an emotional response wrong, you can end up sabotaging positive situations and relationships and magnifying negative ones. For example, men especially tend to mislabel fear as anger, causing them to lash out defensively and make it even harder to find a productive solution. The better you can sort through and identify your emotions, the more effectively you will guide their influence on your responses.

---

1   To learn more about these emotions and their subcategories, check out my book *Being God's Man* at liveupresources.com.

3   Manage your emotional expression.

Even after labeling your emotions, you may still have the urge to act on them in impulsive ways. But doing so doesn't actually help you accurately convey what you're feeling. Instead of always just reacting to your feelings, you must learn to take a step back and assess the best way to respond from both a logical and emotional perspective.

4   Understand the emotions of others.

Because empathy is a key component of the brain that thinks, you must also increase your ability to label the emotions of others, especially those of your child. Besides allowing you to help them express their emotions properly, empathy also helps you read the situation and respond in a way that reflects the other's person emotions back to them without hurting their feelings further. However, you can only recognize the emotions of others when you achieve a certain level of emotional development, which is why engaging with the first three processes is so important. It's also helpful to reconcile your painful memories so you don't accidentally project your emotions onto others, hindering your ability to read theirs.

5   Manage others' emotional responses.

Once you make progress in each of the areas above, you'll be well equipped to find productive ways to use your emotions to acknowledge and appropriately influence the emotions of others. By giving a response that reflects what you're feeling while also respecting their perspectives, you can connect with them at a deeper level and help them process what's going on within them, allowing them to experience personal and relational success.

. . .

Aligning your own brain that feels with these five processes is the first step in teaching your child to do the same. Consistently managing your emotions and expressing them positively will form a predictable pattern of behavior your child can rely on. When they know what to expect from you in any situation, they can emotionally prepare for your responses, naturally teaching them how to label and guide their own emotions.

Having a strong brain that feels will also allow you to recognize and label what your child is experiencing, even when they can't do so themselves. This is especially important in moments where their emotional expression may not reflect their true feelings, like when their anger over a fight with a friend causes them to lash out at you over a minor incident. The more you can understand your child's various emotional responses, the better you can step in and help them sort through what they're actually feeling. In turn, you'll learn to guide them through those experiences and make choices that more accurately reflect what they're feeling.

Most of the time, all this emotional guidance requires is a conversation where you and your child try to talk through what they're feeling and find solutions for them to work through it. As you already well know, part of your job as a father is to simply be present, and that includes showing up during their emotional turmoil. Any type of growth is harder to achieve without relational support, but emotional management is especially elusive when your child doesn't have someone to rely on. A lack of love and support can trigger any number of negative emotions, such as loneliness, disappointment, anger, or even shame. Those emotions are tricky enough to manage as is, and if a child also feels alone, they won't see the point in even trying to navigate their feelings.

For your child to feel emotionally loved and valued, they need to sense that you understand them, which you can only do when you're deliberate about talking with them about what's going on in their life. Many men will say that their children are their top priority, but then they spend all their time at work or go straight to the TV when they get home, indirectly telling those children that they come second to their father's desires and goals.

Even if you *do* have to work a lot, or if your job is physically exhausting, there are always ways you can make sure your child feels connected to you. Make a point to have a conversation with them daily, or plan special time each week for you to be together. Showing them their worth in this way will fuel your child's self-assurance, which will in turn both prevent them from being overwhelmed by any emotion and make it easier to work through what they're feeling, especially since they know you'll be there to support them the whole way.

Sometimes, however, being there for your child and initiating conversations about their emotions simply won't work. If you've already lived through the teen years of your child's journey, you'll know exactly what I'm talking about. No matter how hard you try, your child may sometimes be determined to shut you out, even going so far as to deny anything's going on with them at all. But those feelings still exist, and you'll see them coming out in other ways, whether it's through a door slammed in your face or, if they're younger, a temper tantrum thrown on the floor.

If you find yourself in such a stalemate, and especially if you feel your own frustration rising in response, it may be time to discipline them. I remember a time when Kim was young and was experiencing a particularly intense bout of emotions, kicking and screaming over something relatively trivial. As discipline, I had her spend half an hour on the couch by herself. Even before the time was up, she'd completely changed her attitude, taking ownership of her negative choices and expressing her contrition. I still had her finish her consequence, but I asked if I could sit beside her and talk to make the time go faster. She agreed, and that day we had a great conversation that helped both of us understand each other even better.

Removing your child from the situation in this way and forcing them to take some quiet time will allow both of you to calm down and give your brains that feel the space to regain some control. Once you give your child time to label what they're feeling, you may even find that they're relaxed enough to let you in, giving you a chance to talk them through their emotions and convey the lessons you were trying to teach before.

Above all, the best way to help your child develop their brain that feels is to let them experience their emotions. Too many children, especially young boys, have been taught to suppress both their negative and positive emotions, either because they're "inappropriate" or because the parents find them "too overwhelming" to address. But this mindset only teaches their child to ignore their emotions instead of processing them, which causes them to turn into adults whose emotions still take over their decision-making in unproductive ways.

Your child is complex and very different from you. They may at times be angry or excitable in extreme or unmanageable ways, and they may even experience some of the overwhelming emotions, like depression, that we talked about in Chapter 20. But the solution is never simply to tell them to stop feeling that way, no matter how hard it is for you to understand their perspective. Even if you don't have time in the moment to help them fully work through what they're feeling, do your best to calm them down without being harsh or angry yourself. Then find time later to revisit the situation and help them figure out why that emotion took over.

Yes, it may be tiring, and yes, it may take more than one conversation or one instance of discipline. But putting in the effort now is essential because it will help your child go through that process of emotional management. That way, the next time they're in a similar situation, they won't respond in the same negative way they did before. Instead, they'll be better equipped to take control of their emotions before their emotions can take control of them.

A NATURAL PROCESS

Even though we just spent a lot of time talking about how to develop both our child's and our own brain that thinks, many of you may still be a bit confused about what it actually is. And trust me, I get it! Emotions are incredibly complicated, and figuring out exactly how they work can take some time. In this section, I'm going to break down some of the key tools of our brain that feels along with how it works in conjunction with our brain that thinks. To make it simpler, I'll be talking about it mostly from the father's perspective, but know that everything we discuss also applies to your child. The better you understand these tools and processes, the more equipped you'll be to use them properly and teach your child to do the same.

The first tool is our gut instinct, also referred to as our emotional intelligence, or EQ for short. We typically measure a person's potential for success by looking at their academic IQ, but the truth is that their EQ can actually play just as big of a role in what they can achieve.[2] In fact, our brain that feels actually works faster than our brain that thinks, giving us a sense about our circumstances that we can't always explain or even fully understand. We experience these gut responses about the people we talk to or the situations we're in, triggering a reaction from us before we even get a chance to engage our brain that thinks and decide logically what to do.

Even when we don't have all of the facts about a person or situation or fully understand our circumstances, our brain that feels is still taking in information and working to give us some direction. It's like when you're remodeling your house or trying to get

---

2   Daniel Goleman, *Emotional Intelligence 2.0* (San Diego: Talent Smart, 2009).

a project at work just right. You can tell when something's off, but you can't always put your finger on exactly what. In those cases, your gut feeling doesn't give you the answer, but it still flags your attention so you know that you need to keep looking for one.

However, while our emotional responses are meant to help inform our decisions, letting that gut instinct take too much control can be just as harmful as ignoring it completely. We see the effects of this all the time in young children. Because they don't yet have the ability to regulate the intensity of their emotions or guide their expression in appropriate ways, they throw temper tantrums in the middle of grocery stores or have meltdowns when being dropped off at day care. While these responses may accurately reflect their perspective, they typically don't help change their circumstances like they would want.

One aspect of our brain that feels that can trigger these inappropriate emotional responses is a small but powerful part of the brain called the amygdala. Its job is to vigilantly scan our environment for possible threats to our well-being. When it identifies one, it has our brain release the stress hormone cortisol along with a shot of adrenaline to give us the cheap and quick energy we need to respond quickly and efficiently.

In short, the amygdala helps protect you by telling you to run when a big dog lunges at you or to put up boundaries when you meet someone you sense intends you harm. The problem is, the amygdala isn't always the best at determining what qualifies as a dangerous situation. When we're overly attached to getting our way, it can light up in response to anything that might prevent us from doing so. And when we have traumatic events in our past that created deep, intense negative emotions, it can make any vaguely similar situation feel like impending doom, even when there's no danger at all.

The best way to prevent your emotions from hijacking your decision-making or responses is to teach your brain that feels and your brain that thinks to work in conjunction with each other. They may seem to be completely separate parts of you, but they're actually most effective when they function as one unit. While you may rely on your brain that thinks to know how to provide for your family, get important tasks done, and be a good father, it's your brain that feels that motivates you to follow through. We need our feelings to call attention to problems or to highlight the positive parts of our lives. Only then can we know to engage our brain that thinks to find a solution, deepen a relationship, or create new goals.

Our brain that thinks is also what helps us learn to label our emotions, evaluate them, and then manage our responses. Since not all of our emotional reactions will be based on reality, we can use principles based on God's Word to help us gauge whether our feelings are accurate and figure out how He would want us to respond (Psalm 119:105). We should engage in this type of self-evaluation both before and after an emotionally triggering situation. When we take time to do this, our brain that thinks will provide feedback on how we managed our emotional responses, allowing us to be better prepared to handle them more appropriately next time.

As you can see, we all already have the tools we need to recognize, understand, and manage our emotions as well as to interpret and relate to the emotions of others. It's just a matter of knowing how to manage them effectively and applying them in practical ways to our everyday lives. And it's the same with your child. You may not always feel equipped to handle their emotions, but it's not all that different from helping them develop in any other area. You just need to show them the tools available to them, guide them in building their skills, and instruct them on how to respond well. Then trust that God will give them the strength to handle the rest.

THE FATHER'S HEART

I can't stress enough that the key to guiding your child well in the emotional realm is to first develop your own brain that feels. Children learn best by example. If you strengthen your understanding and management of your emotions and your ability to sense and empathize with your child's, you will find them beginning to do the same just from observing you. But if you instead let your anger get the best of you, or if you dismiss other people's feelings as unimportant, your child will likely grow up to do so as well. It doesn't matter how much you try to teach them otherwise—in your child's eyes, you are giving them permission through your behaviors to act selfishly and let their emotions run rampant.

A big part of setting a good example is being open and vulnerable with your own emotions, specifically your passions. A child who feels their father's heart will be shaped by it for their entire life. I do what I do partially because I saw my own father's heart. Despite his shortcomings in other areas, he openly expressed his abilities to recognize the hurt in the world, to share the Gospel effectively, and to minister to others simply by meeting their needs. And as a result, I grew up intrigued by God, tuned in to human struggles, and inspired to become a counselor to help people through their various issues.

Just as I looked up to my father in these ways, your child loves you and wants to be involved in your life. Share with them what your passions are and what excites you about them. And just as importantly, if your child sees you get angry or upset about something, explain what made you feel that way. Children are more intuitive than we often give them credit for, and they can sense when we're not quite feeling like ourselves. Rather than letting your child try to guess why, tell them what you're feeling and help them understand the reasons. Who knows? They might even be able to cheer you up.

Of course, any sharing you do with your child should always be age appropriate as you don't want to say anything that would harm their development. But letting them into your emotional world, even just a little, can make all the difference in how well they learn to manage their emotions. Not only will you teach them emotional regulation through your explanations of your own emotions, but you will also give them a head start in knowing how to respond in similar situations so they don't have to make the same mistakes you did.

As you learn to share with your child, you'll find expressing your emotions becomes easier in your other relationships as well, and nowhere is this more beneficial than in your relationship with your wife. Like your child, your wife wants to be heard and understood. She wants to be valued, loved, and supported. And she wants to know what's going on inside of you—so share it with her. You two are in this together, and the more emotionally connected you are, the easier it will be to work as a team, both to help each other become stronger and to guide your child to become the best they can be.

So it's time to stop hiding. It's time to be a *real* man who's not afraid to connect with others closely, to share his inner feelings vulnerably, and to teach his child to do the same. Jesus Himself didn't live only in the world of logic. He wept in grief, confronted in anger, and rejoiced in happiness (John 11:35; Matthew 21:12; John 15:11). He expressed empathy for others and let them into His own emotional processes (Philippians 2:7-8). He loved without fear of judgment or rejection (Mark 2:15-17). And now it's time for you to do the same. After all, doesn't your child deserve that much?

ROY'S STORY

Growing up, Halloween was always an unpleasant time of year for me. Having a minister for a father meant that our home was the prime target for local pranksters. Year after year they soaped our windows, flung toilet paper everywhere, and destroyed anything they could get their hands on. Knowing that they were targeting my family on purpose, I couldn't help but feel a sense of rejection, and it made me angry to see how we didn't socially fit in.

There was one year in particular when things got really bad. The pranksters had attacked our house multiple nights leading up to Halloween, and my father had had enough. He snuck out of the back of the house one night to catch the culprits red-handed. He walked several blocks, circled back around, and then took a seat right behind our tormentors. After they were finished, he called out to each of them by name and let them know that this year things would be different.

When I heard my dad had caught and reported those boys to the police, I was thrilled. I had spent years cleaning up after them and was eager to see them get what they deserved. I waited impatiently on the day of their hearing to find out what consequences the district magistrate would give them. But much to my surprise and disappointment, my father told me all he asked for was that they be sentenced to come to church every week for three months. Even more baffling to me was that he didn't even ask that they endure a sermon or Bible study. He simply wanted them to come on Friday nights to play basketball in the church's gym.

The magistrate complied with my father's wishes, and so every Friday night for the next three months, those boys came to the gym. My dad joined them as well, bringing food, drinks, and his support and conversation. And wouldn't you know it? Those boys continued coming to church for the next five years, long after their sentencing had ended.

It took me a while, but I finally realized that my father didn't actually care much about the damage those kids had inflicted on our house. What he was concerned about was the fact that they likely would never make it to church. As a result, they would probably never learn about God and would never experience a positive influence that could change their lives.

The godly tradition he initiated as a result of their pranks changed my life. It's the reason why I write so many programs and books that integrate the Bible into real men's issues, and it's the reason why I specialize in counseling addicts and sex offenders. It's not because I'm a nice guy! It's because I felt my father's heart. He showed me that there are more important things in this world than vengeance. God loves every one of His children, and so sometimes, even when they hurt us, we must dig deep, feel their feelings, and do our best to love them too.

💬 DISCUSSION QUESTIONS

1   Give an example of a circumstance that causes you to experience excitement, fear, aggression, sadness, happiness, or tenderness. How do you typically respond to each of these emotions? How could you better manage your emotional expression?

2   How easy or difficult is it for you to recognize and help guide your child's emotions? What unresolved emotional experiences do you have that can get in the way of empathizing with them? What are some ways you can teach them to manage their brain that feels?

3   How often do you share your heart with those you love? What are some activities, hobbies, interests, or passions you can share with your child? How can you become more emotionally open to your wife?

4   Discuss what Proverbs 4:23 says about the importance of the heart. What impact do emotions have on a man's ability to father well?

Above everything else, guard your heart.
    Everything you do comes from it.

23

A FATHER RELATES

Of all the threats life poses on us, there's one that can wreak havoc like none other on our self-worth, our identity, and our faith—the disease of loneliness. Now, that may sound dramatic to you. After all, aren't men supposed to be tough and independent, never in need of a helping hand or shoulder to cry on? But if you got anything out of the last chapter, you know that this picture of manhood is simply false.

Just like with emotions, our culture has given us a false impression of how relationships relate to manhood. We're taught that loneliness equals self-sufficiency and strength, but it actually has the exact opposite effect. Besides weakening your mental and emotional development, isolation can actually decrease your memory capacity, cause heart problems, increase depression, and alter your brain's functioning.[1] And because it separates you from a strong support system of accountability relationships, loneliness can also make you much more likely to attach to addictive behaviors like food, drugs, alcohol, or compulsive sex in an attempt to find some outlet for your pent-up emotions.

As a father, you must learn to prioritize relationships now, because if you don't, this will become not just your future but also

---

1   Oliver Hämmig, "Health Risks Associated with Social Isolation in General and in Young, Middle and Old Age," *PLoS One* 14, no. 7 (July 18, 2019), https://www.ncbi.nlm.nih.gov/pmc/articles/PMC6638933/.

your child's. After all, you pass on to them what you don't process for yourself. In this chapter, we'll break down the role you play in your child's relational realm, which starts with unpacking your relationship with your child. The better you understand how your relationship affects their ability to connect with others, the more equipped you'll be to both lead by example and directly teach them the many different relational skills they need to develop. Through your intentional influence, your child will learn to establish and maintain the supportive relationships they need to truly thrive.

THE FIRST RELATIONSHIP

To paraphrase a common saying, the only way to make a good friend is to be one, and this concept applies to your relationship with your child too. Now, you may not think of yourself as your child's friend, which makes sense considering you can't guide, instruct, and discipline them as needed when you're focused on making sure they like you. However, that doesn't mean you don't need to learn to relate to them. Just as with the other areas of fatherhood we've talked about so far, your child will learn how to form all types of relationships directly through their relationship with you—and that includes how to be a good friend, a good coworker, and even a good spouse.

As we discussed in Chapter 19, your child needs more than just a positional father who does the bare minimum of providing. They need a spiritual father who takes an active role in their emotional well-being, continually seeks to understand them, and deliberately guides their development. The stronger the foundation of your relationship is, the more your child will trust you, and the better you can influence them in the areas they need it the most, including the relational realm.

Part of guiding your child in this realm is being aware of how you interact with them and the ways these interactions teach them the skills they need to build their own relationships. How you behave in all your relationships, including the ones with your wife and other members of the family, will shape what your child views as normal in a relationship. If you never listen to your wife and disregard her needs, your daughter will not only come to expect the same in her own marriage but will also never learn to demand anything more. And if you hide your emotions from those you love and ignore their need for empathy, your son will also learn to withhold his emotions from those who need him most, limiting his ability to form meaningful connections.

To avoid these negative outcomes, let's start with the basics. Relationships are a complicated concept that I like to boil down to one simple idea, which I call L.A.R.G.E. C.A.R.E.[2] These nine skills embody the way God loves and relates to us and how we in turn are to love and relate to others. By demonstrating these skills in all your relationships, especially the one with your child, you will do more than just strengthen your relationship with them. You will also teach them how to use these same skills to relate to others and what standard they should expect from all their future relationships.

LISTENING

In any interaction you have with others, they will be expressing themselves in multiple different ways. This means that to fully understand them, you must be continually listening to and searching for their messages. True listening requires looking at more than just what a person is saying. You must also learn to recognize why they're saying it and what it means to them.

---

2   For a more extensive explanation of the L.A.R.G.E. C.A.R.E. skills, check out our manhood resource *Being God's Man* at liveupresources.com.

ATTENTION

People always need reminded of their value, which means putting your love for them into action. This includes not only investing time in them but also giving them your full focus when you're together. Then they can feel the true value you have of them.

RESPECT

A fact of life is that other people, including your child, are simply different from you. Instead of becoming upset or frustrated by these differences, you must learn to accept their existence and grow to appreciate others for who they are.

GENUINENESS

Simply being your true self goes a long way toward expressing your care for others. When you can share your heart in transparent, humble, and vulnerable ways, they will feel your love for them behind everything you do.

ENERGY

All relationships require some level of investment, such as time, money, or personal sacrifice. No matter how you spend your energy, putting effort into your relationships will prove to others that you're fully engaged and involved in all areas of their life.

COMMUNICATION

As important as listening to others is, it's equally important that you share with them in return. The more you express what's going on inside of you, the less they will have to guess your thoughts, feelings, and struggles, and the more they'll want to share in return.

AFFECTION

Many men aren't that comfortable with expressing affection, but part of caring for someone means physically showing them you care. Whether through a hug or a compliment, demonstrating affection can help boost another person's mood and encourage them to keep going.

RESPONSIBILITY

When you have a relationship with someone, you naturally care about and want to ensure their well-being. This sense of responsibility will motivate you to help them develop their capabilities, learn to adapt to challenges, and push themselves to succeed in their goals.

EMPATHY

Because others are different from you, you must expend effort to understand them, which means learning to put yourself in their shoes. The better you can view life from their physical, emotional, mental, and relational perspective, the more equipped you'll be to help them through each of those realms.

Now that you have an understanding of the basic skills that will help both you and your child develop your relationships, we can take a look at some of the more specific relational skills you can use to build supportive friendships, work well with others, and manage conflict. Besides modeling these skills to your child through your own actions, you should also help them adopt them in their behavior through direct instruction and encouragement. By guiding them through their relational development, supporting them in their conflicts with others, and confronting them when they veer off course, you will prepare them to build strong, satisfying, and life-sustaining relationships.

IMPROVE YOURSELF FIRST

Just as with becoming a good father, the first step in building any relationship is achieving a certain level of personal growth. Your child's sin nature doesn't make it easy for them to connect or collaborate with others, especially when doing so goes against their natural selfish tendencies. They can get stuck in a "me, me, me" mentality, making it hard to look past their own desires and to see the value of empathizing with another's emotions or contributing to their goals.

In order to overcome their sin nature, your child must learn to practice self-control and build strong internal structures, which you can show them how to do through working on your own development. But beyond general growth, there are also a few key skills and attributes your child needs to develop to combat their selfish tendencies and make any relationship work.

1   Be attractive.

Now, I don't mean *attractive* in the superficial sense. When it comes to relating to others, it really doesn't matter how conventionally good-looking your child is, despite what the culture tries to make us believe. What *does* matter is the impact their physical attributes and attitude have on those around them. For instance, bad personal hygiene can make others uncomfortable, and a constantly negative attitude can exhaust or annoy them. We are all much more drawn to people who take care of themselves and who can make us feel relaxed and uplifted (Proverbs 17:22).

2   Control impulsivity.

Especially when they're young, your child's self-control is virtually nonexistent, which can cause problems in all of the life realms. In the relational realm specifically, giving in to their impulsive desires will make them seem inconsistent and unreliable, causing others to feel anxious around them (Proverbs 25:28). They'll never know what your child might do, and they won't trust that they'll play by the rules or follow through on their promises. The earlier and more effectively your child learns to organize their behaviors and responses, the more predictable and competent they'll seem when interacting with others.

3   Share freely.

Sharing is one of the most universal lessons every parent teaches their child early on, whether it's sharing an object with another child or sharing their feelings with them. However, sharing isn't just a behavior—it's also a mindset. There are typically two views of life when it comes to sharing: a deprivation mindset, which makes us believe there isn't enough to go around, and an abundance mindset, which gives us confidence that there's more than enough for everyone. A deprivation mindset most often leads to unnecessary competition with others, stinginess with our own resources or possessions, and fear of the success of others. An abundance mindset, however, understands that the heart of relationships is mutuality. Your child must learn both how to share and how to value sharing so that they not only willingly give to others but also don't hold any resentment for it. The more you share with them, and the more you explain why it's good to share, the better they'll internalize the value of making sacrifices for the good of others (Hebrews 13:16).

4   Be flexible.

Though flexibility is essential to the constant fluctuations and changes in relationships, we would often rather choose the pattern of behavior or thinking that's the most comfortable, reliable, or interesting. In many areas of life, those patterns can give us consistency that makes it easier to face a challenge, but in the relational realm they often cause even more problems. As your child becomes more social, they'll find that others don't always do what they expect or want, which can cause them to get frustrated and withdraw from the relationship. But if they've already established a certain level of flexibility, they'll be more equipped to take those differences in stride and adjust to a continually growing relationship (Romans 15:5-7).

ENGAGE SOCIALLY

In addition to developing the personal skills and attributes that will prepare your child to relate to others, they also need to learn the basic requirements for building any type of relationship. The first thing they need to understand is how to navigate social interactions in general. Here are a few basic unwritten rules everyone should learn to follow when interacting with others (Colossians 4:5-6).

1 **Acknowledge others.**

Even if it's just a simple greeting like "hello," our acknowledgment of another person's presence demonstrates a polite respect that will set a positive foundation for future interactions.

2 **Use basic manners.**

Besides conveying respect to the person we're talking to, using manners such as saying "please" and "thank you," being polite, and not interrupting demonstrates our ability to control ourselves, which will make others much more eager to engage with us.

3   Control your nonverbal language.

Because we often say much more with our body language and expressions than with our words, we must always be aware of our nonverbal messages. For instance, maintaining good eye contact shows that we're focused on the other person, and respecting their personal space provides a sense of safety and comfort.

4   Control your emotional expression.

There are multiple ways we must learn to manage our emotions on a relational level. Most obviously, we should work to avoid any negative outbursts that could make another person feel threatened or uncomfortable. But just as importantly, we should learn when to be patient and focus on what others may need to express and when to be assertive and let others know how we feel. As with sharing, emotional control will help provide the give-and-take necessary in any relationship.

5   Use humor appropriately.

By learning to laugh at ourselves and life, we can demonstrate confidence and touch the heart of those we're laughing with. At the same time, we must also be able to read the room and know when humor would be inappropriate or insensitive.

6   Know when to disengage.

While conversation is essential to relationship building, people won't always want to talk, either because they have other priorities or because they're just not in the mood. However, it can often be hard for them to say so out of fear of being rude. We must learn to be sensitive to the nonverbal cues of others and end these types of conversations ourselves. Doing so may be disappointing at times, but as long as we remember it isn't personal, that disappointment will fade quickly, allowing us to try again at a better time.

BUILDING BETTER RELATIONSHIPS

Of course, building a relationship requires more than just having a handful of successful conversations. While the above techniques are great for initiating or maintaining surface-level relationships, they don't necessarily help us build lifelong bonds. If your child wants to turn a classmate into a friend, strengthen a working partnership, or deepen a romantic one, they must be deliberate about fostering a connection on an emotional level in order to build a deeper bond.

There are many different ways to do this, but two of the best ones are asking good questions and giving compliments. Seeking more information about another person's life experiences both demonstrates interest in them and allows for a more complete understanding of who they are. Complimenting them then tells them that you do understand their perspective as you affirm what they like about themselves and acknowledge any personal progress they've made.

In addition to deepening relational connections, your child must also demonstrate a commitment to those connections through their actions (Matthew 7:12). Again, there are multiple ways to achieve this, but there are four key behaviors your child must absolutely learn to adopt.

1   Follow up.

Just having a conversation and moving on isn't enough. If your child truly cares about someone, they should make sure to check back in about what they talked about, either by seeing how an upcoming event went, asking what they decided to do about a challenge they were facing, or offering new advice to an ongoing problem. In doing so, your child indicates not only that they remembered what the other person had shared but also that they thought about it while they were apart, showing them just how significant they are to them.

2   Prioritize the relationship.

As we discussed with the L.A.R.G.E. C.A.R.E. skill of energy, deliberately setting aside time and carefully planning social engagements proves to others that they hold an important place in our lives. Of course, making plans means nothing unless you also keep them, which is why your child must also learn to back up their promises with action. If they want others to have faith in them and trust in their word, they must be careful at all times to protect it by following through with action.

3   Practice cooperation.

Cooperation means working well with others as a team and contributing your gifts to work toward a common goal. Your child has amazing abilities, and they should be willing to share what they know or what they can do to help others succeed. Besides contributing to another person's life, doing so will strengthen their own self-confidence and create a sense of trust between them and others.

4   Create balance and compromise.

No one wants to be in a relationship with someone who always gets their way and never considers anyone else's needs. For some reason, we don't find it fun to be manipulated and taken advantage of to fulfill someone else's agenda. For this reason, your child must learn to delay their gratification and say no to themselves from time to time. Rather than winning every argument or always doing what they want, they should engage in a compromise that makes everyone happy, either by agreeing to go with the other person's plan this time and theirs next time or by finding a plan that meets somewhere in the middle.

However, balance isn't just important in the big moments or decisions of a relationship—it should also be there in even the most trivial conversations. Children *love* to talk, but to maintain a relationship, they need to learn how to balance talking with listening. As much as they may not like it, going with the flow of a conversation sometimes means holding back a point that may be distracting or would derail the discussion. In the long run, developing the self-control to wait until it's their turn will strengthen their relationships, because it will help them focus on what they can learn from others rather than only sharing what they already know.

RESOLVING CONFLICT

The difficult truth is that no matter how much effort your child puts into developing their relational skills, they will still find themselves struggling with their relationships at times. Everyone is different, and if both people in a relationship are being authentic, there will naturally be some sparks. One of the most important social skills your child can learn is how to control their frustration when something goes awry, manage the conflict gracefully, and figure how to move forward in the relationship.

Though every conflict will look different, there are a few key skills that will help your child work through any issues that might arise in their relationships. Perhaps the most difficult one to adopt is accepting criticism without being defensive. As hard as they might try otherwise, they will at times hurt, frustrate, or simply annoy others, whether it's by making a selfish choice, ignoring their feelings, or even making a simple mistake.

However, it's usually not these mistakes themselves that damage a relationship, but rather what happens after. The more your child resists admitting fault and defends their actions, the more others will pull away. By instead accepting external criticism and owning up to their mistakes, they will demonstrate that they value the other person more than their pride, allowing them to work together to strengthen their relationship and find a way to move on.

Conversely, when it's the other person who makes a mistake, your child must be willing to constructively confront them. Confrontation is not about anger or revenge but about trying to address a problem and find a solution. Your child must learn to clearly and respectfully communicate their viewpoint, which begins by carefully picking the best time and place for the confrontation. Then during the conversation, they should focus on "I feel" statements that express their perspective rather than "you" statements that might provoke or degrade the other person. And above all, they need to be open to hearing another person's point of view, because it's only through reaching a mutual understanding that they can find the best way forward.

People are often reluctant to confront others out of fear that doing so might cause irreparable damage to their relationship. But if your child's relationship is so tenuous that expressing how they feel will cause a fracture in it, the relationship probably wasn't worth it in the first place. Part of deciding how to confront is deciding if doing so requires ending the relationship. If your child ever feels unsafe or like they can't overcome the differences between them and another person, encourage them to call it quits. Even if it may hurt, sometimes that's the best thing for everyone involved.

Unsurprisingly, the first lessons a child learns about dealing with conflict is through observing how their father handles it in his relationships. Does he hang on to resentment, or can he forgive someone who has hurt him? Does he let his anger get the better of him, or can he do the right thing regardless of the circumstances? How nobly does he accept the consequences of his own mistakes, and does he humble himself to take the steps to make amends? Whatever instruction you give your child, you must also learn to follow it yourself. It's through your example more than anything that they will learn to navigate the tension in their relationships and end the conflict once and for all.

DO YOU MEASURE UP?

As with any life realm, part of leading your child well relationally necessitates that you are willing to continuously and honestly examine yourself in order to see where you need improve so you can be a more consistent, positive, and godly role model (Psalm 26:2). It doesn't matter what kind of relationship you currently have with your child—with God's guidance, it is never too late for you to improve.

The following survey can help you start this journey of relational growth.[3] Each question represents a specific social skill your child will need to develop to be relationally strong, which means you must also consistently practice it. As you read through the list, think about each point and grade yourself on a scale of 1 to 3. By identifying the specific areas you excel in and the ones you struggle in, you can know what steps to take to improve your relationship with your child and become the positive example of relationships that they need.

---

3   For a printable version of this survey, visit liveupresources.com/fatherhood.

_____ 1   I take care of myself so that I'm clean, and I present myself in a way that makes it easy for others to relate to me.

_____ 2   I never behave in a manipulative, dominating, or self-centered way.

_____ 3   I maintain a positive attitude that helps others feel appreciated and encouraged.

_____ 4   I limit my impulsivity and follow established rules, which allows others to rely on me.

_____ 5   I share myself, my time, and my resources with others.

_____ 6   I believe there is enough goodness to go around and am not overly competitive.

_____ 7   I am flexible and able to adjust my preferred patterns of behavior in order to do what's best for others.

_____ 8   When I come home at the end of the day, I take time to greet my family and make myself available to them as needed.

_____ 9   I practice basic manners so others feel respected as we work or play together.

_____ 10   I create a positive environment in the home that allows my family to feel safe and comfortable.

_____ 11   I control my emotional expression so no one feels threatened.

_____ 12   I recognize and accurately express what I'm feeling instead of forcing others to guess.

_____ 13   I use humor and my playful imagination to create an enjoyable experience for others.

_____ 14   I recognize when others are busy and know when to disengage rather than demanding their attention.

_____ 15   I know how to ask good questions that encourage others to share what they are thinking and feeling on a deeper level.

_____ 16   I compliment others to bolster their confidence and demonstrate my value for them.

_____ 17   I follow up on previous conversations by asking questions or offering new suggestions.

_____ 18   I prioritize my family and deliberately set aside time to spend with each of them, both as a group and one on one.

_____ 19   I stick by every promise I make, and if I can't, I take responsibility for it rather than ignoring my error.

_____ 20   I demonstrate an attitude of cooperation by helping others succeed at their own goals instead of only focusing on mine.

_____ 21   I delay gratification and say no to my desires in order to meet the needs of others.

_____ 22   While it might not be my first choice, I am willing to participate in an activity that would make someone else feel valuable.

_____ 23   I respect the viewpoints of others and willingly admit when I might be wrong.

_____ 24   I encourage others to have their own perspectives and to share them with me even when they're different from mine.

_____ 25   I know when to share my thoughts and when to remain quiet and listen to others.

_____ 26   I accept criticism without getting defensive, and I use this feedback to improve myself.

_____ 27 I apologize, ask for forgiveness, and own up to the consequences of my negative choices.

_____ 28 I carefully and respectfully plan how to confront others in a way that they'll hear my message.

_____ 29 I am intentional about respecting others' differences and appreciating their uniqueness.

_____ 30 I intentionally encourage my child to develop their social skills in order to prevent the destructive effects of loneliness.

Your child relies on you for much more than the basic necessities of life, and it's up to you to decide whether you will provide them with all they need and more. Relationships can be a tricky and messy area of life, but they are also what gets us out of bed in the morning, encourages us to do our best, and motivates us to always keep persevering. You have the amazing opportunity to do exactly this for your child, and to teach them how to be there for others in the same way. So take a deep breath, and work on how you relate—starting with your child.

 ROY'S STORY

For one of Kim's birthdays, I went all out and created a competitive scavenger hunt for her and her friends. I split the kids up into two teams and sent them off across our property looking for clues, which would lead them to a treasure box if they followed them correctly.

Well, coincidentally, both teams ended up finding the treasure at about the same time. Now they had to face the next challenge—opening the box up. The team that got there first, by about thirty seconds, immediately raced to open the combination lock using the code they'd gotten from their clues. To the delight of the second team, it didn't work. Needling the first team with taunts that they must not have figured out their clues correctly, they pushed their way to the treasure box, confident that they had the right code. And yet when they put those numbers in, the box still remained locked.

Both teams were stumped. Each took turns putting in their codes again, hoping that they somehow were just putting their combination in wrong. After some time and a lot of frustration, the teams finally discussed the advantages of working together. Eventually they had the idea that maybe the numbers they had were only *part* of the secret code. Maybe they had to combine them in order to get into the treasure. Well, sure enough, as soon as they tried that, the treasure box popped right open.

I know, I know, that was pretty sneaky of me. Kim and her friends thought they were just having a fun, competitive afternoon with some prizes at the end, and instead they got a lesson on the importance of cooperation. I won't pretend that meant she never got into battles with others again, but now that she's an adult, I can see that she did take that lesson to heart. She doesn't try to get ahead at the expense of others, and she loves working on a team. I know it isn't all because of that game I created, but it still gives me joy to see her treating others just like her dad would.

💬 DISCUSSION QUESTIONS

1   Name three of the L.A.R.G.E. C.A.R.E. relationship skills that are the most difficult for you to practice regularly. How can you more effectively incorporate them into your life so you can lead your child to do the same?

2   Which of the various social skills do you feel are most import-
     ant in building relationships? What are some practical ways
     you can help your child develop them?

3   Look back at the survey, and discuss what areas of influence
     you need to improve on. How can turning those areas over to
     God help you become the father your child needs you to be?

4   Discuss what 1 Thessalonians 5:11 says about relationships.
     What are some relational characteristics a father should want
     his child to have?

     *So encourage one another with the hope you have. Build each
     other up. In fact, that's what you are doing.*

24

A FATHER PROTECTS

I'm sure you've seen the videos. A dad grabs his kid just as they're about to smack their head on the pavement. Or he pulls them out of the path of an out-of-control car at the very last second. Or he dives to catch a loose basketball right before it knocks over his toddler. Even though we can't control everything, all fathers seem to have an innate ability to sniff out danger right before it happens. It's like we naturally gain a sensitivity to it as soon as we become dads. The lessons we've learned from experience, which we often ignore for ourselves, become a foundation for our fatherhood, allowing us to take care of our children in ways we never thought we could.

However, although it's great that we're able to instinctually protect our children from many of these unexpected threats, not all danger is quite so easy to combat. As fathers, we have to do more than simply save our children from physical danger. We must also do whatever we can to protect their hearts and minds from anything that seeks to destroy them. And since God has called us to help them eventually grow independent from us, we must teach them to protect themselves as well.

Evil runs rampant in our world, convincing people to live selfish and even predatory lifestyles that harm others, particularly inexperienced and naive children. As they grow up, your child will be under constant attack from those who will attempt to make them exchange godly values for cultural lies, and the fact is that you won't always be there to defend them. To truly protect them, you need to ensure that your child has a full understanding of the many threats that might come their way and how to stand firm against them. As you build up their defenses together, you can be sure of their strength, confidence, and ability to press on no matter what challenges them.

BUILT TO DEFEND

As fathers, it can be tempting to try to shield our children not just from danger itself but also from the very knowledge of danger, especially when it comes to their spiritual well-being. Sinful threats and temptations, such as addictive substances and abusive relationships, are more insidious than obvious physical challenges, and we don't even want to think about our children having to face these kinds of threats. So we put off talking about them at all, convincing ourselves they're too young to understand anyway.

But keeping your child in the dark will only hurt them in the long run. For one, if they don't learn about certain threats from you, they'll learn about them somewhere else, and that information won't be as accurate or helpful. As a counselor, I see this all the time in regard to sexuality. Many parents are slow to talk about sexuality with their children, which means they wind up learning about it mostly from older kids on the bus. And because that's their only source of information, they're more likely to believe it even if it's wrong or sinful and may develop self-destructive sexual behaviors as a result.[1]

Furthermore, you may hope your child will never be abused or offered drugs, but the reality is that it's impossible for you to know what challenges they'll face. It's better for them to be aware

---

1   For more on the importance of sexual integrity, check out my book *All Man* at liveupresources.com.

of the possibility than to have no idea it exists. If they do have to face such threats, being naive and innocent will only make it more likely they won't even recognize the danger, let alone be capable of defending themselves against it.

The best way for you to protect your child is to be open and honest with them about the more dangerous and self-destructive aspects of life. This doesn't necessarily mean getting into the nitty-gritty details of those aspects, especially if they're too young to fully understand them, but even a broad discussion about recognizable issues will help. Talk to them about how not everyone is nice to others or how some people won't have their best interests at heart in order to teach them to be alert instead of trusting blindly. Most importantly, give them good general guidance they can use to handle any issue. This guidance should include:

- Helping them learn to trust their gut, as it's often based on real experiences and the lessons they've learned from you about life.

- Teaching them to slow themselves down and respond intentionally. The better they can think through a situation, the easier it will be to react well.

- Encouraging them to talk with you about what choices are available to them. You can do this by creating an atmosphere of open sharing in the home and asking non-judgmental questions.

These conversations are the first step in actively preparing your child to protect themselves. By instilling within them these important principles and values, you give them the tools they need to be alert against threats to their well-being and feel empowered to withstand their attacks.

There are several specific areas you must prepare your child to defend themselves in, the most obvious being the physical realm.

In addition to learning to avoid risky behaviors that could lead to injury—or at least learning to be more careful while taking appropriate risks—your child also needs to establish a foundation for physical self-defense. Most of the time, this simply means making sure they're physically active. Developing their body will help give your child the strength and confidence to figure out how to deal with those who would harm them.

However, even more important than knowing how to fight is knowing when *not* to. Men in particular often allow their pride or machismo to lead them into unnecessary altercations that risk injury and violate their character. Rather than further instilling this cultural lie into your child's mind, teach them that physical fighting is always the last resort (Proverbs 16:32). Instead, they should learn how to read a situation and resolve it before a fight breaks out, either by finding a way to deescalate the conflict or by simply leaving the room.

While it may be uncomfortable to think about, another important physical threat to prepare your child for is inappropriate touching. That phrase probably makes you immediately think of child molesters, but it can also refer to any type of nonmutual physical experience, such as an unwanted hug, an overly familiar massage, or a disrespect of personal space. Everyone has a right to maintain their physical comfort by setting boundaries, and children are no exception.

To help protect your child in this way, teach them that it's okay to say no to any expression of affection or physical touch, even if it's something they normally appreciate. Let them be honest when they don't want to be close to you, such as when they're unhappy about an unwanted but deserved discipline. Above all, encourage them to come to you for assistance when someone doesn't respect their boundaries. By guiding them in these ways, you prepare them to know what to do to protect themselves in any situation, whether it's facing a child molester or even navigating their future sexual relationship with their spouse.

Another area where others may attempt to harm and control your child is in the emotional realm. Rather than using physical force, some people rely on emotional intimidation or manipulation to get their way. They use their anger to dominate and control others and guilt them into doing what they want. Your child's best protection against such people is to develop a strong emotional IQ, which we discussed in Chapter 22. The more balanced their emotional state is and the more control they have over their responses, the less they'll be swayed by the emotional responses of others and instead will remain calm, rational, and level-headed.

Along with physical and emotional defense, your child will also need to prepare to protect themselves in the relational realm. Throughout their life, they will experience peer pressure and rejection from others, either intentionally or incidentally. They must have a strong internal resiliency and be secure enough in their identity to stand up for what's right. When they develop these pillars, they will no longer base their self-definition on whether others like them or not. Instead of being debilitated by the negative behavior of others, they'll be able to grieve what happened and confidently move on, even if it means ending the relationship and pursuing more positive ones.

Besides alerting your child to the danger in the world, discussing the potential threats to their physical, emotional, and relational well-being will arm them with the resources they need to defend themselves, whether that's a step-by-step plan or simple self-confidence. However, your job doesn't end there. Just because your child has the resources they need doesn't mean they'll know how to use them. To truly protect your child, you must also help them put their understanding into practice in applicable ways, every day and as often as possible.

DEFENSE IN ACTION

Anyone who plays sports will tell you that you can't learn how to play through huddles and locker-room meetings alone. You have to put what you learn from those meetings into action by getting on the field, running drills, and practicing your game plan. It's only by simulating a real game that you can build the skills you need not just to play well but also to win.

Physical self-defense is relatively easy to practice since, as mentioned earlier, there are many classes and sports your child can enroll in to learn physical finesse. Creating emotional and relational safety, however, is trickier because those types of attacks are often less straightforward. The best way you can help your child develop skills in these areas is to work on techniques and attributes they'd need in emotionally or relationally threatening scenarios, such as confidently expressing their viewpoint. By giving them space to disagree with you, like I did with my designated "argument time" with Kim, you can help your child develop confidence in their own perspective and stick up for themselves and what they believe is right.

Of course, the point isn't to always give in to their arguments, since in life they won't always get what they desire. It's also not helpful to let them whine about things they don't want to do. Instead, encourage them to speak up about their feelings, directly state what they think is unfair, and present their reasons why. By allowing your child to challenge you in a safe and balanced way, you help them hone their ability to do the same with less respectful individuals in the future.

All that to say, sometimes the only way for your child to really learn to protect themselves is simply to face the danger on their own. As hard as it may be to stand by and do nothing, it's better for your child to go through certain experiences while you're around to provide unspoken support, guidance, and encouragement, even if it means they end up failing and feeling wounded. By going through this gauntlet, they can develop heartiness and resiliency and discover what they're truly capable of. And with that discovery, they'll gain the confidence to swim through the river of life on their own.

As you make your child aware of the threats in the world and teach them how to protect themselves in practical ways, always keep in mind that these tools and techniques lose their effectiveness when used without the ultimate resource—a personal, day-by-day relationship with God. When you teach your child self-protection, make sure to share your own faith in God and how He actively strengthens each of us. Remind them that even in situations that seem beyond their ability to comprehend or manage, His loving presence means they don't have to be afraid. As long as they're willing to participate in a relationship with God, Jesus will help them overcome all of their troubles (John 16:33).

Part of relying on God includes grounding ourselves in His Word. Besides teaching your child important principles that will help them fortify their character, the Bible contains many specific stories that can show them how to prepare for real-life scenarios. For example, the Old Testament story of David defeating Goliath can both feed your child's adventurous spirit and demonstrate God's empowerment and what they can achieve when they seek it (1 Samuel 17:23-50). It's only by continually growing closer to Him and immersing themselves in Scripture that your child will be empowered to truly rise above any evil the world has to offer.

BEWARE OF THE LIES

Although much of the danger in life comes from external sources, like other people, the media, or false cultural beliefs, external threats aren't the only danger we have to worry about. Many threats actually come from within. As we discussed in Chapter 13, our sin nature and its many distorted ways of thinking can push us toward passivity and undermine our ability to step toward our challenges. And in their innocence and naivete, our children are especially vulnerable to falling prey to their own internal deficits and internalizing lies that lead them down a self-destructive path.

Along with being wary of physical, emotional, and relational threats, you must always stay alert for when your child has accepted an untrue belief about themselves or the world and has integrated it into their identity. It's your responsibility to protect them from themselves by confronting these lies as quickly as possible and directing your child back toward God's truth. Below are some of the most common lies to look out for in your child's thinking. The better you can recognize their warning signs, the more you'll be able to help your child acknowledge the threat, defend themselves from it, and grow stronger as a result.

1   It just happens.

So much of life is outside of our control, and it can be easy to deny any influence we do have over how our lives turn out. When your child believes the lie that "it just happens," they succumb to a fixed mindset, give up on developing themselves, and repress their passions and dreams. They decide risks aren't worth it and instead choose patterns of behavior that feel safe and yet constrict what they can become.

The only way for your child to grow is to learn to focus on the eighty-five percent of life they can control instead of becoming defeated by the fifteen percent they can't. God has given them the ability to adjust to any circumstance. Instead of accepting life as it is, teach your child to acknowledge their responsibility to take action to change what they can. Even if they can't alter their circumstances, they always have the ability to choose the attitude with which they respond.

2   It's too late.

What makes a failure debilitating is usually not the consequences that result from it but rather our own response. We often give unnecessary power to our mistakes and imperfections by turning healthy guilt into self-judgment and shame. When your child internalizes failure in this way, they begin to believe that their mistakes and negative behaviors define who they are. As a result, they disengage from life and choose to be an observer. Rather than participate in creating their own destiny, they become stuck in a cycle of destructive decision-making, not even bothering to make an effort to break free.

It's natural to want to succeed in anything we try, but taking on a perfectionistic attitude will only add to your child's anxiety, make life more burdensome, and increase their chances of failing. Your child can't be perfect, but they *can* continue to grow and improve. When you see them give in to self-pity, remind them of how God loves and values them, and gently encourage them to resolve their discouragement. By engaging in self-forgiveness, they can find new solutions to problems that once defeated them.

3   I'm not valuable.

In addition to convincing us that it's too late to change, failure can also make us feel worthless. If your child begins thinking this way, they can become consumed by their own negativity. Instead of facing the challenges that will make them stronger, they desperately search for quick ways to feel better and make demeaning, self-destructive choices in the process.

No matter how your child feels about themselves, God says they are amazing and wonderful (Psalm 139:14). As His representative to them, you must demonstrate this definition to them. With your unconditional love and support, they can learn to avoid making choices that demean themselves and instead develop positive habits that eliminate the negative voices in their head, allowing them to pursue their true potential.

4   What other people think about me matters more than anything else.

The false belief that we must be liked by others to have value holds us hostage to people who don't deserve that level of influence. If your child measures their success by what people think of them, they are setting themselves up to be miserable. Your role is to help them understand that they can't control others or make others accept them—and that's okay! By finding their true value in God alone, they'll learn that no one can define them except for Him.

5   I need to achieve or obtain something in order to feel good about myself and life.

Thanks to the rampant commercialism of today's culture, it's easy to become confused about what is most important in life. Besides learning to incorrectly interpret all their wants as needs, your child can internalize the idea that success is defined in materialistic terms. To counter this message, take care not to overindulge your child's wants and instead teach them other ways of experiencing gratification. The more they understand that they already have everything they need to enjoy life within themselves, the less their happiness and self-worth will be defined by external success.

6   Life is either completely good or completely bad.

There are always both good and bad parts to life, but the lie that it can't be both at once makes us exaggerate negative experiences, which empowers them to take over more of our lives than they should. To prevent your child from developing such a black-and-white perspective, teach them to celebrate the positive parts of life even during the negative moments. When they can experience a sense of gratitude, they'll have the strength and resources to face any challenge life throws their way.

7   If one relationship isn't working, it means all of life is bad.

Because of the love and support relationships provide, it can be easy for us to become overly dependent on certain people. And if those relationships turn out to be toxic or dangerous, like when a close friend lies to us or a respected peer talks bad about us, we are often quick to see it as a failure on our part or a sign that our lives are going horribly. However, as important as relationships are, they don't define life as a whole. When your child finds themselves struggling in a relationship, instead of becoming upset, they must learn to accept it, search for a way to improve it, and if necessary, be strong enough to end the relationship and move on.

8   If it feels good, do it.

There's nothing wrong with a little fun, but overemphasizing the pleasure of the moment causes us to be controlled by our impulses. Such a mindset will lead us to do whatever we want whenever we want, regardless of the consequences. A hard lesson your child must learn early on is that life won't turn bad just because their wants aren't satisfied right away.

By telling them no, you teach them to say no to themselves, which will prepare them to make the right decisions in the future.

9   **I'm right about most things.**

As much as we need to build up our confidence, we must also learn the difference between positive self-assurance and destructive pride. A narcissistic mindset not only disrupts your child's relationship with God but also isolates them from others, preventing them from recognizing how much they still need to learn and develop (Proverbs 18:2). To continue growing, your child needs to evaluate their thinking processes so they can identify the various cognitive distortions that can get them into trouble, like we talked about in Chapter 21. The better they can recognize the mistakes they've made or the beliefs they were wrong about, the more they'll learn from them, which will help them keep growing toward their God-given potential.

As you work to protect your child from the lies of the world, keep in mind the power of a self-fulfilling prophecy. How your child defines themselves is often what they will become, which means you must be careful when confronting your child about their self-destructive beliefs. It doesn't matter how loving your intentions are. If you make generalized negative statements about them, even inadvertently, you can create the very problem within them that you are trying to help them overcome.

Rather than making statements about who your child is, focus on encouraging them about what they can do. No matter their circumstances, your child doesn't have to accept the negative aspects of life. They can always do something to make their experiences more positive, even if it's simply reframing their mindset to focus on their blessings instead of their challenges. Encourage them to embrace their individual power and amazing, God-given gifts, and help create within them a spirit of learning and growth as they tune in to the daily conversations God has with them. When they recognize what they can do with Him, they'll gain the confidence to avoid the many traps of a sinful world and ultimately become all God intended them to be.

 ROY'S STORY

Between my freshman and sophomore years of college, I ran the youth program at my father's church. One night after the program had ended, I needed to give one of the kids a ride home, but because she lived quite a distance away, I had to fill up my car with gas first. Luckily, we already had some gas stored on the property for the church buses, so I wouldn't have to take another detour on my way home.

I was just about done filling up my tank when suddenly the chief of police pulled into the parking lot. I was a little bewildered to see him, considering it was almost eleven at night and the church was in the middle of nowhere. He got out of his car and promptly asked me what I was doing there. I simply told him that I was the minister's son, expecting that to be enough. He smugly replied, "So it's the minister's son who's been stealing the gas!" Even more bewildered, I stated that my father knew I was there because I worked for the church. The chief replied, "So your dad knows you're the one who's been stealing the gas!"

Now, you should know that it was no secret that this man disliked our church and what it stood for. Years prior, the church had purchased a piece of rural property to build a larger worship center, which the municipal authorities had done everything they could to stop. They'd wanted a business established on that land that could provide a bigger tax base for the school system. But the purchase went through, and ever since then the chief of police had held a grudge against the church.

And now it seemed he had an avenue for some revenge. He was right that the gas stored on the church property would frequently get stolen, but no one had ever been caught. Even though I wasn't the one stealing it, I could see that he was going to do whatever he could to get me in trouble simply because I was the minister's son. He demanded to see my driver's license, which I realized I had left at home. He then told me that if I didn't get off this property in the next thirty seconds, he would arrest me.

I quickly complied, took the girl home, and drove back to my own house, feeling shaken. I had never been treated so harshly before, especially not by an officer. I had always respected the police and the work they did in the community, and I didn't know what to make of the encounter.

When I got home, I told my father what happened. He immediately got on the phone with the chief and asked him a series of questions: "Did you catch my son stealing gas? Did you ask him for his driver's license, and did he have it? Did you then tell him that he needed to leave this property or you would arrest him?"

The chief affirmed what had happened. In response, my father told him that I was an employee of the church for the summer and that I had been approved by the church board to use gas as part of my job. Then he calmly asked him one more question: "Why did you throw my son off of a property that he is part of owning as a member of the church while knowing that he didn't have a license on him to legally drive home?" He heard only silence in return.

I'll always remember how my father stood up for me that night. Even though I was legally an adult, I didn't really have the emotional and cognitive means to defend myself in that situation—but my father did. He could've let me face the consequences myself, but he knew the threat the chief of police posed to me, my family, and the church, which allowed my father to see through his manipulation and figure out the truth. In turn, I learned how to be prepared to stand up against sin no matter what—even when the attack comes from those meant to be pillars of leadership.

💬 DISCUSSION QUESTIONS

1   Discuss some of the threats your child will have to face in life. How have you dealt with these threats in your own life? How can you prepare your child to navigate them well?

2   How can allowing your child to disagree with you increase their ability to protect themselves? What are some other ways you can help your child practice self-defense in practical ways (physical, emotional, and relational)?

3   Review the list of lies we often believe about ourselves. What can you do to help your child counteract these lies?

4   Discuss what Psalm 144:1 says about how God helps prepare us to protect ourselves. How can you show your child what an ongoing relationship with Jesus can do for them?

Give praise to the LORD, my Rock.
He trains my hands for war.
He trains my fingers for battle.

25

A FATHER TOUGHENS

I can still remember when Kim joined the swim team at her school. She was so excited to get in the water and show everyone what she was made of. She worked hard at every practice, doing everything she could to prepare for her first race. When that race finally came, she stepped up onto the block, dove into the water, finished her first lap—and was promptly disqualified for making an illegal turn.

Failure happens to everyone, even the children we try so hard to protect, and it can be tempting to jump in to fix the situation for them. But as we discussed in the previous chapter, sometimes the best way to protect our children is *not* to protect them at all. What happened to Kim wasn't unfair. She made a mistake, and she received the consequences for it. The question wasn't how to get around those consequences. It was how to make sure she would learn her lesson and avoid making the same mistake again.

In this chapter, we'll take a deeper look into one of the most important aspects of self-protection—building internal toughness. Your child will have to face their fair share of adversity, challenges, and pain throughout life. Their ability to not only get past it but also grow from it all depends on how well you help your child build three vital characteristics—perseverance, determination, and grit.

TOUGH LOVE

I'm sure life isn't always easy for you, and the same will be true for your child. Life won't care about hurting their feelings. It won't listen to their excuses. It certainly won't give them a second chance just because they ask for one. Life is tough, and the best way to face it is with toughness in return. As we discussed throughout Part II, hardships and adversity can be gifts for the growth opportunities they create (Romans 5:3-5). Obstacles in your child's path will force them to develop self-control and perseverance to overcome them. Challenges will teach them to work on and contribute to a team to achieve a common goal. And even mistakes and failures will help them learn how to take all their losses in stride, pick themselves up, and move forward.

However, life's toughness can only lead to internal growth when your child is strong enough to face it head-on, push through it, and identify the lessons they need to learn. Unfortunately, such perseverance isn't a skill we're born with. Sure, some people are naturally excited by challenges or have an innate tendency to look forward rather than back. But even they started out as toddlers who exploded in fits of rage when life didn't go their way. Part of our responsibility as fathers is to help our children grow past these tantrums and learn to say no to any escapist tendencies that will detour their character development. Only then can they learn not just to survive life's toughness but also to thrive in it.

In her book *Grit: The Power of Passion and Perseverance*, psychologist Angela Duckworth explores two main approaches to helping a child develop an attitude of unwavering toughness: providing loving support and demanding high standards.[1] A supportive approach means loving, comforting, and reassuring your child when they feel frustrated or overwhelmed by a challenge. By

---

1   Angela Duckworth, *Grit: The Power of Passion and Perseverance* (New York: Scribner, 2016).

acknowledging and understanding their emotions, you can help them calm themselves down and rebuild their confidence enough to either move on or try again.

Alternatively, a demanding approach means encouraging your child to move past what happened to them and answer the question "What next?" By emphasizing independence, self-reliance, and responsibility instead of taking care of everything for them, you can challenge your child to push themselves past their limits in order to find a solution, which will help them strengthen their abilities and develop their full potential.

As Duckworth suggests, supportive and demanding parenting isn't meant to be an either/or choice. To parent your child the way they truly need, you must find a balance between the two. Interestingly enough, God created both fathers and mothers to work in tandem to accomplish this. Because women are naturally more in tune with their emotions, they tend to gravitate toward a supportive approach, feeling that a more demanding one is too harsh and would only overwhelm their child further. Men, on the other hand, are more naturally action oriented and tend to prefer a demanding approach, believing a supportive one would be too soft and more likely to make the child adopt a victim mindset.

Technically, both opinions are right, at least to a certain degree. After Kim was disqualified from her swim race, wiping away her tears, telling her she did amazing, and taking her out for ice cream would've just swept her mistake under the rug without allowing her to learn from it. At the same time, dwelling on her failure, refusing to listen to her perspective, and instructing her to get back into the pool to practice more would've just swept her feelings under the rug instead. In both cases, she would've been equally likely to quit, either to avoid failure again or out of frustration and a sense of inadequacy.

The reality is that your child needs a careful mixture of both comfort and guidance to gain the confidence to try again, because only then can they know you'll be there to help push them through their challenges and love them even in their failures. To highlight the importance of both showing loving support and demanding high standards, let's look at four different combinations of these two strategies that Duckworth covers in her book and the impact they can have on our children.

1   Neglectful parenting

Neglectful parents are neither demanding nor supportive, often too distracted by their own lives or too disinterested in the hard work of parenting to be active in their child's development. Rather than being based on God's standards, their values and responses fluctuate depending on their current desires or moods, which means rules, obligations, responsibilities, and even their relational connection with their child change from day to day, giving their child little consistency to rely on. With no one to teach, encourage, confront, or support them, the child is forced to find ways to take care of themselves, often developing unhealthy habits that stunt their emotional and relational growth as a result.

2   Authoritarian parenting

Unlike neglectful parents, authoritarian parents take an overly active role in their child's development, demanding that they live up to a standard of excellence at all times. Unfortunately, that standard is all these parents care about. Who their child is or wants to be is seen as irrelevant to their development, and any deviation from the parents' perception of excellence is unacceptable, even ones resulting from the child's own interests, strengths, or developmental pace. Additionally, these parents don't help their child break down those expectations into the smaller detailed steps needed to achieve them. Consequently, the child feels relationally disconnected and confused about their identity, even when they manage to achieve success as their parents define it.

3   Permissive parenting

Contrary to authoritarian parenting, permissive parents provide endless support and love but few standards for their child to live up to. They believe that not putting pressure on their child to perform gives them the freedom to define themselves without being constrained by expectations. But while such support may initially feel good, it actually prevents the child from building confidence and perseverance because it allows them to continually choose the easy route of quitting and facing the consequences later. Even with their parents' unconditional love, these children eventually end up looking to peers, cultural role models, or other mentors to find some standard (whether positive or negative) to ground their identity in.

4   Positive parenting

Like with authoritarian parenting, positive parenting (also called *wise* or *authoritative* parenting) provides a child with high standards and an expectation that they'll work hard to live up to those standards. However, positive parents are less interested in making the child conform to their expectations than in providing ways for them to discover and develop their potential, which enables them to live up to godly standards in their own unique way. These parents recognize their child's natural gifts and interests, and they support their child through failures and challenges to help ensure they continue pushing themselves beyond what they are currently capable of. For positive parents, their child's personal growth is more important than anything, and they'll do whatever it takes to help them reach their full, God-given potential.

. . .

God invites all of us to come to Him for rest when we are tired and heavy laden (Matthew 11:28). He also confronts us when we try to take the easy path and directs us back to His purpose (Jonah 1:1-17; 3:1-3). Life's waves will always be there to wash over your child. Your job is to both support and comfort them when they get hit and to challenge them to stand back up amid the turmoil. It's these waves that will test what your child is made of, and it's only by figuring it out that they can develop into all God created them to be.

TRUE GRIT

Part of why positive parenting is so important is that as much as your child may want to be independent, they don't yet have the experience to know what they should work toward, how to work hard to achieve it, or even when it's okay to give up. In their childhood, you act as that pillar of strength they can rely on for support and guidance when life gets a little too tough. However, you won't always be around to hold them up. For your child to learn to turn hardship, failures, and challenges into opportunities for growth even after they leave the nest, they'll have to increase their internal strength and fortify their resiliency now. In other words, they'll have to develop their grit.

Early in her career, Duckworth set out to discover why one out of five cadets dropped out of the United States Military Academy at West Point before graduation. On the surface, it didn't make sense. After all, these cadets had spent two years working hard to get into West Point, whose admissions process is arguably harder than the most selective universities. Even odder, there was no pattern to the dropouts. The highest-ranked recruits were just as likely to leave early as the lower-ranked ones.

So what was the difference? Their internal toughness, or what Duckworth calls grit. In her analysis of West Point and continued research on toughness, she discovered that in all areas of life, a person's natural skills or intelligence are largely irrelevant to their ability to achieve success. In fact, some people who don't seem to have that much natural talent or potential can actually outperform those who have measurable talent in the same area. That's because what matters most is how much passion and perseverance they have—in other words, whether or not they have a sense of direction and the determination to go after it.

If you want your child to be able to successfully navigate the ups and downs of life, you must help them develop their grit. It's this combination of passion and perseverance that will create the strong foundation they need not just to stand firm against life's waves but also to keep taking the next step up any mountain that appears in their path. When your child is driven by a broader passion, they'll be willing to pay any price to become strong in that area and achieve goals related to it. They'll actively appreciate, seek out, and employ feedback, no matter how difficult it is to hear, because they know it will make them better. They'll learn how to establish priorities and make decisions accordingly. They'll take mistakes and failures in stride, too dedicated to their life's purpose to give up. In the process, all of their actions will begin to align with an overarching standard and vision, allowing them to act consistently and become a pillar others can always rely on.

Although grit is something your child will have to develop on their own over time, there are several ways you as a father can encourage its development. First, you can teach them to value effort over talent (Proverbs 13:4). The best way to instill this message is to teach your child to have a growth mindset, as we discussed in Chapter 14. They are constantly growing and are thus able to continually achieve new goals, no matter how limited they may feel at times in their abilities. As they tackle new projects at school or face new challenges in their extracurriculars, focus not on their talents, gifts, or abilities but rather on the hard work they put in. By celebrating their efforts, you will encourage them to endure difficulties and find ways to achieve their goals, even when they're not sure how.

Another way you can help your child develop grit is by encouraging them to focus more on the process than on the end result. Many people only find success or gratification in achievement, but focusing solely on the goal only emphasizes the distance between where you are now and where you want to go, which can often lead to discouragement. The more your child learns to love the process and focus on taking one step at a time, the more they'll develop their potential, and the easier it will be to keep moving toward their goals.

Because it's such a key part of grit, you should also encourage your child to adopt a passion. In this context, passion is more than just infatuation or strong feelings. Grit requires a consistent, sustainable passion rather than an intense, momentary one. It's this type of passion that will help direct your child's goals and define their broader purpose in life. By discovering this direction, they'll always have some goal to go after, ensuring that they never become complacent and instead continually push themselves to grow in an attempt to achieve those goals.

Passion can be broken down into two different elements, the first being personal interest. As tempting as it may be to nudge your child in a certain direction, you must accept their need to develop their own interests. The more personally fulfilling a passion is, the longer it will last. And the best way for your child to discover what they really want to attach to and engage in is to test out different behaviors, choices, and activities and see which fit them best. As they develop, let them play around with anything that piques their interest, keeping an eye out for what seems to excite them most. Then encourage them to pursue it with your full support.

However, it's not enough for a passion to be personally

interesting. Perhaps the most important element of passion is purpose, or the feeling that your work matters and contributes to the welfare of others in some way. As your child begins to discover their interests, encourage them to consider how those interests are or can be connected to the well-being of others. When they're motivated by helping others, they'll always have extra fuel to keep their passion burning, even when the work gets tiring and makes them feel like quitting.

As your child discovers their passion and applies it to a purpose, they will naturally create opportunities to develop perseverance, the other main aspect of grit. This character trait can only be gained by going through the fires of life, as we discussed earlier in this chapter. When your child emerges from the other side successfully, they will have a newfound confidence in themselves along with a new set of capabilities, both of which they can use in their pursuit of future goals.

Sometimes, however, they *won't* make it through, which can cause them to fall into the trap of feeling sorry for themselves instead of trying again. The more they indulge in self-pity, the more it weakens their grit, because it supports the lie that life should be fair. In turn, your child becomes blind to what they're capable of, holding them back from achieving everything they potentially could.

While you should let your child feel their disappointment or sadness about a failure, you must also step in before they fall too low. As they process what happened, help them focus on determining what they can learn from the experience and finding better solutions for the future. By recognizing what went wrong, they can learn to make better decisions next time. And by breaking down a skill or task into smaller steps, they can avoid becoming overwhelmed by the big picture. Then they can feel ready to pick themselves up and try again, and again, and again. If they go through this process enough times, their grit will grow so strong that the next time they fail, starting over won't even be a question—they'll just do it.

GETTING IN THE FLOW

Given that grit largely comes from persevering through challenges and overcoming failure, it can be easy to think of it something that relates only to the big moments in life. However, success is actually the sum total of a lot of smaller decisions, skills, and habits, which means grit also applies to the everyday moments. In fact, the more your child develops and practices their grit in minor ways, the more equipped they'll be to employ it when they need it most.

A great way to develop your child's grit is to teach them to practice what psychologist Mihaly Csikszentmihalyi's defines as *flow*.[2] We all know the expression "time flies when you're having fun." Well, Csikszentmihalyi believes we can apply that phrase to any area of life, whether it's chores around the house, a big project at work, or even a personal hobby. When a person discovers a state of flow, they feel in the zone, energized, and completely focused on accomplishing any task set before them. Achieving such a mindset is just a matter of finding a way to enjoy one's work, which includes ignoring distractions and becoming fully engaged in an activity or task.

Learning to create flow experiences out of everyday situations will help your child develop grit for multiple reasons. For one, being so wrapped up in the moment limits self-consciousness. Your child won't have any spare energy to worry about messing up or about what others think. Instead, they'll be fully devoted to developing solutions under the pressure of the moment, which will allow them to discover and use emotions, ideas, and behaviors previously not

---

2   Mihaly Csikszentmihalyi, *Flow: The Psychology of Optimal Experience* (New York: Harper Perennial Modern Classics, 2008).

considered. These discoveries will in turn enable your child to push through their challenges or a task they don't want to do, because it's evidence that they are capable of growth and achievement. And the better they can persevere through mundane tasks, the easier it'll be to face stressful situations, where grit matters most.

Like with grit, learning to create flow experiences will ultimately be up to your child, but there are a few ways you can help foster that development. The first is to give them structure in the home. Though they may not always like it, it's actually easier for children to engage in tasks when they have clearly defined rules, boundaries, and expectations. That's because they don't have to spend extra energy figuring out how to behave, fighting for control, or worrying about the future. Instead, they can focus their whole attention on discovering their interests and taking risks that challenge them, allowing them to fully commit to their own development.

Another key way to help your child learn to get in the flow is to manage their challenges. The best flow experiences come at the midpoint between what your child can currently do and what they aren't yet able to. Challenges that are too easy for their skill level will only lead to boredom, just as challenges that are too hard will only lead to anxiety. Of course, your child may not understand that concept, so it's your responsibility to guide them to work on either increasing their skill level or increasing the challenge. By finding the right level of intensity for their goals, you can ensure their development continues without being detoured by unnecessary frustration.

Above all, the best way to increase your child's flow experiences is simply to be present yourself. By putting your own self-consciousness aside and temporarily losing yourself in the moment, you can not only better help your child grow stronger through your interactions but also increase the intimacy between you. It's a special thing when you can be so engaged in each other and your time together that you didn't even notice the time going by. Maybe later you won't even remember what you did with that time. But the lessons fostered in those moments and the skills your child learned will endure forever.

Grit, flow, passion, perseverance—no matter what you call it, the toughness you instill in your child now will carry them through the rest of their life. And as you build up your child, always remember to build up yourself too. Dads are meant to be tough, but that doesn't mean we can't continue to work on our own grit and determination. It's only by developing ourselves that we can make sure we're the solid pillar of strength our children can lean on anytime they need help with the many demands of a fulfilling, purpose-driven life.

 ROBERT'S STORY

Aside from being an amazing wife, mother, and accomplished performer, Colleen is also a highly sought-after voice instructor. Every year she loves to hold a recital concert for her students to show off their talent and growth. Naturally, her favorite pupil has become our daughter, Sophia. And those voice lessons and recitals haven't only taught Sophia how to sing. They've also led her to experience one of the most important life lessons she could ever learn.

Everyone gets nervous before they perform. The butterflies in the stomach and accompanying tense energy is simply part of the rush. For eight-year-old Sophia, however, butterflies weren't really the problem—a full bladder was. That year, as she made her way up to the stage, her mother and I could see an underlying layer of distress, and we knew exactly what that look meant. If you've been a dad for a while, you know what look I'm referring to. She only made it two lines in before she stopped, looked down, and rushed offstage. She ran straight to the bathroom and did what I believe came naturally.

When she finally emerged again, she looked mortified. She told us there was no way she would ever go back out there again. I knew this was the perfect moment for a great speech, but I was at a loss. Truthfully, I probably would have felt the same way. For an artist, that feeling of embarrassment can cut deeper than anything else.

But I knew I needed to say something, so riding on pure, God-given instinct, I looked at Sophia and said, "Yes, it was embarrassing. But it doesn't have to be the way you remember this day." Colleen chimed in and reminded her of how hard she had worked to memorize these songs and sing them correctly. With beautiful wisdom she asked Sophia, "Don't you think you deserve to sing your songs? The audience is there. And they want to hear you."

As Sophia stood there contemplating her choice, I leaned in and told her that she was in control of how this story ended, and that no matter what, we loved her. Like a true warrior, this little eight-year-old found the courage to rewrite her ending. She climbed back onto the stage and sang her heart out. With her final note, the audience leaped to their feet and gifted her with a roaring applause. That day, she discovered exactly how tough she is and the great inner strength that can come from failure.

💬 DISCUSSION QUESTIONS

1   Of the four types of parenting, which one best describes your current style? How can you work on finding a balance between a supportive and demanding approach? How would such a balance help your child develop their internal toughness?

2   Describe a present challenge you're facing in life. What motivates you to keep going? How can the concept of grit help you and your child persevere through any challenge?

3   In what areas of life are you most able to lose yourself in flow? How easy or difficult is it for you to create flow experiences for your child? What can you do to engage more fully with them?

4   Discuss how Deuteronomy 1:29-31 relates to grit. How can we rely on God as a source of strength when we feel like giving up?

Then I said to you, "Don't be terrified. Don't be afraid of them. The LORD your God will go ahead of you. He will fight for you. With your own eyes you saw how he fought for you in Egypt. You also saw how the LORD your God brought you through the desert. He carried you everywhere you went, just as a father carries his son. And now you have arrived here."

26

A FATHER CORRECTS

When Nick was five, I conducted a little experiment with him. I knew that some children can have a natural fear of bodies of water, and given that we had a large pond on our property, I felt it was important to know if Nick had that same response, especially since, with his autism, he couldn't make normal judgments and wouldn't be able to learn how to swim. If he was afraid of it, I wouldn't need to be as worried about him entering the pond on his own. But if he wasn't, we'd have to be extra vigilant to keep him away from it.

So one day I took Nick down to the pond with Kim, who was eight, and we watched as he walked right into the water with no hesitation. I quickly pulled him back, satisfied that I had my answer. I now knew just how dangerous the pond was to Nick. And if he ever disappeared outside or walked away, I knew to check the pond first and then work my way back over our property from there.

Well, to my surprise, the next day Kim walked into the house with Nick close behind, once again soaking wet. I asked Kim what had happened, and she explained that she had simply taken Nick down to the pond to redo the experiment. Why? To make sure our results from the day before were still accurate!

To be frank, I was a little puzzled about what to do. Should I scold and punish her, or should I simply tell her not to do it again? After all, though she had done something potentially very dangerous, she hadn't actually known she was doing anything wrong.

If you're anything like me, you've probably run into this same conflict at some point in your parenting career. Discipline is essential to fatherhood, but the best approach to take or punishment to assign isn't always obvious. In this chapter, we'll unpack what discipline really means and some basic principles that can help you respond effectively to your child's misbehavior. By knowing how to apply the right discipline, you'll teach them to recognize their mistakes, learn from them, and make the better choice next time.

THEIR WARNING LIGHT

Remember back in Chapter 13 when we talked about our sin nature and how it affects us and our children? Well, that sin nature is what pushes us into making bad choices, even as a little voice in the back of our heads warns us of the danger. We come across a snake in the woods and have the urge to poke it with a stick. We see a "Wet Paint" sign on a door and have to touch it to be sure. We tell a little lie because we believe no one will know. We just can't seem to help it. We're aware of the potential consequences, and yet we have a strange desire to see if we can get away with it this time.

Unfortunately, our children are even greater gamblers than we are, because unlike us, they don't have the experience or wisdom to truly know better. It's why they run out into the street without considering the cars and put off their homework until they miss their deadline. Because the judgment centers of their brains are not fully matured, they often don't recognize the potential consequences of their actions. And even when they do, they naively believe it won't happen to them.

Luckily, that's what you're there for. As a father, it's your job to act as a warning light for your child to keep them from straying away from the path God created for them. And when they do slip up and take a wrong turn, it's your job to point them back in the right direction (Revelation 3:19). For many parents, that's where punishment comes in. After all, the main goal of punishment is to teach the child that certain behaviors are unacceptable and not to engage in them, right?

Well, not exactly. We tend to think of punishment as pretty straightforward. If your child does something wrong, you take away their toys or send them to their room to teach them a lesson. The problem is, a punishment by itself doesn't always teach the *right* lesson. Your child may make poor decisions for a multitude of reasons, from pure animosity to simple ignorance. To truly make them aware of their mistake and keep them from doing it again, you have to respond in a way that addresses the root of the issue.

That's why many punishments are ultimately ineffective. They either don't relate to the crime or are applied without a purpose, like when a parent simply states that what the child did was wrong, takes away something they like as retribution, and instructs them not to do it again. Such an approach fails to engage the child's brain that thinks to help them see for themselves why their decision was wrong. If you continually punish your child in this way, all they'll internalize is that certain negative behaviors will get them in trouble, not that they shouldn't do them. So while they might obey you in the moment, and even for a little while after, eventually they'll go right back to doing what they want when you aren't around to catch them.

If you want to make lasting change to your child's behaviors, you have to respond in ways that get them to start to think for themselves. And to do that, you must be deliberate about engaging in *discipline*, not punishment. Discipline is the practice of using consequences, instructions, and exercises to train and develop your child in their moral character and behaviors. It requires holding back an immediate reaction and evaluating the context of a situation, your child's perspective and motivations, and any other relevant factors. Then you can use that information to decide on the response that will best help your child internalize the lesson so they'll be equipped to make better choices in the future (Proverbs 29:15).

Proper discipline removes the mentality that you always have to punish your child, which is an approach that can harm your relationship with them. Instead, it allows you to respond based on your child's stage of development, what they did, and why they did it, like with the story about Kim and the Nick experiment.

There were a few key factors that helped me determine that a punishment wasn't the best course of action for Kim. First, I knew I hadn't fully explained the context behind why I was testing Nick's fear of water—that he could get very, very hurt if he went near our pond without supervision—and in her youthful innocence and inexperience, she hadn't connected the dots herself. Second, she honestly thought she was helping me by verifying my experiment. And finally, I hadn't explicitly told her to keep Nick away from the pond after finding out he wasn't afraid of it.

Given all of this, a discipline such as a time-out or a harsh scolding likely would've felt unfair and confusing to Kim, which could've led to an emotional outburst later. Instead, I simply told her I appreciated her thoughtfulness but that she should never bring Nick around water again without an adult because it was unsafe for him.

Now, had Kim had different motivations, my response would've been much different. For example, if she'd repeated the experiment as a way of getting my attention or to be mean to Nick, I would've responded much more severely and certainly would've provided a more serious consequence. But given the actual circumstances, a simple explanation and instruction was all that was needed, and it was never a problem again.

In the same way, any time your child acts out or makes a poor decision, you should avoid jumping right to punishment and instead take a deeper look at the situation first. All behaviors are a message, which means emotional outbursts, misbehavior, and self-destructive choices can actually be signs of another issue your child is struggling with or an area of development that needs more attention. For example, an older sibling who feels ignored in preference of a new baby may start throwing tantrums just to get their parents' attention. Or a child who keeps getting into fights at school might be using their aggression to cover up underlying insecurities that require more deliberate guidance from you.

If you come across a deeper issue like this, you must find a way to address it directly before it grows any bigger. Discipline the behavior as needed, but make sure to do so in a way that also connects with your child emotionally. The preservation of your relationship with your child is more important than any lesson. If you let your discipline get in the way of that, your child may start choosing to hide pieces of their life from you, which will only harm them further. Instead, make maintaining open communication your highest priority. The more aware you are of what's going on their life, the more effectively you can discipline them in a way that helps them work through the true issue they're struggling with.

CREATING CONSEQUENCES

Once you have a good understanding of the reasons behind your child's transgression, you can begin to determine what type of response will best hold them accountable to godly principles and standards and teach them better ways to behave. The most common response is, of course, deliberate discipline, or what I prefer to describe as finding the right type of consequence.

As we discussed in Chapter 13, providing consequences for your child's actions, especially ones that don't naturally have noticeable consequences, can help them see the implications of their negative behaviors and learn to control their sinful impulses. The earlier they internalize these lessons, the less likely those impulses will be to lead them into behaviors with harsher consequences, such as losing a friend, getting fired from a job, or even falling into an addiction.

Depending on the age of your child and their mistake or negative choice, a consequence such as the loss of TV privileges or cleaning up their mess might be enough to correct their behavior. Often, however, a consequence must also be combined with a good question, a time of quiet reflection, a discussion, an instruction, or a task in order to help them actively develop replacement behaviors, which will prevent them from making the same negative choices in the future.

For instance, a teenager who crashes the family car could be both grounded and required to take further driving lessons, or a preschooler who fights a classmate over a toy could be both not allowed to keep that toy and required to apologize. These extra tasks aren't additional punishment, though it may feel that way to your child. Rather, they're about helping them develop the social skills and emotional IQ that will better ensure they don't repeat the same mistake twice or hurt someone else in the future.

As important as it is to pick the right response, that response won't be effective if you don't communicate it well to your child. After all, how can you expect them to learn and grow if they don't even understand what they're experiencing? Whether the misbehavior was a violation of a previously established rule or standard, a violation of an issue not explicitly discussed, or an inadvertent mistake, you must discuss what they did wrong, why you have to discipline them, and how you expect them to behave going forward. By increasing their understanding in this way, you can influence their thought processes so that the next time they're faced with a similar choice, their internal dialogue will point them in a different direction.

Sometimes your child will be receptive to such a discussion, and other times it will feel like you're talking to a brick wall. Especially as they get older, they may be reluctant to admit they were wrong, closing themselves off to hearing your message. In those cases, you'll have to use some creativity to find a way to engage your child and help them understand the lesson, such as through using a parable or analogy as an example or sharing a personal story. Even if they still refuse to open up to you, have them at least repeat back the purpose of their discipline. That way you can be assured that they at least recognize that purpose, which will make it more likely that they follow through on it.

One way to make this communication easier is to preemptively discuss key principles and values and the consequences you'll give for violating them. By learning how to differentiate between positive and negative choices, your child can understand ahead of time what types of decisions will not be tolerated and what will happen if they do choose to make them. This knowledge will give them an internal structure that will help them make good decisions. They'll also know what discipline to expect when they don't, making it more likely they'll understand and accept it (though they still won't necessarily like it).

When you think about it, discipline isn't really all that different from the other aspects of fatherhood we've already talked about. At its core, it's about helping your child develop themselves into all God created them to be—it's just a less desirable way of doing so. But no matter how frustrating or tiring the process may be, you must continue to discipline your child. It tells them that you care, since being passive ignores their ultimate welfare. It also shows them that you believe they're capable of doing what's right. And it's only by being held accountable for their negative behaviors, experiencing the implications of their choices, and learning a better way to behave that they can find their way back to the path they've stumbled off of (Hebrews 12:11).

A MORE EFFECTIVE CONSEQUENCE

Now that we've covered the broader principles of discipline, we can touch on some specific types of discipline. However, I'm not going to go too deep into the details of exactly which types of consequences to use when. After all, most consequences aren't simply "good" or "bad," nor are certain ones always effective or always ineffective. For now, I'm just going to cover one common one that I think is necessary to address—physical punishment.

Physical punishment is one type of discipline that I'm willing to go out on a limb to state does not usually work, at least not at the level of change we would desire. Now, I know that's a pretty controversial statement. Some of you may already be agreeing with me, while others are ready to argue their opposing perspective. I'm not here to pass judgment, and in fact, I'm not even going to discuss the issue from a moral angle because I don't feel it's relevant to this conversation.

Instead, I'm going to unpack the practical reasons why physical punishment is typically harmful and ineffective, even though it might make your child change their behavior in the moment.[1] As you read over these reasons, try to focus on thinking through the concepts described, not on what you've done or what has happened to you. The goal of this section is not to judge the past or create shame. Rather, it's simply to understand the impact of physical punishment so you can make more informed choices about how to discipline your child going forward.

First of all, despite its intention of curbing a child's misbehavior, physical punishment is often less about the child's development and more about the father's authority. When a father is frustrated about his child's misbehavior or disobedience, physically controlling them can feel like it affirms his significance and

---

1   Eve Glicksman, "Physical Discipline Is harmful and Ineffective," *American Psychological Association* 50, no. 5 (May 2019): 22, https://www.apa.org/monitor/2019/05/physical-discipline.

leadership. It can also just feel good to emotionally release his aggression in this way.

However, a father who's developed himself internally and learned to manage his emotions doesn't need this type of affirmation (Proverbs 29:11). In fact, he would actually feel bad if he were to hit the child he loves and guides. He understands that discipline is about teaching them to submit their will to what's right, not about controlling them through the use of physical pain. He can instead focus on his child's welfare and create consequences that will help them grow out of their misbehavior.

Physical punishment can also hurt your relationship with your child in several ways. For one, effective discipline takes time, and a father whose main tool of correction is a quick smack on the butt demonstrates an unwillingness to do the hard work of connecting with his child and helping them work through their issues. And for fathers who have so few daily interactions with their child to begin with, such a harsh discipline can create within their child intense negative feelings toward them, needlessly limiting what the relationship can become.

Another reason not to use physical punishment is that controlling your child's body can send them negative messages. As we talked about in Chapter 20, it's important to teach our children how to protect themselves in the physical realm, which includes setting boundaries to protect their physical comfort and autonomy. But how can we expect that lesson to sink in if we violate those boundaries ourselves through physical punishment? Children learn more through actions than through words, which means if physical punishment is your primary form of discipline, all they'll internalize is that boundaries are fragile and your word can't be trusted, no matter how much you try to teach them otherwise.

Besides breaking their boundaries, physical punishment can also create unintended physical reflexes in your child. You can see this in dogs that have experienced repeated physical punishments.

They flinch at the sound of a raised voice or cower whenever their owner lifts their hands. Such reflexes often become ingrained at a biological level, which limits your child's openness not just to learning from you but also to being vulnerable in other future relationships.

Most importantly, physical punishment simply doesn't help curb misbehavior long term. Spanking your child (or threatening to) may seem to solve the problem because it does get them to stop acting out in the moment. But the truth is that it doesn't eradicate this form of negative expression—it just causes them to hide it. The next time your child feels frustrated or disappointed, they'll just act out in a manner that's less noticeable. They may even decide that the potential of a brief physical consequence is worth it, because at least it's over quickly.

The main reason why physical punishment is only a short-term solution is because it does nothing to help our children understand or manage what's going on inside of them. In fact, the stimulation it provides actually competes with their ability to calm themselves down, understand what choices got them in trouble, and find a better way to cope with their emotions. As we discussed in Chapter 22, God gave each of us an amygdala, the part of our brain that helps us identify and manage threats to our well-being. Unfortunately, even when there's no real threat and we're simply experiencing discomfort or disappointment, our amygdala can make us feel like we're in danger, causing us to react inappropriately and even harm ourselves or others. That's why a toddler can misinterpret being denied a treat in a grocery store as a catastrophic event, leading them to throw themselves on the floor in a fit of rage.

Handling such an outburst by spanking your child or manually making them do what you want will actually further trigger their amygdala, because now they believe they're in physical danger. This belief immediately shuts down any ability they had to think about the situation rationally. Scared people simply do not have the ability to learn or process anything at a deeper level. Even once the physical punishment is over and the fear of danger has passed, your child will likely feel dominated and repressed, keeping them from being cognitively and emotionally available for any productive conversation about the situation.

A child's anger about their punishment can also override their ability to feel responsible for what they did, which means they won't feel true guilt about making a similar choice again. This is especially true after the physical punishment is over, as they can feel like they've already paid for their bad choice and thus don't have to atone for it anymore. As a result, they don't see a need to take ownership of the emotional struggle or negative thinking process that led to their decision, making it more likely that a similar experience will lead them toward even more bad choices in the future.

The best way to calm your child down in these heated moments and truly prevent this type of acting out in the future is to discipline them in a way that teaches them to regulate their emotional responses (Galatians 6:1). Consequences such as time-outs and revoked privileges allow you to engage your child at a deeper level because they directly address the situation at hand. Additionally, while a physical punishment is over quickly, these consequences give your child more time to settle down and experience the implications of their negative choices, which forces them to confront themselves about what they did and why they did it.

Initiating this kind of introspection will also make your child more likely to be present during your follow-up conversations. Because they've already acknowledged to themselves what they did wrong and what they were feeling—even if that acknowledgement is reluctant or ultimately denied—you can jump right into a discussion without having to waste time reminding them of what happened. Instead, you can focus on helping them break down their motivations and feelings and put words to them. The more you can help your child strengthen this internal dialogue, the better they'll be able to think through decisions when the same negative opportunity arises again.

During these conversations, it can be useful to relate their choices to biblical concepts, such as why they shouldn't violate God's expectations with their actions. However, be careful about the language you use. Rather than simply telling your child not to do something because God doesn't want them to, remind them of how much God loves and values them. In most cases, presenting God and His Word as a guiding resource is more productive than giving your child rules He wants us to follow. After all, God has always chosen relationships over rules, and His desire to have Jesus sacrifice Himself is evidence of that (2 Corinthians 5:19). As long as your child knows they can always rely on Him, they will repeatedly seek His empowerment to make the right choices, even in times of uncertainty and turmoil.

As you continually work to find the most effective methods for disciplining your child, you may come across times when physical discipline *is* actually the only option. When a situation has escalated so far or your child's self-destructive choices have become so dangerous, you'll have to make an abrupt change to your usual way of disciplining. That's why I haven't said you should totally remove physical discipline from the table. However, it should only be used in a controlled manner when there is no other positive alternative—and it should never be the only way you discipline your child.

I spanked Kim only three times in her whole life, and all three occurred during different car rides where she was already mad at me about something trivial. She was at an age where she no longer needed a car seat, which meant she could easily reach the door handle, and in her anger, she threatened and even began to open the door while I was still driving. Each time, I pulled over and gave her two swift but fairly gentle swats on her backside. The spankings caused indignation and a bucket of tears, but it allowed us to proceed home safely.

When we got home, I made sure to tell Kim that I didn't like spanking her but had to in order to protect her safety. Then I said I would have to do it again if she couldn't better control her actions. Those conversations opened the door for me to encourage her to strengthen her emotional regulation, which is ultimately what any discipline comes down to—helping our children continue to grow. Engaging them on an emotional and mental level will shake them free from their negative behavior in a way a physical punishment simply can't. Look at it this way. I think we'd all prefer God to give us some wise consequences instead of a spanking. So why should we do anything else for our children?

DON'T REMIND ME

Deciding on the right consequences isn't easy no matter the situation, but it can be especially tricky when your child doesn't seem to be doing a task they need to complete, whether it's homework, a chore, or even a favor for a friend. Part of doing any job is taking on the responsibility of remembering to do it and intentionally following through, but that's not often a skill that comes naturally, particularly when the task at hand is boring or just not fun. The question is, how can you teach your child that sense of responsibility? And how can you use discipline to do so?

Well, I can tell you what almost never works—reminding your child of what needs to be accomplished. It's often tempting to needle your child about a task, especially when they currently seem to be do nothing. But in these moments, pointing out chores they still need to do will only annoy them and potentially offend them. Though it's probably not your intent, your reminder can subtly imply to your child that they aren't adequate or mature enough to handle the task on their own.

And how does a child react when they're frustrated with their father? Well, usually by snapping back at him. They may get defensive and claim they were just about to do their chores, or they may look for a way to make him frustrated too, often by not doing the task or by doing it poorly. But that just shows the father that he was right to remind them, creating a cycle that ultimately leads the two of them nowhere.

The best way to break the cycle and prevent yourself from nagging your child is to lay out clear expectations from the beginning. As we discussed with S.M.A.R.T. goals in Chapter 21, when you give your child any task, you must explicitly state what needs to happen, the standard for how it should be done, the deadline it should be done by, and what consequences they'll receive if they fail to meet either the standard or the deadline. By being thorough in explaining the assignment, you can be confident that your child fully understands what's expected of them, which in turn eliminates your need to continually remind them of it.

Of course, knowing you don't need to remind them and sticking to not doing so are two different things. We often think we're helping our children by reminding them of their responsibilities, but we're really harming their ability to manage their own tasks and, in turn, to become more responsible themselves. I often recommend to clients struggling with this particular issue to give their child a dollar each time they remind them to do the job before the predetermined deadline. The idea is that paying the dollar will trigger the parent to remember they shouldn't be reminding their child, which over time will get them to stop (though some parents were such slow learners I thought they might have to take out a second mortgage).

Interestingly enough, I've found that this strategy can help the child too. You might think it would simply make the child procrastinate further, hoping to gain more dollars in the process. However, I've heard that in many cases when the parent slipped up, their child told them they didn't want the dollar. They knew that if the parent were to pay the dollar, they would undoubtedly follow through on the consequences if the child didn't meet the deadline. It made the child more determined to prove themselves, leading them to work extra hard to make sure they completed the task long before any consequences would come.

Now, let's say the deadline comes around and you've successfully resisted reminding your child at all (or maybe you've given up a couple dollars along the way). If they still haven't completed the task, at that point you must follow through on the consequences you outlined for them when assigning it. While there are several different consequences you can use, there's one I've found to be most effective—positive practice.

The concept is as simple as it sounds. Instead of taking away your child's phone or grounding them for a week, have them practice for a certain amount of time or repetitions whatever task they failed to complete. For example, if they fail to take out the trash on time, instruct your child to walk around the house with an empty bag, pretend to empty all the trash cans into it, carry the "trash" out to the garbage can, and take the garbage can to the curb. Then have them turn around and start all over again, and again, and again.

There are multiple reasons why positive practice is an effective tool for discipline. For one, repeatedly doing the same task teaches your child self-control and helps them internalize the standard they're expected to reach. But more importantly, it forces them to do the same task they tried to avoid in the first place. What better way to get them to overcome their desire not do it once than by making them do it five times in a row? Your child may not like it, but they'll understand that it's the result of their choice to disobey. Even as they grumble, they'll be focused on developing the new behavior, just so they don't ever have to face this consequence again.

Positive practice can also be useful with other types of misbehavior. If your child throws a toy out of anger or runs around the pool when they know they're not supposed to, have them stop, go back, and repeat the proper behavior. Not only will this approach help them begin to build better habits, but it will also encourage them to be more mindful about their behavior in the future. I once had Kim practice closing her bedroom door without slamming it twenty-five times in a row. Well, it was actually more, because I didn't count the attempts where the door wasn't completely latched before she opened it again. It was not a fun afternoon for either of us, but she had much less trouble not slamming doors after that (Proverbs 29:17).

Discipline can be a long and tiring process. It requires time and commitment, something many parents are reluctant to give, either because they can't discipline themselves or because they can't stand to see their children so upset. But investing in your child's growth in the short run wastes a lot less time than discussing and providing the same consequences year after year (Proverbs 23:13). Your child can either learn important lessons through your loving discipline, which will feel like a squirt gun hitting them in the chest, or they can learn through harsh worldly consequences, which will feel like an atom bomb erupting beside them. I think it's pretty obvious which option is more effective and loving.

 ROBERT'S STORY

"You betrayed my trust." These are the deepest, most emotionally slaying words I've ever heard my dad say to me. To this day I can choke up just thinking about it.

When I went away to college, my dad made an agreement with me. As long as I studied well and went to all my classes, he would write me a check each month to cover my normal living expenses. I knew many people didn't have that luxury, so I was initially very grateful.

However, I didn't think about how much I'd miss my high-school sweetheart, Colleen, who I'd be leaving behind to go off to college. She and I had been in a relationship for close to a year at that time, and I was very much in love. I'd fully intended to go to school, stay in school, and study. But tasting the new freedom of independence, and armed with a credit card covered by my dad, I couldn't resist taking secret trips back to my hometown to see my girlfriend, which required money for gas, tolls, and dates—none of which my dad knew he was paying for.

Unfortunately, on one of those secret trips, my father saw Colleen and me driving down the street, though I didn't realize it at the time. How he didn't lose his cool, I'll never know. He did, however, call my dorm and leave a message: "Son, I'd like you to come home next weekend. We miss you, and we'd like to see you if possible." When I got back to school a couple days later and heard the message, I called him back, made up an excuse for not calling right away, and promised to come down.

Upon arriving home the following weekend, my dad sat me down in his living room. He asked how I was doing and how school was going. I responded with acceptable answers. Then, without missing a beat, he asked how long I'd been spending money on secret trips to see my girlfriend. I was in shock—complete, blindsided shock. I couldn't think of anything to say.

That's when he looked me straight in the eye and uttered those heart-wrenching words: "You betrayed my trust." Then he handed me a check and said, "This will cover your credit card. I am keeping my end of our agreement, and I will continue to do so."

Holding that check in my hands, I felt like Judas holding a bag of silver. I was so guilt-stricken that I began to cry. Seeing this, my dad got up and sat next to me. He put his arm around me and said,

"Son, sometimes we disappoint the people we love. Sometimes we fail them. But as long as God forgives, I will too. I must. Someday you'll have to as well. I love you. Just don't lie to me again."

That experience completely changed the course of my thoughts, judgments, and behaviors. My dad exposed me, condemned my actions, and yet never threatened our relationship or his love for me. My dad could not have been more like Jesus in my life at that time. And that is the lesson I want to always be ready to give my girls. I want to be quick to condemn wrong actions, but even quicker to lay a bed of love in the process.

💬 DISCUSSION QUESTIONS

1   Discuss how your parents disciplined you. How helpful or unhelpful was their style in preparing you for life? What can you change in your own parenting style to become a better disciplinarian for your child?

2   Name some mental, physical, emotional, or relational choices your child could make that would require discipline. How could you respond well to these specific scenarios? How might you discuss the situation with your child to help them see for themselves why what they did was wrong?

3   How do you feel about the use of physical punishment? Think of a scenario where you might want to engage in physical discipline. How might an emotional or thought-provoking intervention better help your child learn and grow?

4   Discuss what Proverbs 13:24 says about the importance of discipline. What are some of the long-term benefits of confronting your child's negative behaviors while they're still young?

> *Those who don't correct their children hate them.*
>   *But those who love them are careful to correct them.*

27

A FATHER PROVIDES

One of the simplest truths about life is that in order for it to continue, it needs to be sustained. Whether it's a single-cell organism or one as complex as ourselves, in the deepest seas, hottest deserts, or highest mountains, all living creatures have basic requirements for survival. Some are simple and straightforward, such as how plants need soil, sun, and water. Others are just bizarre, such as how baby koalas need to eat their mothers' poop to get essential nutrients. But in both cases, meeting the need is absolutely vital. Otherwise, life would simply end.

For your child, especially when they're young, their needs are primarily met by you and their mother (Matthew 7:9-11). I've frequently referenced the dependence and reliance your child has on you, from the imprinting instinct that prompts them to follow your every move to the simple survival mechanism that causes a baby to smile and coo in order to bond with their caretaker. However, there is such a thing as too much of a good thing, especially when it comes to taking care of our children. As they grow and mature, their dependence on us should naturally decrease as their personal responsibility increases. And even when they're still small and relatively helpless, there's a fine line between providing for our children and spoiling them.

If you want to give your child the best chance of success, you must find the balance between taking care of them and teaching them to care for themselves. In an age where abuse is way too common and some parents limit their child's development by doing everything for them, we need godly wisdom to know the difference. In this chapter, we'll discuss what this approach looks like in fatherhood and then break down some of the core needs you must help your child meet. The better you address each of these needs, the more equipped your child will be to one day survive on their own in an often cold and unhelpful world.

A FATHER FULFILLS

Just as your child was born to rely on you, there's also an innate part of you that makes you want to give them everything they need and more. And while that fatherly desire helps motivate us to work hard to put food on the table or take time to toss a softball in the backyard, it can also cause us to take things a little too far. If we truly want to care for our children, we can't just fulfill their every request. Instead, we must focus on both understanding and helping them understand the difference between a true need and a want.

Unfortunately, our materialistic culture actively blurs this line, doing its best to make us feel like every trivial, worldly pleasure is essential to our survival or life satisfaction. Companies create ads that attempt to convince us that we absolutely need a certain product to be cool, attractive, or powerful, when in reality we'd be just fine without it. As a result, it can be all too easy to develop misplaced values that distort both what we feel we need in our own lives and also what we feel required to give to our children.

When it comes to fathering, this distortion only increases when we feel that our own childhood was lacking, something you may have uncovered when you assessed your father's influence back in Chapter 9. Not having the clothes other kids had, never experiencing a family vacation, or missing out on an educational opportunity are all losses that can cause real trauma that lasts well into adulthood. From that pain, we often develop a strong determination that no matter what, we will never let our children experience that same kind of disastrous letdown.

Sometimes this conviction can lead us to improve on our parents' approach in positive ways, either by building a stronger relationship with our children or by creating a healthier home environment. But more often, we focus too intently on the concrete details of our childhood disappointments, leading us to put all of our effort into providing our children with the trendiest clothes or the newest toys so they never have to feel the disappointment or discomfort we did.

As tempting as it can be to overindulge our children to ensure their contentment and comfort, I'm sure you can see how doing so can actually cause more damage in the long run. For one, satisfying their every whim and desire can warp their perspective on life. A spoiled child will never truly be satisfied, because they believe they're so special that everyone and everything will go out of their way to please them. The problem is, that's simply not reality. As they grow up and their responsibilities naturally increase, some of their desires will inevitably be denied. And when they've never had to face disappointment or go without, they won't know how to handle it in an effective or healthy way.

Spoiling your child can also demotivate them to put in the effort required for development. As a chick's lungs become stronger as a result of fighting through its shell, your child must also face a certain amount of struggle to develop their capabilities. It's only by being tested through challenge and adversity that they can learn where they need to grow and then push themselves to do so. But when all of their needs and desires are met fully and instantly by their parents, any effort on their part simply isn't necessary. As a result, they fail to recognize how they need to change and develop, leading them into a life of passivity, boredom, and stagnation.

To prevent your child from such a future, you must learn to identify when *not* providing for them might be the most beneficial approach. That's not to say you should deny them every request that isn't an obvious necessity. Wants that are excessively expensive, unhealthy, or distracting should receive a firm no, but others can simply be given conditional terms. Let your child have ice cream for dessert as long as they finish their vegetables. Give them permission to get that new video game as long as they save up the money for it themselves. Grant their request to buy them a car, but only once they get their first job. This way, your child gets what they want, but they also learn the important lesson that good things don't come easy—they'll have to make plans, delay gratification, and expend effort in order to earn them.

This approach will also help you gradually shift the responsibility for meeting your child's needs from you to them. When they're little, they'll rely on you to fulfill all of their needs from the physical, like food and shelter, to the emotional, like love and understanding. Not only will this help them survive, but it will also prevent them from being overwhelmed. Due to their lack of development, many children actually become scared when they're allowed to make more decisions than they're ready for. For their own sake, you should not give your child the power of choice beyond their ability to handle it, at least not while they're still young.

But part of growing up requires eventually learning to meet their needs for themselves so they can continue to survive once they're on their own. As they develop, encourage them to tune in to those needs and identify the steps required to meet them, and work with them to achieve those steps until they're able to do so themselves. Additionally, encourage them to create their own support network outside of you and their mother so they can continue to receive guidance and love even after they leave the nest.

God doesn't intend for our children to get everything they desire but rather to learn to be content with what they have

(1 Timothy 6:6-8). The better they can appreciate life when they have less, the easier it will be to find contentment no matter their circumstances. One way to help them do this is by telling them about or letting them experience other undeveloped societies that are surviving with much less than what we have. This will allow them to appreciate even the smallest blessings they have to enjoy.

Such a mindset will help you too. Instead of condemning yourself for not being able to give your child everything you think they should have, focus on what you *can* give. After all, the most important thing your child needs is simple and always accessible— you. Their secure attachment to a father who unconditionally loves and supports them is what will ultimately determine their ability to adjust to any disappointment or struggle they face.

GETTING TO THE CORE

Given how many frivolous distractions there are in the world, it can be easy to lose sight of what really matters, especially when it comes to differentiating between our wants and our needs. In this section, we'll look at a list of core needs all fathers should help their children meet through both providing for them and teaching them how to meet those needs themselves. You may notice that many of these needs reflect topics we've already covered in different ways in this book, which just shows how integrated they are into so many other life realms, further highlighting their vital importance to living a satisfying, God-directed life.

Learning to identify and fulfill these fundamental needs will not just help your child survive but will also equip them to develop their potential, enjoy life more fully, enhance their relationships, and truly achieve all God has in store for them. And it can do the same for you. As you read through the list, take a deeper look into how they're integrated into your own life (remember, you can't give what you don't have). Think back over your childhood and reconcile any hurt you have about what needs you feel your parents failed to meet. Evaluate your priorities and how well they align with the needs listed here, using the Bible verses to understand what God desires of and for us. When you understand your own past and present in this way, you'll be able to identify what changes you can make to more effectively care for both yourself and your child far into the future.

1   Physical care

No, I train my body and bring it under control. Then after I have preached to others, I myself will not break the rules. If I did break them, I would fail to win the prize. (1 Corinthians 9:27)

Just as your body is a vital aspect of your manhood identity (Chapter 17), physical care is also one of the most important needs we must meet for our children. At the most basic level, this includes providing food, clothing, clean water, and a safe shelter. However, that's only the beginning of meeting your child's physical needs. You should also create a good relationship with a pediatrician or family doctor and consistently follow up on their medical care. That includes prioritizing dental care by making regular visits to the dentist and enforcing good brushing and flossing habits.

Part of why taking care of your child's health is so important is because their brain development is directly impacted by physical factors like how much sleep they get and how well they eat. Without the right amount of nutrients and rest, they'll become less alert, less able to focus, and less likely to remember any lessons they learn. In addition, other external stimulants, such as TV, smartphones, and video games, can impact the structure of your child's brain and hinder their ability to focus, learn, or even read the emotions of others.[1] So if you notice your child struggling mentally or emotionally, take a look at their physical habits. The solution might be simpler than it seems.

2   Safety

Here is what I am commanding you to do. Be strong and brave. Do not be afraid. Do not lose hope. I am the LORD your God. I will be with you everywhere you go. (Joshua 1:9)

As we discussed in Chapter 24, the world is full of domination, abuse, and violence, and our children need us to help protect them from and guide them through many of those challenges. In the physical realm, this requires taking preventative measures like watching for when they walk off in a crowded location or warning them about trusting strangers. And in the mental and emotional realms, it requires consciously challenging any ideas that contradict God's messages, such as limiting TV shows and commercials that overstimulate or emotionally manipulate children. Besides teaching them negative messages, these shows also make it difficult for your child to slow down, think through decisions, and understand what really matters.

Your child will also need to learn to protect themselves, which means you should teach them to have a healthy skepticism about everything they hear. Discuss with them how to discern between unhealthy risks and those that are necessary to achieve growth. Above all, do your best to foster your child's self-confidence. When they can trust in themselves through God, they'll be able to stand firm in the face of any challenge or threat.

---

1   Stephanie Pappas, "What Do We Really Know about Kids and Screens?" *American Psychological Association* 51, no. 3 (April 2020): 42, https://www.apa.org/monitor/2020/04/cover-kids-screens.

3   Security

Our troubles are small. They last only for a short time. But they are earning for us a glory that will last forever. It is greater than all our troubles. (2 Corinthians 4:17)

While safety needs focus on protecting our welfare in the present, security needs look more into the future. Your child wants to feel that they are well-prepared for the next stages of life, whether that's starting school or beginning their career. Unfortunately, because they have so little experience, it can be easy for them to become overwhelmed with worry about what the future will hold. To combat their anxiety, talk them through what they can expect in various future situations and help them create a plan for navigating any potential challenges.

At the same time, you must recognize that life is often unpredictable, and there's only so much we can plan for. Part of establishing security for your child is helping them develop all of their capabilities and adopt an optimistic mindset. The more confidence they have in their ability to manage life's difficulties, the more successful they'll be in actually doing so. With God's empowerment and your unwavering love and support, they can feel secure no matter what the future holds.

4   Certainty

That's because I know who I have believed in. I am sure he is able to take care of what I have given him. I can trust him with it until the day he returns as judge. (2 Timothy 1:12)

Just as we want to feel secure in the present and confident about our future, we all want to feel certain we can handle any challenge that comes our way. But our certainty can take a blow when we encounter a situation we can't comprehend or don't feel we have the resources to adapt to. This is especially true of our children who, in their desire for certainty, can become enslaved by the world's false and short-lived versions of certainty, such as popularity, pleasure, and personal power (Matthew 4:1-11). These avenues can make them feel good for a little while, but they ultimately only amplify their dissatisfaction.

The best way to combat these negative outlets and truly feel certain in life is to have a well-developed identity founded on godly principles. When your child focuses on growing in this way, they can establish the structure necessary to think wisely and make the right choices. Focus on helping them grow internally, teaching them to set goals they can follow through on, and encouraging them to submit to God. After all, only His omnipotence, love, and plan for them can provide the certainty they crave.

5   Relationships

So encourage one another with the hope you have. Build each other up. In fact, that's what you are doing. (1 Thessalonians 5:11)

As we established in Chapter 23, there is nothing more important than our relationships with God and with others. When your child has a strong and supportive community, they'll experience some of the safety, security, and certainty they need, because they'll be surrounded by people they can rely on. Such a community also provides an opportunity for them to use their gifts and contribute to the welfare of others, which will in turn allow them to grow and develop their capabilities, especially when they receive feedback along the way.

Part of helping your child fulfill their need for relationships will require teaching them the L.A.R.G.E. C.A.R.E. skills and other social skills discussed in Chapter 23. However, it also includes developing your own ability to practice those skills and develop strong friendships with other adults. Besides giving your child an example of the types of friends they should pick, building friendships also allows you to model how they should relate to their friends. And as an added bonus, your friends can provide your child with an extra sense of community, serving as additional resources for support, guidance, and love.

6   Esteem

But here is how God has shown his love for us. While we were still sinners, Christ died for us. (Romans 5:8)

Although it may seem like our desire to feel confident, capable, and valuable comes from a self-centered tendency, our esteem needs are actually some of the most important to fulfill. How positively we define ourselves directly impacts the quality of the choices we make. If we instead fall into our sin nature's classic characteristics of pessimism or pride (Chapter 13), we're more likely to turn to demeaning or addictive habits in order to feel better—or toward the false belief that we can handle life ourselves without God's help.

Esteem needs are especially important to meet for our children, because how they view themselves in childhood can impact their self-definition for the rest of their lives. As your child grows up, continually remind them to pursue their own gifts rather than relying on others to affirm them. Encourage them to focus on how God sees them—as a friend, His child, and a person worth dying for. When they live according to His standards, they'll develop a sense of self-respect and will gain the humility, transparency, and vulnerability they need to authentically express who they are.

7   Understanding

God, see what is in my heart. Know what is there. Test me. Know what I'm thinking. (Psalm 139:23)

Deep down, we all want others to understand who we really are. But for your child to truly be known and receive the support and feedback they need, they must learn to express themselves authentically and consistently—and that means being willing to share their deepest thoughts, fears, and desires.

However, it can take time for children to understand how to put words to what they're experiencing, and even more time to find the courage to share it. To help them through this process, make sure your child feels safe enough to share with you both the positive and negative aspects of their life. While it may not always be easy for you to relate to their pain or understand their interests, your child needs you to listen and support them with a nonjudgmental and open heart. Try to reflect what they are saying back to them and respect their perspective even when you see things differently.

In Chapter 22, we talked about how sharing your heart with your child will help them gain the courage to be vulnerable with their own emotions, which means that the best way to help your child learn meet their understanding needs is to vulnerably share your own authentic self with them—the good *and* the bad parts. Telling your child in an age-appropriate manner that you are afraid, angry, or sad about something can help them trust and relate to you even more deeply. In turn, they will better understand the value of connecting with others in this way, leading them to feel more confident about sharing themselves in order to be truly understood.

8   Love

Most of all, love one another deeply. Love erases many sins by forgiving them. (1 Peter 4:8)

As we've seen throughout this book, love is foundational to fatherhood and life itself. It's a simple concept, really. In order to survive in a harsh world, your child needs to attach to a loving father who they can trust to help them process their emotional, mental, physical, and relational challenges. There are many ways to fulfill this need, including the obvious ones of support and nurturance. But as we discussed in the last chapter, you also convey your love by confronting their negative choices and holding them to godly standards. It isn't always easy to create tension with your child, but by doing so, you show them that you love them enough to do whatever it takes to increase their chance of success.

In order to fully meet your child's need for love, you also must be able to take in love, which requires dropping your defensiveness. Your vulnerability is the only way to truly experience the depth of the love your child has to share. In the process, you will reinforce to them that they have something to offer, building up their esteem, security, and self-worth in the process.

9　Leisure

By the seventh day God had finished the work he had been doing. So on that day he rested from all his work. (Genesis 2:2)

As much as your child needs to mature, develop, and persevere, they aren't meant to work nonstop. For one, no child has the attention span for that kind of dedication. But more importantly, they need time to run around and play in order to blow off steam and refuel. And so do you! Putting aside your responsibilities once in a while to laugh with your child or engage in an enjoyable activity with them will help you both experience God more fully. Whether it's spontaneous play or a preplanned adventure, prioritizing your leisure together will teach your child that having fun is essential and beneficial to their well-being. By learning that lesson now, they'll be better equipped to know how to avoid burnout in the future.

10   Learning and creating

To start being wise you must first get wisdom. No matter what it costs, get understanding. (Proverbs 4:7)

Remember the wondrousness of your child's curious mind that we discovered in Chapter 8? Well, that curiosity is actually essential to their survival. By encouraging them to engage with it, you can help your child avoid getting stuck in a single pattern of behavior and instead keep pushing themselves to always find ways to improve. Prompt them to continually seek out new perspectives and information, and then help them figure out how to apply those ideas to their life. The more committed they are to learning and creating, the easier it will be to come up with solutions to any problem that may arise.

11   Growth

Keep on doing these things. Give them your complete attention. Then everyone will see how you are coming along. (1 Timothy 4:15)

This need shouldn't surprise you. After all, it's what we've been talking about this entire book! God created your child to be a hero, not to be bored and directionless. As they get older, they'll move into new environments and circumstances, and they may find that what helped them adjust and adapt in a previous environment now limits them. So keep asking them good questions, encouraging their learning, and providing stimulating challenges. As they build their confidence, they'll become increasingly willing to step outside their comfort zone to find new ways to grow, ensuring that they never get stuck in a limiting and dangerous life of passivity.

12   Evaluation

If anyone thinks they are somebody when they are nobody, they are fooling themselves. Each person should test their own actions. Then they can take pride in themselves. (Galatians 6:3-4)

Part of meeting your child's growth needs is to teach them to learn to continually evaluate themselves. It's only by deliberately assessing the positives and negatives of their goals, efforts, relationships, and decisions that they can discover how to improve. Of course, this isn't a skill that will come naturally to your child, which is why it's so important for you to evaluate them as well and share constructive feedback. Over time, they'll learn to internalize that feedback and begin to find ways to identify their problem areas for themselves before you even need to say anything.

13   Purpose and meaning

"I know the plans I have for you," announces the LORD. "I want you to enjoy success. I do not plan to harm you. I will give you hope for the years to come." (Jeremiah 29:11)

Another theme throughout this book has been your child's need to discover and live out their God-given purpose. Your child wants to feel significant, influence others, and effectively interact with life. And God's unique purpose for them is meant to help them do exactly that. In moments where they're feeling lost or hopeless, remind them of God's greater vision for their life. When they learn to follow His purpose, life will always be worthwhile, even if it sometimes doesn't feel that way.

Regardless of your child's specific path, part of God's purpose for everyone is to leave a legacy that improves the lives of others. Just like it is with you, your child's relationships are truly the only thing in their life that will last when they're gone. That's why your role as a father is so important. Like we talked about in Chapters

9 and 10, what you teach your child will get passed on not only to their children but also to every other relationship in their life. As you relate to your child according to God's standards, you will fulfill your own meaning and purpose and, along the way, help your child fulfill theirs.

THE ULTIMATE NEED

There's one final core need I believe deserves to be covered separately from the list above—our need for God. It's only through our relationship with Him that all of the other needs can be met (Ephesians 4:6). When you focus on strengthening that relationship, both for yourself and your child, you'll find your other mental, emotional, physical, and relational needs all naturally being met. Becoming more like Christ takes time and a lot of effort, but with God's presence, guidance, and love, you'll have everything you need to achieve it.

For this reason, the most important thing you can do for your child and their needs is introduce them to Jesus. Only He can provide them with the perspective and guidance they need to know how to best fulfill their needs. Your job as a father is to take care of your child as well as you can, but ultimately, you are just one person in a giant world filled with evil. Knowing they have a God above who knows them and loves them will make all the difference (Isaiah 44:24).

In the next chapter, we'll continue this discussion on needs, this time from a slightly different perspective. In your fatherhood efforts, you may find that just because you meet all of your child's needs completely doesn't mean they'll automatically grow up and begin making mature decisions. As we discussed in Chapter 13, we all have a sin nature that attempts to distort our thinking, our values, and our motivations. And that means that even as we provide for our children and help them grow, they may still give in to unhealthy thinking and go after negative pursuits. So it's time to be vigilant, use the knowledge you have, and take it just one step further.

 ROY'S STORY

Growing up, Kim went to a rural school that was somewhat entrenched in rigid cultural viewpoints. As a creative child, she was targeted by a group of mean girls who didn't like or respect how Kim was different from them. Unfortunately, this bullying went on for years, and some of the girls' parents even inappropriately got involved.

Jan and I did what we could to make things better for Kim, including putting extra energy into developing social opportunities for her outside of school. But nothing helped, and eventually we had to make the decision to seek an educational alternative. After some deliberation and prayer, we settled on sending Kim to another school in the area. It required extra time and finances to do so, but it also set her up to establish more supportive friendships. Before long, she was flourishing as we'd always hoped she would.

As much as we may want to, the reality is that we can't always take care of everything for our children, simply because we aren't God. But at the same time, we don't always have to leave our children to fend for themselves. When God leads, we can create new opportunities for them that meet their needs in better ways. It may mean sacrificing ourselves in some way, but those sacrifices are worth it if it benefits the greater welfare of the children we love.

💬 DISCUSSION QUESTIONS

1   Think back over your childhood. In what ways did your parents provide well for you? What areas do you feel were lacking? How have those experiences impacted how you father your own child?

2   Where is the line between providing for your child and spoiling them? What are some strategies that could help you find the right balance?

3   Review the list of core needs. Which three do you consider to be the most important? How does God meet these needs? Which should you improve on fulfilling, either for yourself or for your child?

4   Discuss how Philippians 4:19 relates to meeting our needs. How can a relationship with God improve a father's ability to care for his child?

My God will meet all your needs. He will meet them in keeping with his wonderful riches. These riches come to you because you belong to Christ Jesus.

28

A FATHER'S NO

When I was fourteen, my mother took me to see an oph-
thalmologist because my teachers had told her they thought I was
having trouble with my vision. It turned out they were right. After
a series of tests, the doctor concluded that I was nearsighted and
then handed me my first pair of black-rimmed glasses. That's when
I lost it. I erupted into a verbal tirade using all the street language
I had ever heard, insisting that I did not need glasses, that I could
see the #$!*%#! chart, and that I wouldn't wear them no matter
what.

Eventually, I calmed down enough to let my mother to drive
me home. By that point, I was less concerned about the glasses and
more about what kind of discipline I would get from my father once
he heard what had come out of the mouth of a pastor's kid. To my
surprise, after asking me a few thoughtful questions, he gave me a
choice of punishment: I could be grounded for a week, or I could go
to the school's basketball game that night with my new girlfriend,
Barb. He would even pay for our snacks. However, if I chose the
game, I had to wear my glasses all night.

It was a pretty easy choice. I'd rather suffer through one night
of glasses than a whole week of misery. And as it turned out, nothing catastrophic happened because of them. Barb even thought I
looked pretty good in my new glasses. To this day, they have continued to be part of my identity, all thanks to a dad who could see

the true feelings of insecurity, shame, and fear behind my outburst. He sensed my underlying need for affirmation, and he set me up to have it fulfilled.

In addition to their core needs, your child also has other needs that are less developmentally mature and often more directly connected to their emotions, making them much trickier to define and thus fulfill. These "impulse" needs, as I like to call them, are the ones that are most immediately and intensely on their minds. As a result, they're also the ones that most often direct their behaviors and dictate their choices, because they want to do whatever they can to get those needs met and lessen the intensity of what they're feeling.

In this chapter, we'll discuss the concept of impulse needs, how they can cause our children to make illogical or harmful decisions, and how we can help them pinpoint and address them. The better you can recognize the factors that lead to a negative choice, the quicker you can step in before your child makes one and help steer them back onto the right path instead.

THE PROBLEM WITH NEEDS

Let's start by unpacking what an impulse actually is. Generally speaking, it's a sudden and intense desire for an object or an activity, which creates an immediate urge to fulfill that desire. Many of these impulses are small or harmless, like the impulse to kick a rock in the path or pet a dog in the park. Because the desire itself is small, we can manage it pretty well, either by indulging it quickly or dismissing it easily.

Sometimes, however, our impulses can grow to the point where they feel like needs. This typically happens when the impulse results from something missing within us. When our core needs aren't being adequately addressed, or when we haven't fully developed an area of our identity, we can begin to feel an itch that tells us to do something, *anything*, to get rid of the emptiness we feel as a result.

Because impulse needs indicate that something's wrong, they can actually be helpful at times. Our feeling of being less than whole can trigger emotions like anxiety, worry, yearning, fear, or desire that help point us to meeting our core needs or developing ourselves further. For example, if you find yourself trying to undermine your boss every chance you get, it may be because you feel insecure in your position or want to feel affirmed or valued. This could signal your need to work on finding security and certainty in your own identity instead of in your occupational success. By first acknowledging your impulse need for obtaining more power, you can then become better equipped to take the steps to grow more confident about who you are and, in turn, become a more collaborative employee.

However, our impulse needs don't always lead us to do the hard work of developing ourselves or meeting our core needs. Instead, they can cause us to engage in inappropriate behavior, especially if we get carried away by the feelings they instigate or if we attempt to ignore them altogether. For instance, if you don't address your feelings of powerlessness at work, your resentment toward your boss will continue to build, and you'll probably end up losing your job. And if you indulge your impulse needs too much, they can become a pattern of behavior, causing you to engage with them even after the feelings that caused them in the first place have long since disappeared.

Especially for our children, the intensity of an impulse can make it easy to exaggerate the importance of that need. And when that happens, they'll do whatever it takes to keep the need satisfied—even if pursuing it leads to other issues or means that they contradict their core needs. Other times they'll simply put all their energy into finding a way to make themselves feel better, regardless of whether it relates to the need at all or is actually harming them further.

To make everything even more complicated, our impulse needs can also easily be distorted in various ways. As we've already discussed, children often struggle with understanding the line between needs and wants, and their emotions can feel so strong and overwhelming that anything they desire feels absolutely vital to their existence. They're also exposed to media and advertisements telling them that certain products, achievements, and values are necessary for a successful life. As a result, they grow up believing that they need that new toy to be happy, those expensive shoes to be popular, that big-shot job to be valuable—even if those things don't fit with who they are deep down.

Additionally, because impulse needs are so closely tied to emotions, they can be hijacked by your child's insecurities, shame, greed, pride, or selfishness, causing them to prioritize those needs over their growth or fulfilling their core needs. For example, if your child is struggling to fit in at school, they may overlook their need for understanding in preference of their need for control. Friendships take time and vulnerability to build, but in their insecurity, narcissism, or laziness, it may seem easier to just try to force others to like them instead. While acting out in this way may give your child temporary relief because it feels like they're fixing the problem, the core need is still going unmet, which means the negative feelings will return even more strongly, prompting them to try to resolve them with the same unhelpful or even unhealthy behaviors.

Now, this all may seem like a lot of negativity, but don't worry—by learning to understand and recognize those impulses, you can help your child reign in their emotions and express them in positive ways, all while meeting their innermost needs and strengthening their identity.

FEEL A NEED, FILL A NEED

No matter how your child's impulse needs get distorted, they can all lead them to try to meet their legitimate needs in illegitimate ways. Of course, they don't necessarily know they're doing this, which is why you must be aware of times when your child seems to be acting out in inexplicable ways. You should also look at whether any core needs or developmental deficits are being covered up or overlooked as a result. Below are seven impulse needs that most commonly get distorted and lead our children into such negative, irrational behaviors. The better you understand these needs, the more you can guide your child in interpreting and responding to them, ensuring that all their needs get addressed and met in the proper way.

1   Pleasure

Though pleasure sometimes has a bad reputation, it's actually a legitimate need we all must work to fulfill (Ecclesiastes 3:13). Similar to the core need of leisure, the more your child enjoys life, whether they're relaxing with friends or simply eating their favorite kind of cake, the more positive they'll be and the more energy they'll have to navigate their challenges.

Unfortunately, however, the need for pleasure is also one of the easiest to distort and overemphasize. Thanks to the short-term, highly satisfying brain chemicals it triggers, pleasure always results in some kind of a positive sensation, either physical or emotional. In fact, it often feels so good that experiencing it once—even through fulfilling a core need like leisure—can make your child obsess over meeting it again.

For this same reason, when your child encounters emotions or situations that *don't* feel so good, pleasure is often the first thing they turn to in an attempt to alleviate their discomfort. The second life starts to get tough, they'll look for the easy way out, for something that will distract them from their negative or challenging circumstance. Over time, they may even fall victim to sexual acting out, drug or alcohol abuse, or other types of compulsive behaviors.

As their father, you are a voice of reason in your child's life. This means you're responsible for helping them learn two important lessons: that sometimes they must push through hardships and discomfort in order to achieve a greater purpose, and that not everything they think will make them happy is really necessary. By learning to tell themselves no, they'll regain control over their impulses and remove the power their physical and emotional desires have over their decision-making.

2   Material objects

One of the most common ways children distort this impulse need is by learning to overvalue material objects to the point where they believe they need them to have value or to fulfill their core needs. It's true that we need many things both to survive and to develop well, such as clothes, tools, or books. However, when your child loses sight of the line between wants and needs, or when you overindulge them in an attempt to prove your love to them, they can easily distort those needs. Providing them with expensive clothes, fancy toys, or luxurious foods can make them believe they need these objects in order to fulfill their core needs of physical care, security, and esteem. They can even become an easy way to make your child feel better and forget the discomfort of their more painful needs.

The more your child distorts their need for material objects, the more those objects will become an unstable part of who they are, limiting them from developing themselves as God sees them. Even worse, they'll be too focused on getting more that they'll fail to develop an appreciation for what they do have (Luke 12:15). And because they've grown used to obtaining stuff as a quick fix to their problem, they'll never learn to delay gratification in order to work hard to achieve their long-term goals.

As we talked about in the last chapter, the solution to this distortion is simply to regulate the fulfillment of your child's wants and, to an extent, their needs. By saying no to certain requests, you can both deemphasize the importance of material objects and give them the opportunity to earn them for themselves. In this way, your child can learn to understand that their worth has nothing to do with what they have and everything to do with who they are.

3   Control

Being a child is hard. They're constantly faced with new situations, challenges, and relationships they've never experienced before and don't immediately know how to navigate. It's enough to make them feel inadequate to deal with life. But rather than trying to find a real solution, they can let their anxiety get the better of them and distort their impulse need for control.

In itself, control isn't a bad thing. In Chapter 24, we talked about how we need to take ownership for the parts of life we can control, no matter how small they may seem, instead of wallowing in misery over the parts that make us feel powerless. God gave us each the ability to choose, which means we *can* actually dictate how our lives turn out, to a certain extent.

However, your child can easily distort this truth and try to control others or their circumstances through negative means, such as throwing a temper tantrum when things don't go their way or rudely making demands of someone. Even if they don't succeed in achieving control, their misbehavior at least allows them to dictate the situation, which can help remove the feeling that life is out of their hands.

Another way your child can distort their need for control is by believing they can control everything about life. Total control is simply a myth, since only God knows the plans He has for your child. And sometimes what they want won't be His will (Proverbs 19:21). The less your child accepts this truth, and the greater their desire for control becomes, the more inadequate they'll be at handling life's spontaneous changes. They'll feel angry and anxious when things don't go their way, creating an unhealthy sense of perfectionism that causes them to create unrealistic expectations for themselves and others.

The best way to help your child recognize this reality is by setting boundaries with them and sticking to them. Allow them to express their disagreement with you, within reason of course, but then lay down a firm no as necessary. In this way, they'll learn what's expected of them, limiting their need to seek control in negative ways.

Most importantly, make sure your child is continually strengthening themselves mentally, emotionally, relationally, physically, and spiritually. When they develop themselves in all of these areas, they'll have enough self-discipline and confidence that they won't need to grasp for control whenever they feel overwhelmed or anxious. With a positive viewpoint of their own capabilities and a faith that with God all things are possible, they'll be able to accept the realities of life without feeling an anxious need to control it (Matthew 19:26).

4   Power

While the need for control becomes distorted mainly due to feelings of anxiety, the distortion of the need for power most often comes from inappropriate aggression. Like with esteem, a positive search for power begins within, through finding our worth and abilities in God's Word and our own internal strength. However, children often overemphasize their need for power when they feel weak inside and try to compensate for that sense of inadequacy. Anything from being compared to their sibling to getting a bad grade on a test can motivate them to dominate others in some way in an attempt to once again feel competent and valuable.

Ultimately, however, a distorted impulse need for power will limit the level of intimacy your child can achieve with others. For one, it will cause them to believe in a social pecking order where some people are better than others, which will make them miss out on important relationships with those they define as below them. They'll also feel like it's okay to dominate and manipulate others to get what they want, causing people to avoid them for their own safety and leaving your child isolated and alone.

Addressing your child's impulse need for power begins at home. By refusing to tolerate such power performances, you can teach them that they have no place in any positive environment. Through wise consequences, you can show them how to treat others lovingly. And by reminding them of how God values and protects them, they can adopt an attitude of humility and confidence, losing the need to prove their worth through empty displays of power.

5   Attention

Just about every child out there naturally craves attention. After all, for much of their early life, attention comes hand in hand with sustenance, care, and love. However, as they get older, their need for attention often shifts from survival-motivated to self-motivated. They believe that being in the spotlight, or being noticed at all, will reinforce their importance and provide the love they need, so they do whatever they can to get that attention—even if the attention itself is negative, like a punishment or scolding.

The longer this behavior continues, the more your child's sense of well-being will become directly associated with the amount of attention they receive. They'll be unable to appreciate anything about themselves or about life if it isn't also appreciated by others. Additionally, the more they focus on seeking attention, the less likely they'll be to receive it. A distorted need for attention often manifests in obvious and frankly annoying ways. Your child may be loud, refuse to follow the rules, or constantly play the victim. Furthermore, people will sense that your child doesn't really care about them and is just using them for their own gain. As a result, they'll distance themselves from your child, further increasing your child's need for attention.

To avoid becoming dependent on others to validate them, your child has to learn to rely on their internal resources and on God's definition of who they are. One way to help them do this is to guide them to develop their strengths and abilities and in turn build up their self-esteem. However, it should also include helping them find ways to enjoy life even when they're alone. The more quality time they spend with themselves, the more they'll discover and appreciate who they are and what they have without relying on others to notice or validate those blessings.

6   Affirmation

While the need for attention prompts us to want to be noticed no matter the cost, affirmation takes it one step further by causing us to want to be liked and complimented by others. While this need is important as it helps your child bond with others and express their love and understanding, it can also make them so obsessed with external opinions that their identity becomes controlled by them. They can't feel satisfied or proud of their accomplishments until someone else tells them they're worthwhile.

By giving others the power to define them in this way, your child's main motivation becomes to make others happy, even at the expense of their own happiness or other core needs. They grow unable to evaluate themselves honestly or handle constructive feedback, whether it's given lovingly or not, because acknowledging their weaknesses feels like admitting that they're not good enough. As a result, their growth stops, preventing them from fully developing into all God has called them to be.

God wants us to love others, but He also recognizes that not everyone is going to love us back (Luke 6:26). And that's okay! While it's true that we all need external viewpoints, support, and feedback to help us continue to grow, the reality is that they shouldn't define who we are. Your child's identity is ultimately based on who God is in their life. If it seems like they're getting too caught up in their need for affirmation, remind them of this truth. By internalizing His value, they'll be able to accept external viewpoints without overemphasizing them.

7 Dependence

In certain situations, dependence is necessary, such as when your child depends on you for survival or on a community to meet their relational needs. However, dependence can also be easily misinterpreted as love, which causes your child to cling to you or others in unhealthy ways. Whether they feel inadequate and unable to function on their own or are simply afraid of losing someone, they may refuse to allow distance to grow in their relationships, neglecting either the needs of the other person or their own responsibilities.

Often the stronger your child tries to hold on to a relationship, the more likely they'll be to lose it. Everyone has a certain sense of independence, and when your child tries to cling to someone out of fear or insecurity, they violate that person's individuality, which will cause them to pull back or even end the relationship just to regain some freedom. Additionally, your child's dependence can cause them to ignore their own individuality, leading them to attach to others to avoid leaving their comfort zone and developing themselves. But this only places an unfair burden on those people to take care of them, and before long they will become resentful and possibly even hostile toward your child.

The best way to prevent your child from distorting their need for dependence is to consciously shift the responsibility for their welfare onto them. This may cause them to panic at times, either due to an uncertainty that they can handle it or out of fear that you're abandoning them. But as long as you stand behind them as they take on these new responsibilities, they'll soon gain confidence in both themselves and your support. Eventually, that feeling of confidence will extend to all their relationships, allowing them to develop bonds with people who will support them, not control them.

STOPPING THE BEHAVIOR

Because impulse needs aren't inherently negative, it can be tricky to know how to discipline the misbehaviors that result from them. But all you really have to do is recognize the underlying issues, evaluate the impulse's inappropriateness, and discipline those actions like you would any other misbehavior. It's like with my outburst over getting glasses. My father wisely avoided condemning my emotions themselves or my need for affirmation. Instead of slapping on a generic consequence, he made sure the punishment addressed the true issue behind my actions. By similarly assessing both your child's behavior and their motivation, you will help them learn to structure their identity in a way that's more adaptive and consistent with God's divine image of them, ensuring they don't repeat the same negative behavior again.

However, because of the impulsive aspect of these needs, there are two caveats to keep in mind. First, though you should provide consequences for your child's misbehavior or set new boundaries, you should make sure those consequences are not a comment on your child's value. You need to respond to the behavioral choices they make, not what you assume is going on within them. Because the desires and emotions associated with most motivations aren't inherently wrong, punishing your child for having them will only make them believe they are. Even worse, they may simply start to hide those feelings from you, preventing you from helping them address their impulse needs in healthy ways.

Second, regardless of what consequences you provide, make sure to sit down with your child and have a conversation about what led them to make the choices they made to help them discover the areas they still need to grow in. Again, this is not about trying to change their feelings or teach them that having desires is bad. Instead, simply acknowledge your child's feelings and needs, explain why what they did was an unhealthy response, and help them figure out a better way to address their core needs next time. Maturing and structuring their identity takes time, and your child needs to feel your loving support throughout this process. By having these conversations, you show your child that you're here for them, empowering them to better understand both their emotions and needs and making it less likely they'll distort them in the future.

STINKING THINKING

A big reason children create and distort their impulse needs is because, over time, they have developed false perspectives and values that affect their brains that think and feel. In recovery groups, they call this concept *stinking thinking*. These are negative ways of thinking we buy in to about ourselves and about life that undermine our abilities and sense of self-worth. These ways of thinking don't just prevent us from motivating ourselves to take on new opportunities that could further our growth—they also cause us to actively make decisions that hurt both ourselves and others.

We are all capable of stinking thinking, no matter our age, but our children are especially susceptible. Their immaturity means they're less equipped to combat their narcissism and shame, while their impressionability makes them more willing to accept concepts and ideas at face value, even if they're wrong. As a result, they're more likely to be impulsive and to make repeated negative choices.

We already discussed a few of the broader lies our children can internalize in Chapter 24, but there are also several more specific lies that can directly impact their thoughts, emotions, and behaviors. The more aware you are of them, the better you'll sense when your child's thinking is starting to get twisted, especially when it leads to their impulsivity. Then you can step in and redirect their thought processes to a godlier way of thinking.

1 I must win.

Because winning is one of the most obvious indicators of success, it can be easy for children to connect winning to their worth, making them overly competitive and unable to handle life's natural disappointments.

2 I have to hide my pain and mistakes.

Failure and loss are unpleasant, and a child's first instinct is often to simply pretend it didn't happen, blocking them from support and help from others.

3 I can act first and think later.

In their immaturity, children tend to react without slowing down to think through their actions. When this approach gets them in trouble, they often try to backtrack and make up excuses to justify their negative choices instead of taking responsibility for improving their behaviors.

4 I can't trust others.

People aren't perfect, and the potential for rejection can cause some children to withdraw from others, believing it's better to be alone than to expend the time and risk involved in developing trust.

5   I should never cry.

Some children try ignore any negative feelings they have, believing they're inherently bad. They don't want to seem weak or like they can't handle something, so they attempt to act tough and cover up their sadness instead.

6   Others don't deserve my forgiveness.

When a child feels hurt, their first reaction is often to hurt the other person back or refuse to trust them again. They may also seek vengeance and retaliation. Not only do these approaches keep them stuck in negativity, they also hinder them from pursuing forgiveness for their own negative choices.

7   I don't care.

Children also attempt to resolve their hurt or disappointment by pretending they don't care about a person or situation. They believe they're less likely to get hurt again if they can convince themselves or others that nothing matters to them.

8   It's not my fault.

To avoid getting in trouble, children often try to shift responsibility for their actions onto other people or circumstances, keeping them from responding maturely and making amends when necessary.

9   I must strike first.

Children can become aggressive and try to intimidate others as a way to cover up their insecurities or avoid responsibility, allowing them to dodge their true emotions in the process.

10   Life is all or nothing.

Because of the concrete nature of their thought processes, children have difficulty perceiving the nuances of life. To them, everything is either all good or all bad, all right or all wrong—including themselves.

11   Truth can change.

Sometimes children accept what's true only when it's convenient, frequently changing their beliefs in order to fit in or get what they want.

12   Everyone else is doing it.

I'm sure you've heard this one before. In their inexperience, children often overvalue popularity and misunderstand fairness. They act on their fear of being left out or lacking what others have instead of building the confidence to do what they know is right.

13   Money talks.

Due to commercialism and peer pressure, children can learn to value others based on what they have rather than who they are.

14   Criticism is always harmful.

Children can mistakenly learn that if something makes them feel bad, it must be bad itself, which leads them to dismiss negative feedback no matter how helpful it might be.

15   I'm just unlucky.

Similar to the lie "it just happens," this is simply another way of deflecting responsibility. When they believe that life is pitted against them, children feel they can excuse themselves from putting in the effort to make it better.

16 It can wait.

Life isn't always fun, which can lead children to put off the more difficult tasks. But rather than making a plan for doing them later, they just keep procrastinating without thinking about the potential consequences.

17 It can't wait.

Conversely, when it comes to their desires, children can feel like they have to have it right now, further limiting their impulse control and ability to delay gratification.

18 What's mine is mine.

Sharing doesn't come naturally to children, whether it's an object, their feelings, or an opportunity, causing them to value possessions and accomplishments over relationships.

19 I know.

When a child learns something new, they can think that the learning process is over and that they don't need to do anything more. However, without applying that knowledge in practical ways and continually trying to learn more, they'll limit their ability to truly know anything.

20 It has to be done my way.

Children like routine, consistency, and comfort, and all of this can provide a secure environment for them to thrive in. However, children can also become too attached to that security and reject any type of change or opportunity for growth.

21 I don't need help.

Just like us, children can succumb to their pride and believe they can do life all on their own. Even as they struggle, they convince themselves they don't need anyone—not their parents, not their friends, and sometimes not even God.

As with your child's impulse needs, though stinking thinking often leads to negative behaviors, it's more important to determine and address the reason behind those behaviors. Unlike some more neutral impulses, however, these ways of thinking are *not* okay. To combat your child's tendency to succumb to stinking thinking, teach them to instead direct their thoughts toward positive things—things they enjoy, things they want to learn, or people who make them smile (Philippians 4:8). Remind them that God is always present and seeking to communicate with each of us. The better they can tune in to His desires and align their ways of thinking to His standards, the easier it will be to avoid getting stuck in stinking thinking or impulse needs and instead keep working toward achieving His plan.

 ROBERT'S STORY

Children are people without the bitterness. That's what I often think of when I look at my two young girls. Praise God they have not lived long enough yet to be affected by the many negative thoughts and worldviews that exist in society. For now, they are safe and secure under my roof... or are they?

Several years ago I was prepping to catch a plane for a huge event I was going to speak at. The day before my departure, I received a phone call from my agent telling me the event was canceled. I was furious. Not only were there a lot of changes I'd had to make in my filming schedule to make it to this event, I had also invited some family to come help out my wife while I was away. And I had spent weeks preparing for a presentation that would now never happen.

It was precisely in the middle of this frustration that Angelina came up to me and asked, "Don't you want to be with us, Daddy?"

Immediately my soul sank to my heels. My little girl thought I was mad because I could no longer get away from my family. I could *not* let that stand. So I sat down with her and explained my frustration in words she could understand. But what I couldn't explain was my behavior.

Here's the hard truth I had to swallow. My daughters may currently be privileged enough to live lives filtered from the evils of this world, but their lives are not filtered from me. Whatever pain, disappointment, anger, or bitterness I carry, I cannot successfully keep it from them or anyone else in the long run. And if I can't get a handle on my impulsive reactions, I will succumb to behaviors that will teach my daughters to give in to their impulses in the same way.

Thankfully, I'm not alone. There's a reason Jesus asked us to come to Him when we are tired and burdened. It's because He can handle it much better than we can. The best way not to let my bitterness affect my girls is to show them how I take that bitterness to Jesus.

In this way, this interaction with Angelina was a gift from God. It was an opportunity to change myself. I don't want my daughter to feel distant from me because I seem emotionally unpredictable. I want her to feel close to her dad knowing that she can learn from the way he loves and trusts Jesus.

So I took my daughter's hand and asked her to pray with me. And that prayer began with, "Thank you, Jesus, for getting my attention."

💬 DISCUSSION QUESTIONS

1   What are some of your present impulsive desires? How have you distorted your needs in the past? How did those distortions impact your behaviors?

2   Which needs are your child most susceptible to distorting? How can you help them meet those need in healthier ways?

3   Which of the stinking thinking lies are you or your child currently affected by? How can both of you unlearn these beliefs and instead pursue godlier standards?

4   Discuss how Psalm 139:1-2 relates to impulse needs and stinking thinking. How can God help you better understand the root of your child's behaviors so you can lead them toward the best decisions?

LORD, you have seen what is in my heart.
   You know all about me.
You know when I sit down and when I get up.
   You know what I'm thinking even though you are far away.

29

IT'S A ?

I'm sure you remember the moment you found out. Maybe it was in a quiet ultrasound room with your wife, or through a creative and lively gender reveal party. Or maybe it was the old-fashioned way, in the delivery room where a doctor made the announcement with a smile. Either way, one of the most exciting moments of early fatherhood is finding out whether your new baby is a boy or a girl. That's the point when their identity and personality starts to take shape in your mind, and you can begin to cater your dreams and aspirations toward your unique child.

Aside from pink dresses versus blue onesies, however, raising a girl isn't really all that different from raising a boy. That's why so far I've mostly avoided mentioning gender at all, instead sticking with the general term *child* or *children*. When it comes to the fundamental concepts of fatherhood, it doesn't matter if you have a son or a daughter. Both are loved and valued by God equally (1 Corinthians 11:12). Both have potential they need to achieve through developing their gifts and capabilities. And both need your love and support to be able to do so.

That being said, boys and girls obviously aren't completely the same (Genesis 1:27). There are key differences in their biological makeup and cultural experiences that will influence their responses to you and to life. In this chapter, we'll discuss those differences and how they impact your role as a father. Some of these topics are ones we've already covered, but by looking at them through a gender-specific lens, you'll strengthen your ability to understand how you can help your son or daughter through their individual challenges.

Keep in mind that these concepts are still generalities, which means they may not apply to your unique child. In fact, you may find that a description regarding sons actually fits your daughter better, or vice versa. And that's okay! This chapter is not about telling you what your son or daughter *should* be like. Rather, it's meant to help you further strengthen your ability to affirm their amazing individuality and adjust your fathering style to their specific needs.

TWO SIDES OF ONE COIN[1]

I think it's safe to say that the most obvious difference between boys and girls is simple biology. There's the blatant physical differences, of course, but it's the underlying hormonal differences that have the biggest impact. This is most evident in adolescence, when both genders experience a surge of hormones that can cause struggles with self-centeredness, narcissism, sexual energy, aggression, territorialness, and competitiveness. However, because the hormones they're flooded with are different (boys get more testosterone, girls more estrogen), boys and girls experience those struggles in different ways and at different intensities. This means that girls naturally aren't driven by the same desires as boys, and they won't engage in the same behaviors to achieve them.

Even before puberty, though, boys and girls can exhibit clear tendencies that seem to separate them from each other. Boys, for instance, are hyperactive, prone to physical play, and impulsive in ways girls often aren't. The more you understand these biological differences and learn to recognize them in your child, the better

---

1   Much of the research and information referenced in this chapter is taken from: Louann Brizendine, *The Female Brain* (New York: Harmony Books, 2006).

you'll be able to father them. To start developing this understanding, let's focus on two areas that girls and boys struggle with, the different ways it affects them, and how they can learn to handle it well.

The first area is aggression. In boys, aggression is largely physical. They wrestle, punch, and engage in rough play, either as a way to have fun or as a means to get what they want. When guided well, you son's aggression can help him fully enjoy life, serve others, and protect himself. But if left unchecked, it can also easily turn into violence, which violates others and jeopardizes their well-being. Your son will need your help to learn to differentiate between positive aggression and harmful violence. As he grows up, help redirect his aggressive energy from selfish desires to more positive endeavors. When he focuses on using his aggression to develop goals and passionately pursue them, he'll be able to achieve all he sets out to.

Now, while boys are about twenty times more aggressive than girls, that doesn't mean girls aren't aggressive at all. Girls have the same desire to have fun and get their own way, but instead of using physical tactics, they most often rely on words and emotions. If not controlled, your daughter's aggression can cause her to make demands of her friends without considering their perspective, or she may use emotional manipulation to guilt a friend into giving her what she wants. Just like you would with a son, confront your daughter's selfish behaviors as they arise and help her learn to put her positive aggressive energy toward helping others. When she does, she'll find she gains much more fulfillment from service than from control.

The second area that girls and boys struggle with differently is sexuality. In adolescence, a boy's testosterone can cause him to become single-mindedly focused on sex. His mind is consumed with fantasies, his eyes are continually drawn to girls' bodies, and he's completely overwhelmed by a desire for pleasure. It's your job to prepare your son to learn how to guide these urges, ideally before they even begin to arise. It may not be comfortable, but you must have direct and clear conversations with him about pornography, masturbation, and treating women with respect.[2] After all, it'll be easier for him to understand how this important desire fits into his identity if he hears it from you instead of somewhere else. By internalizing these lessons ahead of time, your son will be much better prepared to manage his sexuality once he hits puberty. At the very least, he'll know he can come to you when it feels too hard to handle—and before he makes a big mistake.

Girls don't have nearly as much testosterone as boys, which means they aren't as driven by sexual desire in adolescence. However, their behaviors are still influenced by their sexuality in other ways. For example, during puberty, a girl's main objective is to become sexually desirable to boys. This doesn't necessarily mean she consciously wants to have sex, but rather that her hormones cause her to judge herself against her peers and obsess over her appearance. On some level, she's driven by the goal of getting boys to notice her, whether she realizes it or not.

Unlike with a son, you don't necessarily have to be the one to have the sex talk with your daughter, as she'll likely be more receptive to another female's guidance in this area. But that doesn't mean you're totally off the hook. As her father, your role is to provide understanding and support as she goes through these changes. And though you've never experienced the same journey, you can still share your perspective with her, as it will help her better understand the opposite sex. Discuss with her what to expect of her male peers and how to prepare for their behaviors. After all, no one knows better than you what goes on in the mind of a teenage boy.

The struggles with aggression and sexuality highlight how biology can lead to a lot of differences in behaviors between boys

---

2   *Bull* and *Being God's Man* are great resources with discussion questions to help fathers guide their sons through difficult topics like these. Check them out at liveupresources.com.

and girls, but remember that they're not the only struggles your son or daughter will face. There's another area where the genders differ, one they can't avoid, one they'll need your careful and direct guidance in—the realm of relationships.

LET'S RELATE

As much as we may not understand them, and as much as they may frustrate us to no end, we can't get out of relating to people of the opposite sex. We live with them, work with them, buy our groceries from them, and yes, even parent them. Despite this reality, most men still get along better with other men, and most women prefer to hang out with other women. It's all due to those biological differences we've been talking about. Men and women are simply wired to relate to others in separate ways. As fathers, it's important to be aware of exactly what those differences are and how they can affect any relationship. Then we can better tailor our guidance and adjust our own style of relating to fit our children's needs.

One of the main factors in how boys and girls relate to others is that girls are generally more socially-oriented than boys. Girls' brains are dominated by estrogen, which drives them to form harmonious relationships and avoid conflict. They also have free access to the feel-good bonding hormones of dopamine and oxytocin, which produce stress-reducing effects that encourage intimacy. Testosterone, however, limits these effects in boys. Consequently, they care less about relationships and more about power, social rank, and physical strength. And socializing primarily interests them only when it involves sports—or sexual pursuits.

Another factor that impacts boys' and girls' relational abilities is the reality that girls are more naturally in tune with their own emotions and the emotions of others. The hippocampus, the part of the brain that stores emotions, is larger in women, as is the section that controls language and observing emotions in others. At a young age, girls can read into nonverbal emotional cues, such as a look or a touch, and can hear a wide spectrum of emotional tones in a way boys can't. And though the amygdala, which triggers feelings of fear, aggression, and anger, is larger in boys, the control center for those emotions is larger in girls, meaning that even as the feelings are stronger in boys, they're less inclined to manage them well.

On top of all this, girls are also generally better communicators. As we covered in Chapter 16, boys tend to rely on movement both to understand the world and to interact with it. Girls, conversely, prefer to use words. Even as young as twenty months old, girls can have almost triple the number of words in their vocabulary than boys, which isn't surprising given that they tend to start speaking sooner. Additionally, girls tend to use two to three times more words per day than boys, in part because they often speak much faster, especially among friends. In fact, at only seven years old, a girl is more linguistically similar to an adult women than she is to a seven-year-old boy.[3]

Now, I don't present all this information to imply that girls are somehow better than boys for being more naturally gifted in the relational realm. They're just different! And that means your relational approach should be too. With a son, you actually need to be *more* relationally focused. Your son may not be naturally inclined to prioritize relationships, but that doesn't mean he can't or doesn't want to. By strengthening your relationship with him, you can instill in him the value of relationships and teach him important social skills, preventing him from succumbing to isolation.

A key part of strengthening your son's relational skills is helping him develop his emotional IQ, which we unpacked in Chapter 22. Unfortunately, many boys learn to stuff down their emotional

---

3   Deborah Tannen, *You Just Don't Understand: Women and Men in Conversation* (New York: Ballantine Books, 1991): 245.

responses and hope they go away, either because they're afraid of appearing weak or because emotional expression simply feels unnatural to them. But the refusal to learn to process his emotions will only disrupt your son's ability to develop long-lasting, committed relationships. Others want to hear what he's feeling, and they won't appreciate being lashed out at when he lets his emotions control him. And as a result of his emotional withdrawal, he won't receive the feedback he needs for further identity development. The better you teach him to label what's going on inside him, the easier it will be for him to work through it, convey it to the ones he loves, and allow them to love and support him in return.

Of course, it's just as important for you to guide your daughter relationally. Just because she's more in touch with her emotions doesn't necessarily mean she's good at controlling them. She needs a father who can relate to her on her level, one who can empathize with her and help her organize what's going on within her. And that means you'll need to become comfortable with expressing your own emotions and engaging in more conversation than might feel natural to you. But that's not as difficult as it may sound. Simply ask your daughter questions about her day or her relationships to encourage her to share her heart with you, and then make sure to listen. Not only will this level of sharing allow you to adjust your support to what she needs, but it will also create a strong and intimate interaction that she'll appreciate and trust.

Another thing to keep in mind with a daughter is her ability to read emotions via nonverbal cues. Besides helping her relate to others, she also uses those cues to determine her own worth—in other words, whether others perceive her as lovable, valuable, or just annoying. Even when you're tired or in a bad mood, be careful not to unconsciously direct those feelings toward your daughter. Even more than a son, she can read into them and internalize them in negative ways. Especially when confronting her about her misbehavior, try to stay calm and rely on your words. This approach will allow her to take in the lesson you're conveying rather than instilling the false belief that she just isn't good enough.

THE BOY-GIRL RELATIONSHIP

In addition to how the relational differences between boys and girls impact your fathering, you should also be aware of the issues these differences can cause between your child and people of the opposite sex. Due to the relational and emotional gap, boys and girls often have more difficulty creating deeper friendships with each other, mostly because such a gap makes basic communication even harder. I remember Kim coming home in tears one day because a boy had hit her during recess. Why? Well, they'd gotten into a verbal altercation, and the boy couldn't keep up with Kim. So instead, he decided to express his emotions the best way he knew how—physically.

To help prevent some of these issues, take the time to explain to your child the differences that exist between boys and girls. That day, I sat Kim down, dried her tears, and explained that even though hitting others is bad and should never happen, she should try to think about why the boy might have done it. I told her a little bit about boys and girls and emotions, and I gave her some advice to avoid issues with this boy in the future. For instance, she should try not to yell at him, especially in front of other kids, as it would only make him more embarrassed and thus more likely to lash out physically.

And if I had been the boy's father, I would have had a similar conversation, helping him understand how girls and boys talk differently and encouraging him to better express his feelings with his words and positive actions. By increasing our children's knowledge about the opposite gender, we give them the tools they need to have supportive, successful interactions—or at least to avoid a fistfight.

Besides direct instruction, your relationship with your daughter in particular will go a long way in helping her better understand the quirks and tendencies of boys. Your unique perspective on romance, sexuality, friendship, and dating, shared in an age-appropriate manner, will help expand her perspectives and understanding. Even more importantly, your intimate connection with her will build up her confidence in knowing how to express herself in her relationships with men in the future. By seeing in you the kind of relationship qualities she should expect and accept from men, she'll be better able to navigate her relationships and interactions with men—and keep herself safe in the process.

Of course, you can't necessarily help your son understand how women think in the same way, but his mother can. By encouraging her to be open with him, he will gain a similar insight into the other side, which will help him relate better to his female peers. And as he learns to respect and treat his mother well, he'll gain the ability to give the same respect to every woman he meets.

Above all, you should find ways to create opportunities for your son or daughter to develop relationships with both genders. Due to the communication differences between boys and girls, it's vital that they have places where they can connect with people who think and act just like them so they can further hone and develop their strengths in those areas. At the same time, relationships with members of the opposite sex will help them better understand the differences between them. Even better, they'll be challenged in brand new ways, pushing them further toward developing all of their potential.

THE CULTURE'S ROLE

Along with being aware of the biological differences between boys and girls, we must also be sensitive to the different ways the culture harms our sons and daughters. We've already discussed much of the damage it inflicts on men in Chapter 16. Growing up, your son will be bombarded with commercials and ads that instill the false idea that men are simple, sexual, and aggressive. He'll watch shows and movies that portray men as unemotional, teaching him to suppress his feelings instead of processing them. And from these messages, he'll grow to believe that his value comes from his muscle size, sexual prowess, and perceived toughness— not from who he is in God.

While the culture distorts a man's value in these ways, it diminishes a woman's worth entirely. We live in a world dominated by an unhealthy hierarchy that places men's value above women's, defining women as subservient and confining them to the established roles of mother or caregiver. It emphasizes external appearances, causing every day to feel like a beauty contest to your daughter and distracting her from what really matters—developing her internal strengths through God.

Besides hurting our sons' and daughters' self-definition and sense of self-worth, our culture's lies can lead to external challenges as well. For instance, women have historically been unequally paid for equal work simply because they're women. And as we discussed in Chapter 16, boys are often forced to be still by teachers who don't understand their natural aggression and need to move, making it harder to learn to guide it well, or even to learn at all.

However, the biggest problem that can arise from the culture's definition of men and women is that of abuse. Women are already physically vulnerable given that they generally have less upper-body strength than men. Combined with the cultural belief that women are meant to serve men, and that men are meant to be sexual and aggressive, they're made even more susceptible to abuse. The testosterone-influenced, self-centered motivations of many men lead them to care more about how a woman can please them than about who she is as a person. Even worse, some men believe "might makes right," which helps them feel justified in hitting their wives or children when they don't get their way.

Of course, women aren't the only ones who can be victims of abuse. Many women also internalize the culture's lies about men, which can lead them to try to harm men in several ways. Some women see men as sex objects who they can express power and control over through their sexual attractiveness, in turn depersonalizing what is meant to be a gift from God. Furthermore, because of their mistreatment, some women believe that men can't be emotional, or they want men to provide everything for them. And when those men express vulnerability or fail to provide in some way, these women may reject them emotionally or even become physically abusive.

Unfortunately, the prevalence of these negative cultural messages means your child is going to hear them no matter what. That means your job is not to try to shield your child from these lies but to prevent them from internalizing them. Consciously counter them with God's truth and biblical standards, both through your example and through your actions. For your son, build up your own manhood identity, like we discussed in Chapters 16 and 17, in order to show him how to do the same. Help him recognize the negative definitions that exist around him and to understand what God desires of him instead (1 Corinthians 16:13-14).[4] Teach him to respect all women and see them not as objects but as partners in life. Challenge him to pursue God-given goals that require him to express himself fully and develop all of his capabilities. In other words, accept nothing less of your son than becoming the man God has called him to be.

And for your daughter, use your relationship with her to teach her how men should treat her and how to protect herself from overly aggressive males. By building trust and intimacy with

---

4   Besides the other resources mentioned so far, my book *Basic Warrior Training* is an excellent guide to help your son internalize godly principles. Find it at liveupresources.com.

her, you will help her learn not to be intimidated or manipulated by a male's aggression. Discuss the difference between a healthy style of loving and a selfish, sinful one, using your strong connection with her and with her mother as examples. Teach her to trust her gut when something doesn't feel right and to take immediate care of herself by getting out of an abusive situation. And make sure to let her know you're always there to help any time she feels unsafe.

Along with guidance and protection, your daughter also needs your help to forge her identity and become internally strong.[5] As with manhood, the culture is steeped in traditional views of femininity that could potentially limit her capabilities. Point her instead to God's Word and guidance so she can determine for herself how she wants to define her identity. Along the way, counter the culture's negative messages and teach her to do the same. You can affirm her efforts to be attractive, but don't let them impact her sense of value. Help her understand the challenges she'll have to face as a woman, but direct her away from a victim mindset that will only give her an excuse to fail. Encourage her to think strategically, plan her goals carefully, and then go after them with all her heart. When you do, she'll be able to reach her full potential as God defines it.

A WIDE-OPEN FUTURE

Unfortunately, the culture doesn't only distort our sons' and daughters' self-definition and sense of value. It also has a lot of outdated and confining rules about what are acceptable education and career paths for men and women. For example, a common belief is that women shouldn't work in construction because they're not strong enough or because it's not feminine. And men shouldn't be hairdressers or nurses because, well, those are jobs *too* feminine. However, God created each one of us with unique skills and abilities

---

5   For more on developing a strong father-daughter relationship, check out *Dad, Here's What I Really Need from You* by Michelle Watson at liveupresources.com.

that have nothing to do with our gender. More importantly, He intends for us to use them for a specific purpose, one only we can achieve, even if it doesn't align with cultural expectations.

There are many different ways to assess which career path might be most suitable for someone, but I prefer the Holland Occupational Themes model.[6] Based on the theory of John Holland, these six categories outline different personality types and match them to certain occupational environments and characteristics. Just like with your child's passions, which we discussed in Chapter 25, these themes are likely to become apparent at a young age, long before your child ever thinks about picking a career path. The better you can recognize them early on, the more effectively you can guide your child toward God's specific plan for them—no matter what the culture says.

1 Realistic

A realistic person gravitates toward physical and practical work. They prefer to engage with things rather than people or ideas, and they embrace challenges that have concrete solutions, whether it's repairing computers, learning how to use a new tool, or even tending a garden. Typical careers include mechanics, carpentry, law enforcement, and other manual or protective professions.

2 Investigative

Unlike realistic people, an investigative person is drawn to abstract challenges over concrete ones. They are intrigued by deep questions and complex puzzles and enjoy researching, studying, and analyzing various data to find the answers. Typical careers include biology, chemistry, doctoring, and other scientific or medical professions.

---

6   John L. Holland, *Making Vocational Choices: A Theory of Careers* (New Jersey: Prentice-Hall, 1973).

3   Artistic

An artistic person is motivated by some kind of creative pursuit, whether it's writing, music, fine art, or theater. They tend to be flexible and nonconforming, preferring the inspiration and imagination that can come out of ambiguity. Typical careers include journalism, culinary arts, music, and other creative professions.

4   Social

A social person is enlivened by helping others in some way, either through counseling, training, teaching, or some form of caregiving. They appreciate being a part of a team and get immense satisfaction from connecting with others. Typical careers include teaching, social work, ministry, and other service professions.

5   Enterprising

While realistic individuals are task oriented, an enterprising person is goal oriented, always strategizing to find a better way of succeeding and capitalizing on new opportunities. They gain energy through managing, persuading, and leading others, especially when it propels them toward accomplishing a job that benefits both themselves and their team. Typical careers include sales, marketing, politics, and other business professions.

6   Conventional

A conventional person loves organization and structure. They primarily enjoy working with data and information, whether it's creating schedules, managing inventory, or editing a newspaper article. Typical careers include administration, accounting, information technology (IT), and other organizational professions.

. . .

Regardless of your child's individual interests or what career path they decide to pursue, there is one truth that applies to every child—God created them to be a leader (1 Peter 5:2). Now, I don't mean that everyone is meant to become a CEO or motivational speaker. I simply mean that we all influence the people around us, whether we realize it or not. Even when we feel like we can't change anything about the world, we still have the ability to lend a helping hand and contribute to the welfare of others. At the very least, we can always demonstrate God's love to them, reminding them of their value when they seem to have forgotten.

Every day of their lives, our sons and daughters will have countless opportunities to demonstrate their leadership. They'll be called upon to give their opinions on how to accomplish a task, whether it's getting a Frisbee out of a tree or solving a math problem in class. They'll need to organize an effective plan to achieve these goals, even when they don't feel up to the challenge. And they'll have answers at times that others don't, just as they'll have unique skills others will rely on to help work toward a mutual goal.

As their father, it's your responsibility to help your child recognize their leadership capabilities so they can maximize these opportunities. This begins by teaching them that leadership is a behavior, not a position. It's about choosing to live by godly standards in every area of life. When they do, they won't just increase their ability to serve others effectively. They'll also become an example others can look to and rely on to help them in turn become better leaders themselves.

The only way your child can truly rise to such a challenge is by knowing who they are and constantly seeking improvement. Use your relationship with them to show them through both instruction and example how to strengthen their natural skills and abilities in order to act more responsibly and communicate more clearly. As they continue to develop, they'll increase their ability to help motivate others to be more productive, optimistic, and successful.

God has called each of us to be His representatives in life (2 Corinthians 5:20). But your son or daughter can't do that unless they are their true, authentic self. As you learn to adjust your fathering approach to your unique child, whether due to their specific personality or their gender-specific traits, always make sure to let them define themselves. Though you play a big role in shaping your child, who they become ultimately isn't for you to decide. Boy or girl, God created them for a specific purpose. And when you do your job well, when you love, support, and guide them to the best of your abilities, they'll have the very best chance to live up to it.

 ROBERT'S STORY

Growing up, heated arguments between my parents were the norm. It's not that they hated each other. Far from it, actually. It was just their dysfunctional way of communicating their emotions. Basically, the louder you got, the more heard and validated you felt. So that was what I thought communication between a husband and wife was supposed to look like—that is, until Colleen introduced me to an entirely new approach. We called it *stop, think, and speak*.

Whenever one of us feels frustrated or angry, the first step is to simply stop talking and quit moving physically so as to not get worked up. The second step is to think about what you're feeling as opposed to just reacting to it. This was the hardest for me to learn. I *hated* when Colleen would encourage me to label and identify the emotion and then pinpoint the root cause, because doing so made me feel like I was giving up my power position. It took time to understand that there's no such thing within a biblical marriage. Once

I did that, I also realized that by thinking this way, I was sabotaging any chance of growing intimacy and trust with my wife.

When I finally gave this technique a real shot, I was surprised by the relief I felt and the sense of satisfaction I was experiencing. Putting words to my feelings allowed me to enter into the same arena as my wife and communicate in a way she could understand. Suddenly, even my deepest frustrations brought us closer, because we could work through my pain together. I discovered that my wife (my once perceived enemy) was actually my greatest ally, partner, and friend.

From this position, the third step became a breeze. Now my words had weight and meaning to them instead of unbridled emotion. I could express myself without attacking anyone. Even better, I gained a deeper way to connect with my daughters. Controlling my emotional expression has allowed them to better understand the male mind, and I hope that one day it will equip them to better understand their husbands. The benefits of following this process has enhanced all of my relationships and especially my marriage— no power position needed.

💬 DISCUSSION QUESTIONS

1   Discuss how fathering a daughter is different from fathering a son. What are some specific issues you have to be prepared for with a daughter? How would you help her feel understood and valued despite how the culture defines her?

2   What specific strategies would you use in fathering a son? How could you help him learn to manage his testosterone, overcome the culture's sinful messages, and develop godly manhood?

3   Do you consider yourself a leader? How do you demonstrate that leadership in all areas of your life? What leadership concepts do you want to teach your child?

4   Discuss how Ephesians 6:12-13 (NIV) relates to the different struggles boys and girls face in our culture. How can a father help his child prepare to battle these cultural threats?

For our struggle is not against flesh and blood, but against the rulers, against the authorities, against the powers of this dark world and against the spiritual forces of evil in the heavenly realms. Therefore put on the full armor of God, so that when the day of evil comes, you may be able to stand your ground, and after you have done everything, to stand.

30

TRANSITIONS

Fatherhood is one of the most spectacular journeys a man can take, but like all journeys, it must eventually come to an end. Well, maybe *end* isn't quite the right word. After all, once you become a father, you're a father for life. But that doesn't mean your fatherhood will look the same that entire time. As your child grows and develops, certain responsibilities and requirements will naturally change, forcing you to transition into new phases of fatherhood to keep up with your child's needs. It happens when they start school for the first time and are no longer under your constant care. It happens when they make their first friends and don't rely on you as much for social support. And it certainly happens after puberty, when they seem to want nothing to do with you at all.

The biggest transition, however, happens when our children officially become adults. Children were designed to eventually become strong and independent enough to take care of themselves, whether they go to college or start a career, move out or stay at home (Isaiah 43:19). On one hand, it's gratifying to see how much they've grown, and it's certainly nice not to have to always be responsible for them anymore. But at the same time, it can feel disconcerting to have our fatherhood role be diminished so quickly and so jarringly. Even as many fathers celebrate their children's growth—or getting them out of the house—they still find themselves looking around and thinking to themselves, "So now what?"

For some of you reading this book, your child's transition to adulthood is a long way off. For others, it's right around the corner or has even already happened. Either way, it's important to consider it now so you can be prepared to handle it with strength and wisdom. In this chapter, we'll talk about some of the shifting dynamics that occur when a child becomes an adult, along with the important conversations you can have before, during, and after that transition to help you navigate these changes successfully. Through open vulnerability and communication, you and your child will be able to look back at your past together, learn from it, and then build a new type of relationship—one that will last a lifetime.

A TIME OF TRANSITION

With many transitions that occur in fatherhood, no matter what else changes, the father still remains in charge of caring for and instructing the child. However, that's no longer the case when the child becomes an adult. Through deliberate effort, careful guidance, and unconditional love, you'll have helped your child develop the skills and abilities they need to provide for themselves and stand on their own. And that means that whether you're ready for it or not, your time as their caregiver and instructor has come to an end.

And you know what? That's one of the best things that can happen to a father-child relationship. Because the child no longer has to listen and obey, and because the father is no longer obligated to take care of the child, they both become free to truly be themselves. The power dynamic that previously existed is exchanged for a more balanced relationship, giving us the gift of relating to our children more like peers. In this new context, we can get to know them, and they us, in a whole new way.

However, that doesn't mean this transition will be smooth. Any time change happens, conflict naturally emerges. For one, your child may not actually be interested in making the transition at all. It takes money and effort to be responsible for yourself, and some children decide it's easier to stay home where their parents can continue to take care of them. Once on a boat trip down a beautiful Wyoming river, the tour guide told us a story about two bald eagles. Their offspring had refused to head off on its own, and so they moved the nest, which they had spent years building and now weighed several tons, to a different part of the river, just to force little junior to fend for himself.

Now, I'm obviously not telling you that you need to move out of your house if your child won't. But what this story shows is that a child who's relying on their parents' support and refusing to grow up can cause tensions in the home, ones that can limit the relationship. Whether it's charging them rent or setting new house rules, you'll have to find a way to encourage their growth and independence—and unfortunately, that can lead to even more conflict if your child doesn't accept it.

More often than not, however, children are thrilled to become adults. And as your child embraces their independence, meets new people, and tries new things, they will begin to clarify their perspectives on topics like money, politics, faith, work, and ethics. Some of those perspectives may build on what you taught them, and some might differ completely. Not only can this create tension in your relationship, but it can also leave you questioning how much you should give your opinion or guidance, especially now that you're no longer in charge. And even if you do give input on your adult child's beliefs or decisions, they may refuse to listen to you at all. In fact, they may distance themselves from you entirely, due to either their disagreement, a desire to prove their independence, or even mere busyness, leaving you feeling hurt and uncertain of your role in their life.

Along with refining their viewpoints, another part of adulthood that can complicate your relationship with your child is their marriage. No matter how likable their partner is or how well they fit into your family, it's not always easy to accept that you're no longer the most important person in your child's life (Ephesians 5:31). When they have someone else to support, love, and work together with them, the already limited time you spend together will likely shrink even further. And if you believe your child's partner *isn't* actually a good match, well, all of these conflicts can create even more frustration.

Tensions can also arise in the next phase of the adulthood journey, when your child has children of their own. They and their partner may make parenting decisions vastly different from the ones you chose, and they won't necessarily be open to hearing your opinions or advice. Or they might want you to be *too* involved in your role as a grandfather, either by watching their kids all the time or by badgering you with questions or requests they should be handling themselves. In either scenario, boundaries need to be drawn and compromises made, which, unfortunately, can create a different kind of tension.

Of course, these potential conflicts may happen, and they may not. It all depends on your specific circumstances and how prepared you and your child are to face the unknown together. And that means that at different points in your relationship, you have to have a conversation about your relationship. Whether it's a once-and-done chat before they move out of your home, a series of talks conducted throughout adolescence, or multiple discussions held at each major stage of your child's life, these conversations are essential for understanding your shifting relationship. By taking the time to lay it all out and clear the air, you can ensure you both stay on the same page about the nature of your relationship and your expectations for it going forward. In turn, you can set a promising course for the future of your lives together.

LOOKING BACK

One of the biggest tenets of achievement is to keep moving forward, which many people interpret as never looking back. However, as I've repeated several times throughout this book, the only way to create a better future is to review the past. While we form bonds with others through shared experiences and emotional connection, we strengthen them through mutual grief or celebration over past circumstances. Whether it's laughing about fond memories, healing old wounds, or learning from our mistakes, unpacking the past with our children gives us the opportunity to instill our victories, repair our failures, and rebuild the foundation of our relationship into something better and stronger than ever before.

The approach to these types of conversations matters less than making a point to have them, regardless of where your child is at in life right now. If they're still young, you may want to have a series of smaller discussions over the years, or you could sit down with them during each new life stage to have a bigger conversation. If your child is already grown, you may just want to have one comprehensive discussion about their entire life and your relationship thus far. But no matter when or how you do it, there are three specific areas you should make sure to look back at together at some point during your child's life to make sure nothing negative tags along on their eventual transition into adulthood.

1   Positive memories and observations

Every family has at least a few moments where they simply enjoyed each other and laughed together. Remembering those times with your child will help instill in both of you a sense of the love shared and the fun experienced, creating excitement for all the future memories you'll make together.

You can also use this time to affirm your child in their growth and the specific developments and achievements you're proud of.

Hearing your encouragement will build their trust in you and their confidence in themselves. It might even inspire them to return the favor by thanking you for all your guidance and support. From this open sharing, you and your child both get a moment to appreciate all you've accomplished. They can feel good about how hard they've worked and how far they've come, and you can be proud about what you did right. Most importantly, you gain a sense of hope and optimism in imagining what you can achieve together in the years to come.

2   Confusing memories

Due to a young child's innocence and lack of understanding, they often experience situations they misinterpret or don't fully comprehend but that still have a lasting impact on them. When I was about five years old, I accidentally saw my father in his underwear with what looked like blood all over his legs. He quickly ushered me out of the room, and I was left on my own to interpret what in the world I just saw. As you can imagine, that was a little traumatizing for me at such a young age. Years later, I finally got around to asking my dad about that night and why he'd been covered in blood. And it turns out, he wasn't—he'd had a hernia operation, and the medication they gave him to fight the infection was a cream that was bright red.

Children are more observant and perceptive than we often realize, and your child has likely seen or picked up on something that is still lingering with them. No matter their age, giving your child the opportunity to bring up any confusion or questions they have can help you give them context for these memories and resolve any misunderstandings. Then they'll be able to process any negative feelings the memories had caused and finally move on.

3   Negative memories

No relationship is perfect, even when it comes to the most adoring, supportive father-child bond. Over the course of your child's life, you will get into fights with each other, both over important issues and over trivial ones. You will clash over personality differences and aggravate them with your stubbornness, distractedness, or other natural weaknesses. And unfortunately, you will hurt your child from time to time, either by overlooking one of their needs or by failing to be there for them in some way.

All of this is normal, and it doesn't necessarily have to have a long-lasting impact on your relationship—that is, as long as you address it. Either due to passivity, insecurity, or fear, many fathers avoid bringing up issues that have already passed, especially if their present relationship with their child seems to be going fine. However, when pain, sadness, or frustration is allowed to linger, it will limit the intimacy you can build with your child. You never know what old resentments or guilt might be impacting their willingness to trust you or ability to connect with you.

By bringing these feelings out into the open instead of brushing them under the rug, you can take responsibility for your negative choices and mistakes and understand where you need to improve (Proverbs 28:13). More importantly, when your child feels safe enough to admit to their hidden or suppressed feelings, they can take control over those past pains and begin to accept some responsibility in your relationship, equipping them to have more success in all of their future relationships.

Kim and I had several conversations like this over the years. During one of those talks, she shared with me how my overinvolvement in my work had hurt her as a child. It was tough to hear, but I knew she was right. Through my tears, I affirmed her feelings, apologized for my choices, and asked for her forgiveness. And as a result of my willingness to be vulnerable and resolve the past, we both became free to strengthen our relationship in the present. Of course, we still have our differences, and things aren't always perfect. But by simply having the conversation, we can now work through these differences together and learn to appreciate them, which I have to tell you feels really, really good.

APPROACHING THE PAST

Of course, these conversations about the past won't always be easy to have, especially when the emphasis is on negative memories rather than positive ones. To help keep the process as smooth as possible and limit unnecessary tension, you should try to adhere to a few key guidelines. First, it's your obligation as a father to initiate and take the lead in these conversations, like we discussed in Chapter 18 and the refathering process. Your child may now be an adult, but that doesn't mean they won't still be hesitant to bring up issues themselves, either because they don't think it's worth it to potentially instigate conflict or because they're afraid of your response. It will be up to you to both invite your child into a tough conversation and to help lead them through it.

To get this process started, you can first acknowledge some of the ways you know you've failed your child and the areas you still need to improve on, making sure to apologize when necessary. Then ask them how you've hurt them or what you could've done differently to be a better dad. And after they're done sharing, make sure to reflect back what you hear them say and ask follow-up questions to ensure clarity. By being open in this way, you demonstrate a desire to understand their perspective, which will not only help your child open up but will also begin the process of healing so you can both eventually move on.[1]

---

1   To help facilitate this conversation, consider going through the survey from Chapter 9 with your child. You can print or download additional copies of this survey at liveupresources.com/fatherhood.

However, keep in mind another concept mentioned in Chapter 18—be sensitive to your child's pacing. While you should be the one to initiate the conversation, you should never push them into sharing more than they're ready for. For the most part, the topics of these conversations won't be too heavy, since most issues discussed will just require a few adjustments and boundaries going forward. Sometimes, however, a sensitive topic will come up that neither you nor your child will be capable of unpacking with each other, at least not in a constructive way.

At this point, instead of trying to force an emotional conversation, it can be helpful to approach the topic cognitively. Ask your child what rules they want to set with you to avoid being hurt in the future. If you know you've been absent from their life in the past, you could suggest promising to come to at least two of their games or other events per month to show your commitment now. This approach can help create a general sense of safety for both of you that allows you to gradually build the trust that will lead to deeper emotional conversations in the future.

The second guideline regarding having these tough conversations is to make sure they happen between you and your child alone if possible. Though it may seem better to include your wife in sharing your memories or in hearing what your child has to say, it will actually limit your ability to fully connect with your child. When it's just the two of you, you can focus solely on each other, giving you a chance to define your unique relationship together and ultimately reach a deeper level of intimacy.

However, that doesn't mean intimacy will come easily. That's why the third guideline is to enter the conversation with complete vulnerability. We all have a natural fear of facing difficult truths, especially when it requires either sharing our deepest emotions or empathizing with the complex emotions of others. But the only way to process these emotions is to get them out in the open. You have to be courageous and say what hasn't been said. You have to share your perspective and exactly how you feel. Otherwise, this interaction and any others you have in the future won't be fully authentic. And without authenticity, your trust will be limited, leaving your foundation too weak for a real relationship.

The fourth and final guideline is to make sure you remain nonjudgmental and nondefensive, which will also help encourage the vulnerability described above. As your child shares their perspective, don't assume any motivations or try to interpret why they made certain choices. You will only come across as accusatory, which will make them feel like they aren't being heard. The more you let each other talk without interruption, the better you'll each express your full viewpoint and help the other person see your perspective.

Additionally, your child may make statements you don't like or feel hurt by, and you may feel a desire to immediately make excuses for your past behavior. However, regardless of the intention behind your actions, the impact on your child is real. If you ignore that impact and focus on yourself, they will grow even more distant and distrustful of opening up to you. No matter what they say or how you feel, make sure you truly listen and affirm your child's emotions first. Then you can work together to reach a mutual understanding about what happened and figure out how to move forward from there.

It's important to note here that while much of the focus of these conversations should be on your own mistakes because of the impact they had on your child's development, you are not on trial as a father. These discussions are largely about mutual understanding and healing, which means that you should also leave space in them to address your child's negative choices and need for improvement. Children are just as capable of hurting their parents and violating your trust, and it's important to bring those issues to the surface so you can work through them together. Not only will it free your child of any guilt they might still be holding on to, but it will also ensure your relationship can get a fresh start on *both* sides.

MOVING FORWARD

Facing old wounds and mistakes won't be easy, but it's a vital step in walking with your child into their journey toward adulthood. Combing through the past and picking out the relational lice will allow you to stop them before they can burrow further and create even greater issues. And once they're out of your hair, you'll gain the ability to actually do something about them. Then you can fully begin the process of transitioning into being a father of an adult—and building a relationship that matches.

However, as important as it is to look back and sort through the various relational bumps and bruises that have occurred, the success of your future relationship with your child will be determined by what you do next. You are both beginning a new chapter in life and in your relationship, and making that transition will require more than just acknowledging the past. It will also require taking the following four action steps to both reconcile with that past and adjust to your changing roles together.

1   Apologize and ask for forgiveness.

We talked a lot about forgiveness in Chapter 18, and it's an important part of fatherhood regardless of whether you've messed up in big or small ways. We all need to continually assess our relationship with our children and make sure to atone for any hurt we've caused. Whether the mistake you committed was less significant, such as missing your child's middle-school championship baseball game, or deeply impactful, such as repeatedly losing your temper over bad grades, engaging in the forgiveness process is essential. By taking responsibility for your actions, you acknowledge how you've hurt your child and express empathy for what you've put them through. Not only will this demonstrate your love for them, but it will also show your willingness to change and to treat them better in the future (James 5:16).

As with discussing the past, you must be sure to be sensitive to your child's pace during the forgiveness process. Depending on the circumstances and their level of grief, your child may not be able to forgive you right away. While it may hurt to realize that, it's ultimately better for your relationship in the long run. You don't want your child to forgive you just because they feel obligated or pressured to. The only way you can both move forward is if your child grants true, willing forgiveness. That may mean they need more time to process some of the memories your conversations uncover. But when that forgiveness does finally come, it will be all the more healing, because you can know that they truly mean it.

Keep in mind as well that this process of forgiveness should go both ways. Though your failures may be bigger and hurt deeper, your child will also have made mistakes they need to admit to and make amends for. Whether they ask you for forgiveness or not, make sure to give it to them for any negative choice they bring up (Matthew 18:21-22). These conversations are about a fresh start, and the only way to truly achieve that is if you both can get clean slates. Don't excuse your child's actions, but don't hold them over their head either. Talk them through what happened, discuss how they can do better, and then forgive them so you both can let it go.

2   Commit to restoration.

Restoration doesn't mean simply forgetting any past transgressions, as many people think it does. Rather, it means beginning the process of letting go of any guilt and shame associated with your past mistakes so you can move forward with your relationship. It also requires taking ownership of your negative choices so you can learn where you need to continue to grow yourself and avoid repeating the same negative patterns. Periodically ask your child for feedback in order to help you identify what you still need to work on, which will allow you to continue to grow and develop into a better father.

However, improving yourself will only fix the relationship to a certain point. To achieve true restoration, your child will have to meet you halfway. It won't always be easy. Even after forgiving you, they may still find themselves reliving those painful moments in a fruitless attempt to achieve a different outcome. But spending your energy repeatedly trying to make up for something you can't change will only create an imbalance between you and your child that will limit what your relationship can be. Eventually, your child will need to find a way to redefine what happened, identify the strengths that can come out of it, and open themselves up to hope for the future.

3   Establish expectations.

After working through forgiveness and committing to restoration, you should ask your child what specific kind of support, guidance, or mentorship they would like from you as they enter the world of adulthood. Just before I left for grad school, I paid my father a visit. Jan and I were about to move all the way across the country, and I was scared that it would all be for nothing. I knew I had several weaknesses that had always made education difficult for me despite my love of learning, and I knew those weaknesses could cause me to fail no matter how hard I worked.

So that night, I told my dad that I needed to be able to call him anytime and that I needed his support if I had to come back without a degree. We cried and prayed as we sat together thinking about the future. Then, after I moved, he followed through on my request. For years he wrote me a weekly letter of support, slipping a twenty-dollar bill into the folds. His words and contribution helped me and my wife weather the storms, and I made it through school in one piece.

The thing is, his support never would've happened if I hadn't asked for it. Thanks to that conversation, I got exactly what I needed from him. That being said, it's the father's role to initiate this conversation before the child's needs even arise. Make sure to continually ask your child both in specific and general ways how you can support them. If the hurt you worked through together was due to your emotional distance, ask them if there's anything they want you to do to be more present now. If they're getting married, ask how they picture your involvement in their new life with their spouse. If they've always struggled with shyness and making friends, ask how you can help guide them relationally even after they've flown the nest. Not only will these conversations help your child in their moments of need, but they'll also assure them that you'll always be there no matter the situation, struggle, or grief.

As part of establishing expectations, you should also decide how to handle certain types of disagreements. You will always have your differences, and for the sake of the relationship, you must consciously decide together to both accept and affirm each other's right to make separate choices. At times, this may mean agreeing to disagree, as long as the issue isn't causing anyone harm. The most important thing is that you don't allow the past to influence your present arguments. That means dealing only with the issue at hand and that once your child is an adult, you don't fall back into your old parenting role of caretaker. You have to accept that you can't control them anymore—and that any attempts to do so will likely lead to even greater conflict.

4   Set boundaries.

In order to ensure you don't unintentionally hurt your child again in the future, you must be sensitive to their relational needs by working to accept their boundaries and not pushing past them in any way. Like expectations, these boundaries can be specific to a certain area of life or past pain, or they can be more general. For instance, if you have a history of being overly protective of your child and restricting their natural independence, they may set the boundary that you can only give them advice when they ask for it or that you must stay out of a certain area of their life entirely. More generally speaking, if your child lives close by, they may request that you don't come over unannounced so they can have their own space and independence from you.

It may not always feel natural or easy, but you must respect your child's wishes. It's only by intentionally setting clear boundaries and respecting each other in this way that you can focus fully on the new experiences you're sharing together without worrying about stepping on each other's toes. Then you can continue to build up your relationship more and more as the years go by.

It's never easy to realize that your child is all grown up. You may start to feel like they don't need you anymore or like you no longer have a place in their life. But I can promise you, the opposite is true. Your child will always need you—they'll just need you in different ways than they did before. As you work to transition with your child through their new life stages, make sure to include God in your difficult conversations and pray to Him for their well-being. It's His love working within us that brings us together with others, and nowhere is this more true than in fatherhood (1 John 4:19). With His guidance, you and your child will grow closer and closer every day, no matter how far away they may fly.

 ROBERT'S STORY

Puberty is the worst time to be a dad. Not only are you visually reminded of the hidden countdown to the day your child will leave you, but you can also sense a shift in the role you play. Where being a dad meant playing tea time or jumping rope, now it means you have to talk about sin, sexual identity, and shame. It's like your innocent little child suddenly becomes tainted overnight. I *hate* it.

But at the same time, I've realized I need to see this change as a beautiful thing. As much as we may want to believe our blossoming children aren't thinking about adult stuff, they are. And they're struggling like the rest of us. If anything, that reality should make us feel even closer to our children, as we now share even more similar struggles, sins, and temptations with them.

I've learned that when I stop seeing my preteen daughter as a little innocent toddler and start seeing her as a sinner in desperate need of Christ, I begin to better equip her and myself for the next phase of our journey together. When I take the time to listen to her words and feel the struggles in her heart, I can relate simply by looking at myself. This shows my respect for her as a young adult, and it earns greater respect from her by revealing that I desire (and am not afraid of) authenticity.

So I've put aside idealism for something better—truth. I have become more purposeful at reading scriptures with my girls and hearing their applications. My wife and I are free to teach the need of repentance and the joy of forgiveness. Most of all, we can experience the infinite acceptance of a loving Savior who makes all things new, including our relationships with our daughters.

💬 DISCUSSION QUESTIONS

1   How did your relationship with your own father change as you grew up? Discuss what you would say if you could sit down and talk with him about the positive, confusing, and negative parts of your past together.

2   As you reflect on your time with your child, what are some positive experiences you shared together? How can you build upon and celebrate them as your child transitions into adulthood?

3   Name some of the negative moments you need to discuss with your child. What do you need to ask forgiveness for? What boundaries or expectations might you need to establish to restore your relationship?

4   Discuss what Proverbs 16:3 says about the role God plays in building better relationships with our children in the future. How can you rely on Him to help you successfully transition with your child through life's many stages?

Commit to the LORD everything you do.
    Then he will make your plans succeed.

conclusion

THE GIFT

Toward the end of his life, my father was in and out of the hospital several times as his mind and health started to go downhill. During one of those hospitalizations, I was sitting beside him when all of a sudden he screamed out, "Macaroni! Macaroni! Macaroni!" I was alarmed to say the least. I had never heard him use that loud, shrill voice before, and he'd never shouted something so meaningless.

Later, after he was back home and recovering well, I asked him what had been going on inside of him at that moment. He replied that in his confused state, he was afraid people in the hospital were going to kill him. Then he added that he felt safe when I was with him. He told me, "I know the kind of dad I was to you over the years. But I knew that you have forgiven me for that. I knew you would protect me and do what's right."

In that statement, my father took ownership of how he had hurt me in a way he never had before. I thought carefully about how to respond. I could have made him feel better by saying, "No, Dad, you were a great father." But that dishonesty would've prevent us from ever becoming real with each other. So instead I responded, "You're right, Dad. And I did forgive you."

When I saw how receptive he was to this statement, I decided to ask another question: "Can I tell you how you hurt me the most?" He quickly replied yes, and so I said, "I know it was hard for you to deal with Mom's mental health issues, but it was hard for me too. At least you were an adult and could leave. But that meant that as a young child, I not only had to face her alone but also had to protect my siblings. It really hurt me when you threw yourself into God's work and didn't protect your kids. It would have been nice to see you support me and my siblings, to spend more time with you, and to not have to face Mom alone so much."

With tears in our eyes, we continued to talk about our relationship. For the first time, we openly discussed my mother's mental health issues and the impact she had on both of us. As my father took ownership of his choices, the forgiveness I'd already given expanded even further. And even though he passed away shortly after, I'll never forget that conversation and how it has helped with my personal restoration and growth.

Isn't it amazing how one conversation between a father and child can change their entire lives and their feelings toward each other? Just as my father had on me, you have a tremendous impact on your child's view of themselves, others, life, and God. Through your behaviors, relationships, and sense of identity, you model to them the standard they will use to determine how they should live their life. And through your interactions with them, you give them the words and perspective they need to begin labeling and establishing the various parts of their identity. From all these different resources, your child will be equipped to discover who they are and understand their value, allowing them to develop into a wholly unique individual.

And what was true for my father is true for you as well: it's never too late. No matter your fears, insecurities, or past failures, when you choose to walk with God and pursue continual growth, your influence will be a gift to your child. In Mark 7:15-23, Jesus reminds us that our negative behaviors stem from an internal spiritual immaturity. For this reason, the only way to change and fully develop your greatness is to deepen your relationship with Him.

God knows every thought and feeling deep within you, including your harmful and sinful ones—but it doesn't change His view of you. He knows the plans He has for you, and He knows you have the capabilities to achieve them. But you must first accept His omnipotence and guidance. It's only by developing a humble attitude and turning everything over to Him that you can begin to step toward fulfilling your potential and becoming the father He created you to be.

Even by reading this book, you've already taken the first step toward becoming that man, whether you're a brand-new father, one who's trying to make up for his mistakes, or one who simply recognizes his need to continually learn and grow. You've unpacked God's definition of fatherhood and worked to understand what it takes to truly be a godly father. You've reconciled your own father's legacy and put in the effort to develop your strengths, shift your perspectives, and overcome your weaknesses. And you've delved into the specific areas you need to help your child grow in, taking the time to process the details and see how they apply in your own fatherhood.

You may not have the money, status, or power to give your child what they would consider the gift of their dreams. But through your relationship and with God's help, you *can* help them fulfill everything He has in store for them. The experiences and lessons you provide through your affirming presence will create a permanent image your child can build upon for the rest of their life—and that's a gift that will last long after you're gone.

Remember, more than anything, God is a God of relationships. By strengthening the one you have with Him, you strengthen the bond you have with your child. And when that bond is strong, they'll have all the support, confidence, and love they need to make it through anything.

MORE RESOURCES

The following resources include discussion questions at the end of each chapter or in the back of the book to guide conversations about the various lessons. You can purchase these products or learn more about them at liveupresources.com.

VIDEO SERIES FOR MEN

The Heroic Man's Journey
A 5-part series that teaches men to recognize their God-given design and unique potential. Each part contains 24 lessons.

Following God in the Raw
A 14-lesson series that emphasizes the importance of brotherhood and relationships with others.

The Genesis of Manhood
A 6-lesson series that explores God's original plan for manhood and encourages men to rediscover their life purpose.

Real Men (Volumes 1-3)
A 15- to 16-lesson series that brings together a group of dynamic speakers to lead males toward becoming real men of God.

Fighting for Your Manhood
An 8-lesson series that redefines manhood to reflect God's view of the characteristics and actions that make up a true man.

VIDEO SERIES FOR WOMEN

The Genesis of Woman
A 3-part series that takes a deeper look into God's original plan for women and helps women take hold of their God-given strength. Each part contains 9 lessons.

Living Better
A 2-part series that leads women to join together to uncover their great value and unique purpose. Each part contains 18 lessons.

BOOKS FOR YOUTH MENTORING

The Campfire Gang (10+ Books)
(Recommended age: 5-13)
A character-building fiction adventure series for boys that explores God's plan and valuable life lessons.

Jillian Dangerous
(Recommended age: 8-16)
A gripping 2-book adventure series for girls about finding friendship, overcoming challenges, and experiencing God's Word.

Pass It On
A guide for mentoring, counseling, and coaching for both men and women.

Bull
(Recommended age: 12-15)
A coming-of-age book for fathers and sons that covers the most foundational aspects of manhood.

Being God's Man
(Recommended age: 12+)
An in-depth look at godly manhood that can be studied by fathers and sons or by men's groups.

Basic Warrior Training
(Recommended age: 16+)
A true story of a male's search for manhood through his experience of becoming a United States Marine.

BOOKS FOR ALL AGES

All Man
A no-nonsense exploration of the God-given gift of sexuality and how to manage it according to His plan.

Why Not Try to Hit the Real Target—Men
A step-by-step guide for building and sustaining an effective men's ministry.

You're Not Dead Yet
A book to help men over the age of fifty discover the purpose God has for the second half of their lives.

Off the Page and Into Your Life
Inspirational stories of how seven different women discovered how to relate to God's Word in new and wonderful ways.

HELP MORE SERVANT-LEADERS SUCCEED

Our goal at LiveUp Resources is to lead as many servant-leaders as possible toward discovering their God-given value and potential. That's why we partnered with Servant's Oasis, a 501(c)(3). This nonprofit organization uses donated funds to provide LiveUp Resources books and video programs to men's and women's ministries in inner-city churches, community centers, rescue missions, prisons, and other countries.

Servant's Oasis is also currently working to meet their greatest goal—to create a retreat center where servant-leaders can come and be refreshed spiritually so they can continue effectively ministering to others. Thankfully, Servant's Oasis has recently obtained the perfect property to create such an environment. With some major renovations and maintenance, it will become a refreshing oasis where servant-leaders can take time away to reflect, reset, and then go forward in their ministry.

But to achieve this mission, we need your help. Even the smallest donation can go a long way toward funding the retreat center or providing godly materials to men and women. If you aren't able to help us financially, we ask that you support Servant's Oasis with your prayers as we pursue our mission to empower those in need to discover their identity, full capabilities, and true, God-given worth.

You can make your secure tax-deductible donation online at **servantsoasis.org/give** or by mail to:

Servant's Oasis
Attn: Treasurer
200 North 7th Street
Lebanon, PA 17046

ABOUT ROY

Dr. Roy Smith has worked for nearly forty years as a psychologist and counselor to men and their families. Pennsylvania Counseling Services (pacounseling.com), which he began out of his home, offers a variety of services in eleven counties in south central Pennsylvania. Roy is also an ordained minister with the Evangelical Church Alliance. He developed LiveUp Resources (liveupresources.com), a ministry that produces books and video series to guide men, women, and youth toward their God-given potential, contributing to the overarching goal of positively changing our culture.

Roy has written several books in the areas of men's issues and mentorship. He recently began writing *The Campfire Gang* series, which now includes more than ten published volumes, to teach young boys biblical leadership and character-building skills through an engaging storyline.

Roy has a master of divinity degree and a master's and a doctorate degree in clinical psychology. He is married to Jan, who is also a psychologist. They have two children, a son-in-law, and two grandsons.

ABOUT ROBERT

Robert Amaya is a family man with a love of film and musicals. He first won audiences' hearts as Javier, "the Snake King," in *Courageous*. He has since become a favorite in many uplifting films including *October Baby*, *Moms' Night Out*, and *Family Camp*. Robert is a former vocalist for the critically acclaimed Walt Disney's Voices of Liberty. He used the experience he gained there to help launch and direct FamJamz, a program through his church where families could worship together and parents could be equipped to lead their children's spiritual development.

In 2019, Robert became the executive director of LiveUp Resources and is helping develop the associated LiveUp Studios and LiveUp Films. He speaks at both English- and Spanish-speaking churches, schools, and organizations as a minister of the lifesaving Gospel of Jesus Christ. He is passionate about Christian artistry and enjoys helping and mentoring others to unleash their artistic freedom without compromise. He is equally passionate about fatherhood and the significance of such a calling, believing that it is a father's duty to call out the men in their sons. He is married to his high-school sweetheart, Colleen, and is the father of two beautiful girls, Sophia and Angelina.

"GOD HAS BEEN MOVING THROUGH *THE CAMPFIRE GANG.*"

—John C.

An adventure-packed, character-building book series for kids of any age!

While the campfire gang adventures through worlds full of excitement, strange creatures, and new friends, they figure out how to deal with emotions, challenges, leadership issues, teamwork, relationships, and more.

Order at

THECAMPFIREGANG.COM

info@thecampfiregang.com | 1-800-777-0305